BILL
NICHOLSON
FOOTBALL'S PERFECTIONIST

BILL
NICHOLSON
FOOTBALL'S PERFECTIONIST

BRIAN SCOVELL

JOHN BLAKE

Published by John Blake Publishing Ltd,
3 Bramber Court, 2 Bramber Road,
London W14 9PB, England

www.johnblakepublishing.co.uk

www.facebook.com/Johnblakepub facebook
twitter.com/johnblakepub twitter

First published in hardback in 2010
This edition published in paperback in 2011

ISBN: 978-1-84358-390-5

British Library Cataloguing-in-Publication Data:

A catalogue record for this book is available from the British Library.

Design by www.envydesign.co.uk

Printed in Great Britain by CPI Bookmarque, Croydon, CR0 4TD

1 3 5 7 9 10 8 6 4 2

Papers used by John Blake Publishing are natural, recyclable products made from wood
grown in sustainable forests. The manufacturing processes conform to the environmental
regulations of the country of origin.

Every attempt has been made to contact the relevant copyright-holders, but some were
unobtainable. We would be grateful if the appropriate people could contact us.

To Grace 'Darkie' Nicholson.
Bill had a lifelong love affair with football but his most endearing love affair was with Darkie. Their marriage lasted 62 years and her love, devotion, laughter and fun helped make it one of the happiest in British football.

CONTENTS

Acknowledgements

This is my twenty-fifth book and in many ways, it has been the most pleasurable. So many people have helped me, mainly because Bill Nicholson was a great manager but also because he was a decent man and loved by so many. He wanted things done the right way and luckily, I had an enormous amount of help from his daughters – Jean and her husband Steve and Linda Feldeisen. They checked all the references to the family and supplied all the valued pictures that constitute most of the photograph section of this book.

In March 2009, I spent a very rewarding week in foggy, blowy Scarborough, where Bill grew up, and those who kindly assisted me with their contributions include Paul Nicholson, Derek Megginson, Frank White, Geoff Nellist, Ron Anderson, Steve Drydale, Tony McKenzie, Geoff Hillarby, Doreen Procter, Gordon Jackson, David Duggleby, Jimmy and Beryl Johnson, Tommy Johnson, the editor and staff of the *Scarborough Evening News*, the South Beds News Agency, who supplied me with a full report of the murder that took place in Keith Burkinshaw's former house, and Colin Appleton, captain of Leicester City in the 1961 FA Cup Final.

At Tottenham Hotspur, John Fennelly and Andy Porter pointed me to the best avenues to reach former players and others. Alan Leather and Peter Barnes also had considerable input and I thank everyone for their time.

All the players, managers and colleagues that I spoke to talked admiringly of Bill. They never called him 'Boss' or 'Gaffer' – they thought of him as a friend. They include Les Allen, Ossie Ardiles, Jimmy Armfield, Ron Atkinson, Peter Baker, Phil Beal, Ted Buxton, John Barnwell, John Bond, Liam Brady, Norman Burtenshaw, Bobby Campbell, Eddie Clayton, Ralph Coates, Terry Dyson, Olaf Dixon, Hunter Davies, Gerry Francis, Jimmy Greaves, Bobby Gould, George Graham, Tony Galvin, Tommy Harmer, Don Howe, Ron Henry, Glenn Hoddle, Pat Jennings, Cliff Jones, Joe Kinnear, Doug Livermore, Dave Mackay, Alan Mullery, Terry Medwin, Paul Miller, Maurice Norman, Steve Perryman, Martin Peters, John Pratt, David Pleat, Sir Bobby Robson, Graham Roberts, Gary Stevens, Peter Shreeves, Jim Smith and Terry Venables. When the book was published, four of Bill's finest servants died in the space of 77 days: Bobby Smith, aged 77, Mel Hopkins, 75, Eddie Baily, 85, and Ralph Coates, 84.

Several of my journalist friends were extremely co-operative and they include David Miller of the *Daily Telegraph*, Brian James, formerly of the *Daily Mail*, Ken Jones, formerly of the *Daily Mirror*, and in particular, Laurie Pignon of the *Daily Sketch* and the *Daily Mail*.

Two people who made major contributions were Keith Burkinshaw, the manager who had many of the same qualities as Bill, and Eddie Baily, Bill's former teammate, coach and friend. He and his wife were married on December 20, 1952 at Clapton Church and, after a quick peck on the cheek, two Tottenham directors gave Eddie a lift to White Hart Lane where he played in the day's 2:15 kick-off.

I have read many of the books of that time and the list which I set out below might well be too short but if any others are left out, sincere apologies to the authors concerned: *Glory, Glory* by Bill Nicholson (Macmillan), *And the Spurs Go Marching on* by Phil Soar (Hamlyn), *Football Managers* by Dennis Turner and Alex White (Breedon), *The Glory Game* by Hunter Davies (Mainstream), *The Beatles, Football and Me* by Hunter Davies (Headline), *Football Players' Records 1946–84* by Barry Hugman (Newnes), *The Double and Before*, by Danny Blanchflower (Nicholas Kaye), *Greavsie* by Jimmy Greaves (Time Warner), *Clough* by Brian Clough (Partridge), *A Man for All Seasons* by Steve Perryman (Arthur Barker), *Pat Jennings – An Autobiography* (Collins Willow), *Right Back to the Beginning* by Jimmy Armfield (Headline), *Chelsea – the Real Story* by Brian Mears (Pelham), *The Ghost of '66* by Martin Peters (Orion), *The Real Mackay* by Dave Mackay (Mainstream), *Double Bill* by Alan Mullery and Paul Trevellion (Mainstream), *Yours Sincerely* by Ron Greenwood (Collins Willow), *Bob Wilson – My Autobiography* (Hodder and Stoughton), *Jimmy Hill Story* (Hodder and Stoughton), *Tottenham Hotspur Football Book No. 4* edited by Dennis Signy (Stanley Paul), *The World Cup 1930–1990* by Ian Morrison (Breedon), *The History of the World Cup* by Brian Glanville (Faber), *Revelations of a Football Manager* by Terry Neill (Sidgwick and Jackson), *Portrait of a Footballing Enigma – Don Revie* by Andrew Mourant (Mainstream), *Spurs Supreme* by Ralph Finn (Robert Hale), *The England Managers* by Brian Scovell (Tempus), *Football Gentry – the Cobbold Brothers* by Brian Scovell (Tempus), *Whose Side Are You On?* by Norman Burtenshaw (Arthur Barker), *Time on the Grass* by Bobby Robson (Arthur Barker), *The First Voice You Will Hear Is...* by Ted Croker (Collins Willow), *Sir Alf* by Leo McKinstry (Harper Sport), *White Hart Lane Legends* by Keith Palmer (Keith Palmer) and many volumes of *Rothman's* and *The News of the World Football Annuals*.

Finally, immense thanks to Morris Keston, Tottenham's greatest fan, for checking the manuscript and saving me any embarrassment with facts, like the fact that Dave Mackay's second broken leg happened at White Hart Lane, not Shrewsbury FC!

CHAPTER ONE:
THE RIGHT IMAGE

'The great fallacy is that the game is first and foremost about winning. It is nothing of the kind. The game is about glory. It is about doing things in style, with a flourish, about going out and beating the other lot, not waiting for them to die of boredom.'
DANNY BLANCHFLOWER – THESE WORDS SUM UP BILL
NICHOLSON'S FOOTBALLING PHILOSOPHY

When Bill Nicholson left Tottenham in 1974 after 33 years on the payroll, he was eventually paid £10,000 in compensation. The highest annual salary, plus bonuses, he had received was £14,000. He had to go on the dole for a while, until his great friend Ron Greenwood took him on as a consultant at West Ham. Bill was never sacked, he never had a contract with the club, never asked for a pay rise and he never took, or paid out, a 'bung'.

Each year he would meet the chairman and he would offer him a modest increase, which he always accepted. He didn't have an agent, or a lawyer, to handle his affairs – he did it man to man. Steve Bell, his son-in-law, said: 'I never knew how much he was paid, but I was under the impression for much of that time he didn't earn more than a working man's salary.' Bill wasn't concerned about money, only about how his team performed in front of their fans. He wanted the fans to be excited so that Tottenham's anthem, 'Glory, glory, hallelujah', kept ringing out loud and clear.

As today's moneymen move in from all around the world and take over the clubs, they want victories and profits, not so much style and class – although if their teams all played like today's Barcelona side, their reputations would be enhanced. But just as Hungary beat England 6-3 at Wembley on 25 November 1953 to change attitudes about the game, another date emerged to open the eyes of the faithful – Wednesday, 27 May 2009, when Barcelona beat Manchester United 2-0 in the Olympic Stadium in Rome in the final of the Champions League. Josep Guardiola, the young Barcelona coach, spoke of 'the how being important'. Award-winning sports writer Paul Hayward, now with the *Observer*, wrote: 'They [Sir Alex Ferguson's men] collided with a side substantially more literate in the art of moving and retaining the ball at an intoxicatingly high tempo.'

Tottenham's Arthur Rowe gave push and run to the world, his successor Bill Nicholson refined it to a new level, and now a generation later it is being played by Barcelona. They are the trendsetters, the ones to copy. Bill was the man who urged Keith Burkinshaw, one of his most loyal successors when he was in charge at White Hart Lane between 1976 and 1984, to buy Ossie Ardiles and Ricky Villa in 1978. Tony Galvin, one of the many players Bill discovered, said recently: 'He loved Ossie. When Ossie managed the side his team talks consisted [of] only a few words – push, push, attack, attack!' Arsène Wenger believes in beautiful, winning football too and once said: 'Life is important on a daily basis because you try to transform it into something that is close to art. And football is like that. When I see Barcelona, to me it is art.'

Contrast that with today's managers in England with their image rights and their insistent quest for trophies. Some spend more time promoting themselves than coaching at the training ground, so much so that they are bigger names than the artists on the field. Bill was reluctant to give too many interviews to the media after being let down by one journalist who quoted his off-the-record views about a certain player and he probably found it hard to understand the phrase 'image rights'. To many people, his image was that of a dour, uncommunicative man – but that was a totally false impression. He was cautious about the press because he was more interested in the way football was played than in personalities and their public comments about each other.

Those who knew him well recognise that he was a man of principle and a family man, who was deeply loved and revered. His whole life was conducted in the right way, without courting controversy and without trying to outwit the tax authorities. There is a generation of Tottenham fans who idolised him and it is doubtful that there is another manager in the history of English football who equalled, or bettered, his close affinity with the paying customers. As he often said, 'The fans pay your wages so don't let them down.' Unfortunately the fans don't pay the players' wages these days, only part of them. The rest comes mainly from television but also sponsorship, corporate entertainment and other sources.

Nearly all of today's top managers and players use their image rights to reduce their tax bill. If they earn more than £300,000, they can be taxed at 31 per cent, and 20 per cent under that amount. A manager in the top third of the Premiership can make around £1.5m a year from his image rights. It is looked on as a tax-efficient way to conduct their affairs, but recently the Inland Revenue has been investigating the matter. When it was revealed that Joey Barton, a former jailbird, had earned £675,000 in image rights at Newcastle, they stepped up their inquiries. Had Bill Nicholson been offered image rights, he probably would have turned it down because of his innate honesty; he never cheated anyone and deplored cheating on the field. Today's managers keep talking around the subject, or even lie. They are similar to politicians and they waffle instead of informing the public, the people who help sustain the game with their cash and their vocal support.

There was no press officer when Bill was manager and his telephone number was easily obtained but he rarely granted interviews over the telephone, telling journalists: 'I might be available after training, or after the match.' He was the last manager who said, on occasion, 'no comment' when asked a question by a journalist. If a transfer deal was finally concluded, he would confirm it, but not before.

These days, there are three press officers at White Hart Lane and like most of their colleagues at the other leading clubs, they organise the manager's and players' interviews to suit the club. Brian James, the former *Daily Mail* football correspondent who went on most of Tottenham's trips under Bill, recalled: 'He was wary of us, but the ones he got to know were the "Okay Men" and he'd talk about football with you. He didn't tolerate sloppiness and he was very emotional about the game. If he saw a player making an obvious mistake, he would be upset about it. He was a hard taskmaster. I think he had a sense of humour because we sometimes heard him guffawing about something. He wasn't going to be the star, but he wasn't that sort of person.'

Some of Bill's successors make money from their image rights, although their image has been trampled on. A number of managers including Harry Redknapp and Sam Allardyce of Blackburn Rovers have had their affairs investigated by the Crown Prosecution Service. Brian Clough, one of the few who shared Bill's views about fair play on the field, only missed prosecution because he was terminally ill. Don Revie was an outstanding manager, but he was corrupt.

Recently a Premiership higher-up asked me: 'How many managers today are like Bill Nicholson?' It was hard to think of any, apart from perhaps Arsenal's Arsène Wenger. Bill was one of the last Corinthians in modern-day professional football. After his death in 2004, hundreds of messages were sent to the club and one supporter, David Richardson, said: 'They say the game now lacks honesty and integrity. It's true, but understandable. Bill Nick so cornered that market in those virtues that there was none left over for anyone else.' David Pleat, who managed Tottenham between 1986 and 1987, said: 'Conscientious is the word I would use to describe Bill. He was one of the very few managers who put his club before himself. Many of today's managers want to make as much as they can from the game. They're greedy.'

Today's rich club owners want properly trained and qualified coaches, often from abroad, which is why fewer English managers are being chosen. Towards the end of Bill's playing career in 1955, he coached Cambridge University to gain experience and earn some extra money. A number of others did the same but today's top players are millionaires and don't need to go into coaching to earn extra cash on the way to becoming a manager. The supply of talent is decreasing at a rapid rate.

Bill had two great inspiring educationalists helping his career: the athletic coach Geoff Dyson, with whom he worked in the Army in Udini, Italy in 1945–6 and Sir Walter Winterbottom, founder of the FA Coaching scheme. He learned a lot about fitness from Dyson and from Winterbottom, the thinking way the game should be played. Bill detested the offside game that so many clubs still employ – pressing up to the halfway line to catch out opposing players. He regarded it as tantamount to cheating. Cliff Jones said: 'I can't remember seeing us doing that. Bill wanted to play it simple and quick, and get the ball forward.'

Another Spurs manager, Terry Venables (1987–91), took the offside tactic to a new level and at one game, an opposing manager observed: 'I see you've chalked up 18 free kicks from it today and it must be pretty frustrating for the crowd.' Terry said: 'Oh no, our crowd were clapping. They love it.'

Keith Burkinshaw believes Spanish football is the world's best, far superior to England's £2 billion Premiership, which paid out £1.2 billion in wages (the agents took £66m) in the season 2007–08. 'You know why?' he said, 'Because their players are extremely fit and they use all the pitch. They use space better than we do and they get far more shots in. It's more entertaining and Barcelona is the best club side in the world. They've got fantastic, skilful players. Bill believed in using space. He told his players to keep possession and use the ball simply and quickly.'

In his trainee days, Bill learned a lot from coaching young, aspiring footballers at Cambridge University. Sports writer David Miller, a right winger who was one of his pupils, wrote in the *Daily Telegraph*: 'In the old days many men – schoolmasters, bank managers, doctors, soldiers – were cast in the same Victorian mould as Bill Nicholson: strict but fair, dogmatic but logical, austere but open-hearted, wilful but almost perversely modest. Nicholson was all these, yet additionally a crusader, a man with conviction.

'His anomalous, almost subconscious mission was to take the bricks of the simple game of football and fashion them into jewels for the benefit of public entertainment. In this pursuit, he devoted a literal lifetime to Tottenham. More even than Matt Busby with Manchester United, Bill Shankly with Liverpool or Jock Stein with Celtic, he was the embryo of Spurs' greatness during a 16-year reign. A man of unlavish lifestyle, living a convenient short walk from the ground in a semi-detached, he spent the club's money extravagantly, but shrewdly.

'With his passing, I confess a light has gone out of my life. In his formative coaching years, he spent an afternoon a week with Cambridge University where, besides working us to the point of physical sickness, he chastisingly entrenched the fundamentals of the game: simplicity, to eliminate error, repetition of moves, to breed familiarity, honest sweat, so as to leave the field wholly spent. He would afterwards share toast and honey round the gas fire back in our digs. He spoke quietly of the game being nothing without integrity and discipline. He had several players who became amateur internationals. We loved him like an uncle and when he brought glory to White Hart Lane, it would be for us no surprise.'

When Bill was at his peak as a manager someone asked him: 'Why do you still live round the corner? You could live in a mansion out on the outskirts.' Bill's reply was: 'Because I want to get to work on time, that's important.' John Pratt, who played for him between 1968 and 1979, said: 'That was a very apt comment. Bill was never late – first in, last out, and he didn't waste time travelling.' Bill had almost total control of Tottenham for 16 years basically because the directors, mainly small-time businessmen, recognised they had little expertise about football and left it to the expert.

But his disillusionment set in by the early seventies when the stock of emerging footballers was in decline and he was forced to try and buy second raters for over-inflated prices. The directors, chairman Sidney Wale, vice chairman Charles Cox, Godfrey Groves and Arthur Richardson and his son Geoffrey, all questioned some of his choices and that, together with the stress he felt after working 16 years, was why he offered his resignation. The Board members were well intentioned but they were not really football people. Terry Neill, whose appointment in place of Bill was greeted with derision by most of the players and the fans, recalled: 'The board meetings were long, drawn-out affairs and it needed considerable stamina to stay awake. Mr Groves senior sometimes nodded off and as the tea lady came in with the tea and biscuits, conversation stopped, as though they were discussing state secrets.'

In 1984, Bill was persuaded to put his name to an autobiography by Irving Scholar, the Tottenham chairman. The book was entitled *Glory, Glory – My Life with Spurs* and Harry Harris, my friend and former colleague at the *Daily Mail*, collaborated with me to compile it. Harry's ambition was to play for Tottenham and his mother wrote to Bill Nicholson to ask if he would give her son a trial. But Harry never went for the trial because he realised he wasn't good enough. His prowess was aptly summed up by Malcolm Macdonald when a Football Writers' team played against QPR staff on the Omniturf, the artificial surface pioneered by Terry

Venables at Loftus Road in 1981. Said Malcolm: 'Some people can kick with one foot, or two, but H can't kick with either!'

Harry wasn't a star footballer but he was one of the best news gatherers of his era. He had the same persistence as Vic Railton, the late *Evening News* football writer, who once got hold of the telephone number of a hotel suite where Sir Matt Busby was presiding over a disciplinary hearing. Vic dialled the number and as Sir Matt picked up the phone, he asked: 'What's the verdict, Matt? My deadline is only five minutes away!' Matt told him the verdict. 'I admired his cheek,' he said.

Like Railton, Harry Harris was one of the few journalists who could ring Bill Nicholson on his private line when he started his career at the *Tottenham Weekly News*. Vic would call Bill's wife Grace, known to everyone as 'Darkie', at 8am on some days and ask with a laugh: 'Where is that old so-and-so?' 'You ought to know,' Darkie would wryly say, 'He's at work as usual.'

In Bill's first chapter of his autobiography he spelt out his concerns about the future of the game. 'It is a cornerstone of my beliefs as a player, coach and manager that the basics of the game are all important,' he said. 'The simple elements that go to make up a football team, such as passing techniques, striking the ball, controlling and trapping it and movement off the ball, are on the wane today and that makes me feel sad. I watch countless junior matches and trials, and I find there is a lack of players who have these skills.

'The root cause of the problem is the inadequate preparation at the lower level. The emphasis is on stamina, height and power rather than technique and skill. I always thought that the really gifted footballer – a Jimmy Greaves or a Bobby Moore – was born, not manufactured. However, that type of player still needs to practise his skills. Not enough work is done today by young players. Certainly not enough is done at schools, where matches are overly competitive, physical encounters, which discourage the skill factor. If youngsters don't have the basic skills, there are no foundations on which to build teamwork. Moves will keep breaking down. It is easier for the other team to defend and the game becomes boring and fragmented.

'When I was with Tottenham, our approach was to concentrate on attacking football. I was striving for perfection, though rarely achieved it. But as I said to one player who complained, "Look, when I have no interest in you as a footballer, that is the time when you start worrying." Danny Blanchflower had faults but by working on them he became a better player. No sportsman is so good at his sport that he cannot improve some aspects of it.'

Bill also believed the inflated scale of salaries would ruin the game and he was proved right. 'I believe the players are taking too much out of the game and not putting enough back in,' he observed twenty-five years ago, when he went into temporary retirement and worked as a scout for West Ham before Spurs recalled him. 'Wages rose too quickly and the economies of the clubs became unbalanced. Transfer fees were too high. It is a miracle that 92 Football League clubs still survive. Ultimately, some clubs will go bankrupt.

'It amazes me that there is nearly always an entrepreneur waiting to come to the rescue of an ailing football club at the time when it is about to go out of business. You seriously question the motives of such people while at the same time being grateful to them for saving a club that serves a great many people in its area. Astronomical wages at a time of recession have created a social gap between players and the man on the terrace. 'There used to be a time when the spectator could identify with the footballer, who was not earning much more than he was. Today's players stay in their private lounge before driving off to their homes a fair distance from the ground. Players no longer live round the corner, as I did when I was a player and manager.'

He was suspicious of agents and wanted a curb on their activities. 'There isn't as much honesty in the game today as there ought to be,' he said. 'Admittedly football is all about competition, but cheating has become intense. The more difficult it becomes to succeed and the more pressure on the manager to be winner, the greater the risk of corruption. An aspect which perturbs me is the payment to managers of a percentage of fees. These rogue managers may prefer to deal with agents as that is a good way of obtaining a cut. I question the morality of such payments.

'Could some players be transferred at much higher rates than they are worth because of the benefit coming to the manager? There is also the danger of a manager dropping the price for a quick sale because he needs money, so the club may suffer. I believe that these payments – and the agents – should be outlawed. The best managers are not necessarily the ones who finished the season with a trophy. They are many around who succeed in keeping clubs alive against the odds and still entertain, but unfortunately they are not given the recognition they deserve.'

In another prophecy that turned out to be true, he said, 'Some years ago I told another manager: "The players will soon be running the game." I believe we are close to that now. The players and their agents make the demands and the clubs are forced to comply. In my day, managers told the players what money they were to be offered. Today it is the reverse. The player and his agent come up with a list of demands and the club has to decide whether it can afford them. If it can't, the player is touted to another club, often abroad where wages are higher because transfer fees are lower.

'The money paid to players goes out of the game but money paid in transfer fees circulates among the clubs, keeping them alive.'

He was not strictly accurate about players being sold to clubs abroad and the wages offered by most Continental clubs. Hardly any English players go abroad because few speak another language and technically they are inferior in skills. Premiership clubs can afford to buy the world's best players and when they are no longer wanted, they sell them off abroad.

No one from the FA, the Football League or the major newspapers of the time made proper efforts to clean up these irregularities and restore some credibility to the game. Twenty-seven years later, little has been done. In many instances, managers have a clause in their contract allowing bonuses if players are sold for big profits and the get-out excuse is 'well, it's in the rules'. MPs used the same excuse when they were caught overcharging on their expenses and, like politicians, managers know it's against the spirit of the game. Most earn enormous salaries, so why do they need the money? Richard Scudamore, chief executive of the Premier League, told Neil Ashton of the *News of the World* in 2010: 'I'm convinced the game is clean. We scrutinise transfers more than ever after the Lord Stevens inquiry. Sven-Göran Eriksson claimed corruption in the game was rife, but we did a right trawl and we couldn't find any compelling evidence.'

Portsmouth's affairs have been scrutinised on a number of occasions and at the start of the 2009/10 season their chief executive Peter Storrie told a fans' forum at Fratton Park: 'We all know that all managers tap players up. It is not right, it's illegal and it is against the Premier League's rules, but it happens all the way around.'

'Tapping up' players can be traced back to the time when the Football League first kicked off in 1888. The trainers or chairmen of clubs were continually trying to recruit the best players from rival clubs and approaches were usually made secretly through friends, relatives or journalists. In Bill Nicholson's heyday, one of his best contacts was the Scots football writer Jim Rodger, who had a good appreciation of talent north of the border, but Bill was scrupulously honest about his own transfer deals, always going through the right channels.

Shortly after Storrie made his comments about tapping up, FIFA banned Chelsea from buying players until January 2011 after they signed 18-year-old winger Gael Kakuta from Lens. FIFA has a regulation, Article 17, which prohibits poaching players in these circumstances and two other clubs, Roma and Sion, were also found guilty. Progress has been painfully slow but the worldwide clean-up has now started, with UEFA joining the campaign in 2009 by charging Arsenal's Eduardo with 'deceiving the referee' by diving.

Bill was unerringly correct about the lack of skill of many players, the inflated salaries, the growing gap between the overpaid performers and the supporters, plus the unwholesome activities of many agents. The game was losing its appeal and it was only the intervention of BSkyB, buying up the televised rights at a gigantically high price for the new Premiership when it replaced the old First Division in 1992, that prevented a footballing version of a tsunami. Sky devoted large sums to promoting the product – and it worked. The pendulum swung forward to better grounds, pitches like bowling greens, fitter and stronger players, as well as livelier, more informative coverage. But on the downside, some of the new owners were global entrepreneurs who were running up vast borrowings – almost like Robert Maxwell, who wanted to take over Manchester United but had to settle for Oxford United and then Derby County.

Whereas Maxwell was found out and committed suicide in 1991 before he was charged, today's owners stay on the right side of the law, but they have still created empires which may collapse, like a number of banks in the latest recession. After Norwich City were relegated at the end of the 2008/9 season Delia Smith, their incorruptible director and leading backer, commented: 'You can't run a club and succeed if you are a millionaire, or even a multi millionaire, but only a billionaire.' Norwich are on the way back, which proves that honesty is still the best way forward.

Bill was critical of the work rate of the players when he spoke in 1984 because his generation of players, most of whom served in the Armed Forces, were subject to severe discipline. If they slacked, they were put on jankers (punishment duties). His generation has now passed by. They grew up kicking tennis balls against a wall to master the art of control and played in small-size kickabouts in the streets or on patches of grass. Their successors have less self-discipline and money has tended to corrupt some of them.

'A footballer is now in a different class from that of the man who pays his wages,' said Bill. 'Some people argue that they should be paid a relatively low basic with higher bonuses related to success. In a sense, that already happens. They even get a bonus for staying up. My argument is that the only real incentive for players is to seek to play to the best of their ability in every game because of sheer pride of performance and personal satisfaction.

'There are times when I see highly paid players taking a breather and that angers me. They have no pride in their performance. Ninety minutes isn't a long time to be running about, but some want to take it easy. They are cheating themselves, their teammates, their employers and the public. Managers in Italy fine players for not trying and there is no reason why it should not happen here, because the contract of service specifies that a player must play to the best of his ability. There were times when I accused my players of not trying, but I never fined them. I would leave them out of the side, if need be.

'There is no reason why the gifted players shouldn't work hard for the whole of the game. That is one of the problems of the game today: they do not work hard enough. Players soon become complacent and many will duck out of work, if given the chance. Often I was accused of not handing out praise, or concentrating more on finding fault. I may not have complimented players after matches, but I did it on the training pitch. That is the place where I experienced my greatest happiness in the game. That is where great football teams are produced and to achieve that goal, much work is needed.'

Bill was one of the first to ask a centre forward to take over as a centre half, reversing roles to understand the other man's approach; he believed in wide, attacking players to open up defences and he was in favour of flexible formations. He advocated the use of the now outdated WM formation – four rows of men; three defenders at the back, two defensive wing halves, two attacking inside forwards and a centre forward with two wingers. 'It means a more open game,' he said. 'It is very fluid and the man off the ball has to be the playmaker, the man who dictates the next move.'

These days many of the big clubs use only one striker, a sign that the game has retreated because of the fear of defeat. Cliff Jones, the youngest-looking of the 1960/1 Double survivors, said: 'Bill knew more about the game than anyone in it.'

Some commentators called him grumpy, but his observations have proved spot-on. He forecast a top four or five Super League at the top, including Liverpool, Manchester United, Arsenal and Tottenham, making it extremely hard for the other clubs to survive. He was wrong about Spurs and should have anticipated the arrival of Roman Abramovich at Chelsea. It was more convenient, and often cheaper, for managers to import foreign, ready-made players instead of rearing their own English players, and now less than 40 per cent of the Premiership's stars are available to be picked by England. These players, particularly those from Africa, work harder because of their poor background and have more skill, and so the overall standard of matches has gone up. Not many of them drink alcohol either. Too many of the young English players still make exhibitions of themselves, in and outside of night clubs and bars, disgracing their profession. Bill insisted that his players showed respect to the referee at all times and if he was alive today he would probably condemn Wayne Rooney's rushing up to supporters and twice screaming 'F*** off!' in a weird 'celebration' of a hat-trick in April 2011.

After yet another instance in 2009 – when Tottenham's Ledley King was charged with assaulting a 22-year-old bouncer – Harry Redknapp said he was in favour of a ban at White Hart Lane. He condemned David Bentley's latest car crash (luckily, no one was injured) and he told the *Mail on Sunday*: 'Just ask anyone who has lost someone in an accident. In 1990, I lost my best mate [Bournemouth's Brian Tiler] and four people got killed because a young kid was drunk and driving the other car.'

Bill Nicholson drank, but always in moderation. He entertained his many relatives and friends at home, not in pubs or clubs. As an essentially private person, he preferred to spend his time at home rather than being in the limelight. Foreign players are taught at a young age to avoid alcohol and most of them follow this advice but there is still a big drinking culture in English football and the Premiership continues to give out bottles of champagne to their Men of the Match. A better idea would be a cheque, which the Man of the Match would be asked to present to a hospice or school. Not everyone drinks in football, though. One exception is Owen Coyle, the Scots manager of Bolton. 'I've never had a drop,' he admits.

Many millions watch Premiership matches around the world and it is the most-watched league of any country. Bill would certainly agree with Harry Redknapp about the decline in the number of English footballers available to be selected for their country, which is reflected in the international side's results. In 2007/8 the top clubs had debts of £3 billion and Michel Platini, the UEFA President, talked sense when he said: 'There is anarchy and I want to save many clubs from bankruptcy because when the TV rights stop in England, what happens?'

Throughout his life Bill was known as a perfectionist and his daughter Linda confirmed this: 'Definitely. He never deflected from that. He wanted us to do our very best and when I started to learn to drive a car, I sometimes parked the car six inches or so from the kerb. He told me it should be two inches, not six, and I had to do it.

'His lawn was immaculate and he put a lot of care and love into it, and it was like a putting green. We had a beautiful garden and it was his pride and joy. He had our putters close to hand so we could practise our putting skills. You couldn't blame the lawn for a bad shot as Dad spent a lot of time nurturing it to perfection. He had one of those old push lawn mowers that cut the grass beautifully and it was probably his way of relaxing.

'He was a loving father who brought us up the right way and we were very proud of him. There were things he expected from us, like giving a hand in the house. He was a real Yorkshireman and believed that certain things were the women's responsibility, although he nearly always did the washing up. He used to whistle or sing when he was washing the dishes and we'd be drying them with the best tea towels. Sometimes we'd all sing along together, which made it a lot of fun.

'He really was a very happy person at home. I failed my GCE in English one year and that disappointed him, and he said he wouldn't pay for driving lessons until I did it. When I passed, he always came out with me until I passed the driving test. He gave us a time for coming home at night and he was very fair about it. He expected us to take a Saturday and summer job to teach us the value of money. He didn't give us pocket money as such – we had to earn it. But if it was a special event and we told him about it, he would give us the money to go. When he came back from his football trips, he would bring back presents and we have lots of them still around. He certainly didn't spoil us.

'He took us to matches, particularly the big matches. We preferred sitting high in the back of the stand and we didn't see him until he got home. Sometimes we went to Cheshunt, the training ground. Afterwards we would be talking about the game and giving our views, and sometimes he'd say, "You're talking rubbish!" He didn't take his worries home. If we won, the atmosphere was fantastic. He thought it was important to be playing sport. He didn't mind what sport it was as long as you played something and he encouraged his grandchildren to play sport.

'When Spurs lost he wouldn't dwell on it. He'd get the cards out to play – he loved solo. Very often we would have ten or more people round for dinner and they were happy family occasions. If he was ill, he would go into the ground and I can only remember one occasion when he was really sick and had to stay in bed for a day. Even then, he was on the phone talking about his work. He was a very fit man and he liked walking home to and from the ground, and when people spoke to him, he would always have a chat – he never ignored anyone.'

Andrea Fraser, a fan, recalled: 'My dad had a sweet shop near

White Hart Lane in the late seventies and Bill was a regular customer. He would stand in the shop for ages, chatting to my dad about football. My dad felt his comments were valued by Bill and that gave him the biggest buzz, as you can imagine; he was my dad's hero. Bill loved the club with all his heart. He is one of the few managers, past and present, who genuinely respected the fans' views.'

One of the most-quoted of Bill's remarks was uttered at Linda's wedding in 1970, when he said: 'I never saw her growing up.' It seemed to suggest he was guilty of neglecting Jean and Linda. 'He did say that and it was true,' recalls Linda. 'He had tears in his eyes when he said it to Mum and he was a pretty emotional man. I think we were both a bit anxious but I was so happy to have him beside me on the journey to the church, even though he told me not to fiddle with the flowers as I'd spoil them! His life revolved around football and football was always first. And he missed a number of events at our schools but living nearby, he sometimes popped home more than most football managers, like lunch times. He was a wonderful father.'

So how would Bill Nicholson fare today, managing one of the global clubs owned by corporation tycoons who know little of the game? One of his club's best-known internationals from a previous generation, said: 'He would have found it very difficult, basically because players today have great egos. You can't speak to them the way Bill spoke to his players.'

CHAPTER TWO:
A REAL NICE GENTLEMAN

Bill Nicholson was born and brought up in a house in Scarborough, next door to a garage where a woman was later murdered. It turned out to be one of the longest and most unsolvable crimes of the century, and no one was ever charged. On 26 March 1943, two brothers named Johnson – Tommy, aged 8 and his brother Jimmy, aged 7 – were playing in the deserted garage alongside the Nicholsons' rented house when they discovered the body.

Tommy, who was a well-known boxer in the North and still works as a boxing coach, remembers: 'We always used to sneak into the place and play football, and we used to swing on the pump across the pit. This time my hat fell in and I went to get it back.'

In the middle of the garage floor was a four-foot deep inspection pit, covered in oil. To the boys' horror, a naked woman was lying inside it and Jimmy, a football coach, said, 'We thought it was a dummy until we started poking it and I said, "That's flesh!" We went home and told our Mum and she said, "Don't take any notice, it's a dummy." But Tommy said, "The first thing I did was to run down to the police station and told them, and they came back to the garage and they confirmed that the woman had died in suspicious circumstances.' As a reward, the boys were each given five shillings.

The victim was thought to be a prostitute but Tommy said: 'Oh no, she was married to a soldier and they ran a grocery shop in Prospect Road. She must have been walking down the road and met this man in the War, and there were no lights showing so there were no witnesses. It was an offence to leave lights on because of the risk of bombing.

'We were told that she was strangled in our road, Trafalgar Road West, and the murderer dragged the body to Vine Street and threw it into the pit. The Army parked their trucks in the garage, but a few days before they evacuated and the regiment, which was based at Berniston Barracks, went abroad. It was easy to get into the garage. I knew someone who told me that the murderer went off with his unit and that's why they couldn't trace him. There were rumours that he was killed in action.'

Jimmy, a confirmed Tottenham Hotspur fan, knew Bill Nicholson and observed: 'He was a very nice man, a real gentleman. Once we wrote to him, asking if he could let us have a couple of tickets for a Spurs game at Sunderland, and he sent them by return of post – that's the kind of man he was.' Jimmy's wife Beryl was a long-time secretary of Sir Alan Ayckbourn, Scarborough's best-known resident. 'Bill and Darkie often watched Sir Alan's plays at the Scarbrough High School,' recalled Jimmy. 'That was in the early days before Sir Alan's theatre, The Stephen Jones Theatre, was built.'

David Duggleby, who owns the auctioneers and valuers in the revamped garage building, said: 'A young girl was strangled and dumped in the pit and a soldier was suspected as the murderer but no one was charged. In the War it wasn't easy to check up on soldiers who were being moved around. If it was a soldier, he might have been sent off to Northern Africa, or anywhere. This street is better known for our infamous murder than as Bill Nicholson's birthplace, I'm afraid.'

Bill said in his book: 'I was born in 15, Vine Street, a house which no longer exists.' When I started writing this biography, I went to Scarborough, not knowing about the murder, and knocked at the door of one of the terraced houses in the cul de sac not far from the Scarborough Cricket ground. A young woman opened it and I asked her if she knew where Bill Nicholson, the famous football manager, was born. She laughed and said: 'Never heard of him.' 'He came from a family of nine,' I said. She laughed again. 'You wouldn't get nine kids in these places,' she told me.

The day started with a pea soup of a fog, which apparently is not unusual in that part of the country, followed by continuous rain for most of the day. I turned back down the street, carrying my red and blue Sky brolly, similar to the one used by Steve McClaren when his fate as England manager was finally sealed, and I saw a bald-headed man in a fawn raincoat, who looked a bit like Charles Hughes, the former FA coaching supremo who preached the long ball game. I put the same question to him.

'As a teenager, I used to collect Mrs Nicholson's rent at Quarry Mount where the family moved to,' he said. 'So I know all about the house.' Pointing to the end of the road, no more than twenty yards away, he said, 'Number 15 is on the right of the Duggleby's offices and that was where Bill was born. It is still there, as you can see.'

Now 68, Gordon Jackson spoke with enthusiasm and affection for Mrs Nicholson, Bill's mother. 'She was a lovely, cheery lady who always wore an apron, as mothers did in those days,' he remembered. 'She was always on the dot with her rent. She always offered me a cup of tea. Her husband died quite young and I never saw him.'

As I was about to leave, he asked: 'Do you know about the murder?' I didn't. Throughout my visits to interview Bill at his house close to White Hart Lane, he had never mentioned it. The local newspaper called it 'The Garage Crime'. Gordon couldn't remember the name of the victim, but scouring through the files of the *Scarborough Evening News*, I discovered that she was 33-year-old Mary Elizabeth Comins from Middlesbrough. Her husband was serving in the 8th Army in Northern Africa and she was in the habit of entertaining a number of soldiers after working as a barmaid. There were no leads for the police to follow and Coroner Dr D.L. Sutherland said her clothing – a black lambswool coat, a black shirt and top, plus gloves – was found; also her handbag. After a five-hour autopsy, the Coroner said the only apparent cause of death was superficial bruises to the throat. Mrs Comins lived alone at 7 Wrea Lane and took casual jobs at a pub and a grocery shop. More than 2,000 interviews were conducted and although Scotland Yard detectives were called in, eventually the case had to be filed away. Several witnesses had seen the victim in Dean Road earlier in the day, not far from the former prison, and heard her laughing and joking with a soldier.

Some months later, it was reported that Mary's husband was shot and killed in Northern Africa, but Jimmy Johnson thought that wasn't true. Other rumours were circulating, one saying that the murderer had died in the fighting in Africa. In 1943, the Scarborough police reported 386 crimes in that year and 80 per cent of them were solved, but the most infamous was never solved.

Forty-seven years later Keith Burkinshaw had a similar experience: he once owned a house in the posh part of Bengeo, a suburb north of Hertford, but the man who bought it off him was murdered and the house partially damaged by arson. 'I was working abroad at the time when it happened,' he recalled. 'It was a large house, five bedrooms, and I met this man a couple or so times and we agreed over the sale. He was an accountant, I think, around 50, and he had been married several times. I was shocked when I heard that he had been garroted and the house was burned down. I don't know the full story but I think he might have been involved in organised crime. No one was charged.'

The driveway to the house was shared by the residents of two flats and caused a lot of arguments. On two occasions, the BBC's *Crimewatch* featured the case, once reported on by Jill Dando – she herself was murdered in Fulham in 1999. Barry George was tried and convicted for shooting and killing the presenter, but he appealed and was subsequently released in 2008.

South Beds News Agency reported on the murder which took place in the early hours of 1 December 1990, saying: 'Patrick Hurling, 45, was brutally murdered in his £250,000 mansion home in Bengeo and he had been battered and eventually strangled, probably with a wire flex. His killer, or killers, later set fire to the body. Expensive jewellery, including a diamond-encrusted bracelet and rings were taken from the body. Detectives have always ruled out that he was a victim of a burglar and there was no forced entry. The evening before he left his firm of Hurling Roberts in Waltham Abbey to drink with colleagues in a nearby pub. He left about 10pm in his £30,000 BMW accompanied with a woman with dark, long hair, who was never traced. Twenty minutes later he had a fish and chip supper on his own. It was around 5am when neighbours spotted a fire raging in his garage.

'In a downstairs bedroom the body of Mr Hurling was found slumped in a praying position against a bed. It had been wrapped in a blanket and duvet and set on fire. The body was badly burnt beyond recognition and it was later identified from dental records. A post-mortem showed he had died from strangulation from a ligature.

'Mr Hurling was an accountant who led a high profile life and was married three times. Friends said he was a sociable man with an eye for the ladies. Fifty detectives were assigned to the case and 1,700 people were interviewed and 600 statements were taken. Police thought they had enough evidence to charge two suspects but the Crown Prosecution Service disagreed and no action was taken.'

There were disturbing similarities with the murder case at 15 Vine Street, Scarborough. It was extraordinary that two managers of Tottenham Hotspur lived in houses where someone was murdered and no one was charged.

Bill Nicholson was born on 26 January 1919 and was the second youngest of nine children – five boys: George, Fred, Joe junior, Bill and Ted, and four sisters: Doris (known as Dolly), Edith, Ida and Nellie, all deceased. They were hardy people and seven of them lived past the age of 70, five surviving into their eighties. As children, they had just one scooter between them and they used to queue up at the door to take their turn.

Their father, Joe, was born with a congenital defect to a leg and walked with a limp throughout his life before he finally succumbed to cancer of the bowel in 1938, aged 61. Edith Gowan, their mother, was living at 23 Vine Street when she married Joe in 1899. The driving force of the family, despite a tough life in desperately poor circumstances, she lived long enough to see Bill holding up the FA Cup at Wembley in 1961. 'That must have been her proudest moment,' said Bill. 'Unfortunately, she wasn't fit enough to see the match in person and saw it on TV.' The 9-inch TV set was black and white.

Bill was just 19 when his father died (Edith died at the age of 83). Joe had always found it difficult to earn enough to keep a family of nine children and so Edith had to go out to work as a cleaner. The older brothers and sisters were expected to look after the younger ones; it was the only way to cope. When Bill became a manager, he observed: 'A football family is no different to a proper family: everyone has to help each other.'

All the children were born in a large, rented three-bedroom house with a sitting room, a scullery and a front room that was only used on Sundays. With an impressive archway, the building was part of the livery stables next door and Joe worked for a hansom cab company. Bill shared his father's love of horses and enjoyed mucking out the stables, often accompanying his father as he drove the carriage along the Scarborough's promenade in the summer months. He polished the brass harness, cleaned the carriages and rubbed oil on the horses' hooves.

Bill must have been kept busy because in those days, as today, the town was always under aerial attack from indiscriminate seagulls. In the winter, however, there wasn't quite so much work and it was hard to pay the bills. In the early thirties, when the horse and carriage became obsolete, the stables were turned into a garage, where charabancs (the posh word for coaches) were parked and it became a motorcar business.

Joe senior instilled his own willingness to work hard into his children and never once complained about the problems with his leg. 'No one ever talked about it,' said Bill. 'Yorkshire people in those days were private folk and it was looked on as bad manners to discuss other people's ages or their disabilities. I used to go out with him on the horse and carriage from a very early age. Every Sunday the cab would be used to take people to church in their best clothes and during the summer it would parade up and down the promenade and take customers to and from the station. It was hard work for a young boy, but I enjoyed it. Though I liked the horse, I was frightened of falling off when I was put into the saddle and never managed to ride it.'

Years later, Linda spoke of his love of big horses: 'He really loved them. When he and Darkie came over on a vacation to New Hampshire we went to see the Budweiser Clydesdale horses not far from where I live and the lady grooming them said she could tell he had worked with horses by the way he stroked one particular horse named Willie. He had a certain rapport with the horse and his eyes were smiling. I am sure it had nothing to do with the fact that Mum called him "Willie!"'

Scarborough, a hilly borough with a population of around 100,000, is thought to have been founded in 966 AD when a Viking raider named Thorgils Skarthi arrived in that part of north-east Yorkshire, although there is evidence that the Romans were there first. Famous inhabitants include Sir Alan Ayckbourn,

Hollywood actor and film director Charles Laughton, Sir Jimmy Savile, the Sitwell family, actors Ian Carmichael and Sir Ben Kingsley, TV journalists and presenters Selina Scott and Jon Snow. World War I poet Wilfred Owen convalesced there and Yorkshire fast bowler Freddie Trueman lived there for 17 years.

But the town has had few famous sportsmen and hardly any footballers of any class. Bill was probably the best. Next in line was Colin Appleton, the former wing-half who captained Leicester City in the 1961 FA Cup Final, which Bill Nicholson described as 'One of the worst Cup Finals ever played.' The other is Jonathan Greening, the West Bromwich Albion forward and captain. For someone like Nicholson, brought up in a far-off seaside town and sheltered from the stresses and strains of the big cities, to be plucked from that environment and sent to London on his own for a trial at Tottenham six weeks after his seventeenth birthday was an extraordinary and courageous story.

He loved Scarborough and leaving the town must have been a wrench for him. Besides his work alongside with his father, Bill did a newspaper round before going to school each day. He had to get up at 5am and earned 30p a week. 'It was a straightforward upbringing with the emphasis on hard work and reliance,' he recalled. 'We made toys and games for ourselves and simple things brought the greatest pleasure, like playing marbles or riding scooters. Scarborough was a good place to live.'

The town was built around two wide, sweeping bays and the castle, constructed in the 12th century on a headland, was constantly fought over and changed hands seven times during the Civil War. On 12 December 1916, two German warships, *SMS Derffliknger* and *SMS Von der Tann*, landed 500 shells on it and the surrounding area suffered widespread damage. After Elizabeth I died, Scarborough's fortunes changed and it became a fishing village. In 1627, local gentlewoman Mrs Farrow noticed that spring water was seeping through the side of the cliffs and showed signs of magnesium sulphur. An expert in the field informed her that the water was a cure for constipation, an ailment suffered by most people of the time. Suddenly Scarborough became a fashionable spa, attracting wealthy folk from all over the country. Unlike Bath, Tunbridge Wells or Buxton, it had the advantage of being on the coast and taking the waters had been introduced.

When Bill was growing up, food was relatively cheap. He recalled: 'There was little money to spare but we ate vast quantities of food, particularly on Sundays. The day started with a large traditional English breakfast, followed by a roast beef and Yorkshire pudding lunch, with tea later in the afternoon and then supper, the remainders from lunch served cold in the evening.' His parents were too busy to attend church themselves, but the children went to the Salvation Army Sunday School and later, an Anglican church. Jean Bell, Bill's younger daughter, born in 1948, said: 'My dad wasn't really religious, but he led a very moral life.'

Despite living next to the sea, Bill never tried swimming. 'My parents couldn't afford bathing trunks for us,' he said. 'So none of us were swimmers.' But he told his daughters that his grandchildren should be encouraged to swim and so Richard, Colin and Shaun started swimming after a year.

'Scarborough was a pleasant place to grow up in and we took advantage of living near one of the best beaches on that part of the country,' said Bill. 'I spent many happy hours on the beach and when the sun was out, it was very crowded. The ladies were dressed in long, black dresses and hats and carried parasols. The men wore suits and bowlers, or cloth caps. No one sunbathed and you never saw a naked torso. And there weren't many deckchairs either.

'The ugly-looking mobile huts on wheels were still there and were used to take people out to the boats or to swim, but not many people swam. The children would burrow away with their buckets and spades and we were encouraged to enter sand-building competitions. Sand artists used to build elaborate castles and replicas of all kinds of things. Horses were a speciality and people threw coins as a token of their appreciation.'

The huge Grand Hotel dominated the beach. In Bill's younger days, boys with a poor background might gaze wistfully up at the building, but they would never go inside. Jean said: 'I am pretty certain my father never went there. Most of his holidays were at Scarborough and when his mother was alive, we stayed with her. Later we stayed at one of the sisters, or sometimes at a small hotel.'

Bill once went on holiday to Israel, a rarity from the normal pattern of going back to his birthplace but in later life, he visited Spain, Portugal and Greece. He liked staying in good hotels – the kind denied him in his youth. The once grandiose Grand Hotel, which later became a Butlins, was completed in 1867 and the owner wanted it to represent a calendar so the property had four towers to show the seasons, twelve floors for the months and 365 rooms for each day of the year.

'I remember how cold it was when we went to Scarborough for our two-week holiday,' said Jean. 'It was always two weeks – my dad never took any more. When the tide went out, the sand was firm and he organised running games to keep us warm. We played all kinds of sport, including cricket. Dad played a few charity cricket matches, but he wasn't a club player.' Her sister Linda remembered: 'He always got us involved in as many sports as possible, even bowls. He thought it made you fitter and that's right, because my parents both lived into their eighties. He did find some time to relax in a deckchair, but the weather wasn't always kind in Scarborough but even then we'd play badminton or kick a ball about to keep warm.'

Her husband Steve, paying tribute at Bill's funeral in 2004, said: 'Bill was raised in a happy, close and loving working-class family, all in a small, terraced house, where his beloved mother ruled the roost. Bill spent any free time with his mates, kicking about a tin can or anything else that they could afford, usually in the alley behind the backyard. The neighbours must have been irritated, but the skills he learned obviously bore rich harvest. These same back alleys are now clogged with cars.

'Bill always enjoyed returning to his roots to see the Nicholson family and re-acquaint himself with Yorkshire. He knew the local streets like the back of his hand. The whole family knew the best fish and chip shops, greeted Auntie Mary's donkeys by name – just like old friends – and either got stuck into cricket on the beach, built sandcastles against the tide, investigated rock pools, or followed our most well-practised pursuit, sheltering from the rain. Sundays were spent up on the Yorkshire moors with a picnic near Goathland, always in the same spot.

'After he became a famous football manager, Bill tolerated having his picnic food presented on a paper plate on such occasions, but we all knew that he would rather have had it sitting at a decent dining table with a knife and fork. Evenings were often spent in the family home, where his older sister Edie continued to live. They played cards for pennies and Edie kept the change in an old tobacco tin. We were creatures of habit.'

CHAPTER THREE:
NIGHT TRAIN TO LONDON

Bill Nicholson was a late starter in 'proper' football – at the age of seven, he was presented with a rubber ball by a relative. It was 1926, the year of the General Strike. Jimmy Greaves said of his youth in east London: 'If you had your own ball, you were the king.' Similarly, Bill was captain in kickabout matches, usually played in narrow passages between back-to-back houses or on the hilly slopes around Scarborough. Two skippers tossed up – one had a stone hidden in a hand behind his back and asked 'Heads or tails?' The boy who won the toss always picked to play down the hill.

Every day they played on until it was almost dark. In those times, they made up their own rules and the strongest and keenest ended up on the winning side. There were no organised games for youngsters that age and later on, when the older boys were invited to attend clubs, coaches were scarce so these early practice sessions helped them to master the ball.

Amazingly, Bill never played senior football in the Scarborough League, only junior football. And the ground where he played organised football, Falsgrave Park, was on a slope with a drop of more than 30ft from one side to the other and unsuited to any activity except perhaps kite-flying. Frank White, a former footballer and now administrator, recalled: 'There was always a shortage of flat land in the town and Falsgrave, which is close to the reservoir, now has big white stones around it like Stonehenge. I think motorcyclists used it and that was probably the reason why they put the stones there.'

Children's entertainer Ron Anderson, who was born in the same year as Bill, said of him: 'I wasn't much of a footballer but one day the team was short and I played, and I soon recognised that he was much better than anyone else in the team. He was brilliant. I thought then he could be a professional.'

Bill admitted to not being an academic but after gaining above-average marks at the Gladstone Road Primary School, he was awarded a scholarship to the Scarborough Boys' High School at the age of 11. He was soon chosen as a centre half for the U14 side. Despite not being very tall, he was able to jump higher than most of his opponents and was more determined to reach the ball first. Geoff Hillarby, one of his nephews, recalled: 'The High School had a very good record and had some exceptional teachers. Bill could have gone on with his education, but I think he wanted to go into football. He was a very educated man.' His daughter Linda adds: 'He was very good at maths.'

Doreen Procter, a family friend whose brothers knew Bill well, spoke of his almost copperplate writing on Christmas cards. 'He wrote beautifully and I still have a letter from him,' she said. 'I also have one of his autographs. Today's footballers make a scrawl and you can't read it. Bill always took time to write his autograph so as people could read it. He was a very kind man and never forgot his family and friends.'

Eddie Wright, who met Bill occasionally around White Hart Lane, remembers: 'He always had time to talk to you about the club. The last time I met him was in 2004, in the car park inside the ground. I had my Double winning autographs with me and wanted him to sign. Although he had difficulty in writing, he stuck at it and it took about ten minutes to do it. God bless him, he eventually finished it. I have collected many autographs over the years, but this one will stay in my family forever.'

Bill's nephew Tony McKenzie said: 'He had the shakes towards the end and he would apologise for not giving an autograph but would say, "What about a shake of the hand instead?" and people thought that was wonderful.'

In the 1930s the leaving age for the High School was 14, but Bill stayed on for almost a year before starting work. He wasn't selected for the district side because he was still playing for his school, and he had to travel to similar institutions in faraway towns and cities such as York, Hull, Whitby and Malton. At this stage, he had never travelled beyond Scarborough and the boys had to pay their own fares. A match would usually cost a few shillings and one day his mother told him she couldn't afford it. The man who organised the team, C.B. Bradley, paid his fare. Bill bought his first pair of boots from the proceeds of his paper round and he knew they would have to last a long time. He repaired them himself, hammering away on his father's last in the stable.

Not having matriculated, he was forced to accept a menial job on leaving school: drying the clothes in the Alexandra Laundry for a weekly wage of £2. A photo taken of 16-year-old Bill has survived and it shows a serious young man with his arms crossed, wearing a tie and an apron, his sleeves rolled up ready for a hard day's work. He looked mature and older than his years. At that point, he hadn't considered a serious career and certainly not being a famous footballer.

Another character who loved football came into his life around this time: a dentist called Herbert Basil Jones, who ran the Young Liberals FC team, which played on Saturdays. No one in the Nicholson family admitted to supporting a political party but Bill fancied the yellows and he would soon become their best player.

According to Ron Anderson: 'The man who recommended him to have a trial with Tottenham was Albert Hollowood, who worked with me at Mr Jones's working-class dental practice as a dental mechanic. He came from Tottenham and was a Spurs fan.'

Early in March 1936, a letter written with a pencil dated 29 February and signed by Ben Ives, Tottenham's chief scout, arrived at 6 Quarry Mount in Scarborough – the family had moved from Vine Street – addressed to Mr and Mrs Nicholson:

Dear Sir or Madam,
This morning I have had a letter from Mr Jones re: your boy. I was very sorry I could not see you on Tuesday last week when I met your son and Mr Jones. He and I had a good chat with him and I expect you are awaiting a letter from me. I should put your mind at rest as regards to the welfare of your son. At present we have about 20 boys of his age and we get them good lodgings with personal friends of mine. Mr Jones will put him on the night train at York and I shall meet him at King's Cross, or should Mr Nicholson like to bring him down himself, he would be welcome. The boy seems to be very bright and I am sure he will get on here and in any case, I trust you realise that he must have a far greater chance of making headway in London than elsewhere.

Steve Bell, Bill's son-in-law, treasures that letter.

Years later, Bill admitted that he had no recollection of the meeting with the dark-haired, handsome Ives. 'My parents had never seen me play,' he said. 'They knew I was keen, but they had no idea whether I was any good or not. We weren't even sure where Tottenham was.' In those days, agents as such hadn't been invented and with his father unable to take the day off to travel with him to London, Mr Jones accompanied him to York and put him on the overnight train to London. The shy young man found his way down to the London Underground and made his first trip in the tube, getting out at Manor House before changing to an omnibus that took him up the High Road to White Hart Lane, where the main stand was still being built.

Bill's great adventure had begun. He had come from the far end of England, he had no video to show off his skills to a prospective boss, no letters of recommendation, nothing except a mysterious letter of recommendation from a man he had never met or even heard of. As Steve Bell observed: 'You can't see a boy, barely 17, travelling alone on a journey like that today. He was a very single-minded young man.'

Tottenham offered him a month's trial and he performed so well that he stayed with Spurs, a club he knew only vaguely, for 59 years as a player, coach, manager and consultant and ended up as the club's President. He was the one-club man par excellence, devoting his life to Spurs. The *Tottenham Weekly Herald* of 31 March 1936 announced his arrival: 'Spurs are giving a month's trial to an amateur, Wm. E. Nicholson, an inside right of Scarborough Working Men's Club. He recently celebrated his 17th birthday. His height is 5ft 8ins and weight 10st 12lbs.'

Ron Anderson was secretary of the Young Liberals FC (not the Working Men's Club FC, as reported) and some time later Spurs sent a donation of £25. It turned out to be the best bargain in the history of the club. Ron said: 'I remember Bill's headmaster telling him not to sign for Spurs. "There is no future in playing professional football," he said.'

Bill was soon kitted out for his first game in a Midweek League match against West Ham, a club to which he would later have a close affinity, and he was delighted to see that the pitch was heavily sanded – it reminded him of Scarborough's South Beach. Among the West Ham side he met a very chatty, charming East Ender named Dick Walker, later West Ham's chief scout. They became good friends and years later spent thousands of hours watching talent around the country with a view to signing the best. The club found nearby digs for Bill and after playing in the London

Combination reserve side over the Christmas and New Year holiday of 1937–8, he was given a professional contract with their nursery club, Northfleet United. Ron Burgess, Ted Ditchburn and Les Bennett were also loaned out. He was paid £2 a week, the same wage as the Alexandra Laundry. At the end of the season he won a Kent Senior Cup winners' medal in the final against Dover.

There were 48 professionals on the staff at White Hart Lane, a much higher number than most Premiership clubs today, plus eight ground staff boys. The boys were not permitted to enter the dressing rooms and there was hardly contact with the seniors. Juniors trained only twice a week, Tuesday and Thursday afternoons, but if their other work was finished, then they kicked a homemade ball – a bundle of old cloth tied into a ball – around under the stands. Much of their time was spent painting the grandstand and pulling the 6ft-wide fly roller in a wooden frame over the playing pitch. Often the mud was so deep that it was almost impossible to move the roller. By the end of the season, there was no grass on the pitch and the boys had to help the groundsman to reseed it.

Bill found painting a chore: 'I dreaded having to climb up the girders to do it,' he said, 'because I had no head for heights.' At school, he had lessons in carpentry, which came in useful when he was asked to build a shooting box for the players. It was an 8am to 5pm day, with a brief rest for a sandwich and a cup of tea, which is of course in marked contrast to today's young professionals with their sports cars and designer-clad girlfriends. As Frank Lampard Snr observed 60 years later: 'They should learn how to clean the senior players' boots to learn some respect.'

Every summer, Bill went home to Quarry Mount to stay with his mother. Frank White, who lived next door, remembered: 'They kicked small balls about between the back-to-back houses. People always came in from the back door, not the front, which was the posh end, with its lawn and brick wall.' The reason for this, apparently, was because Richard III introduced a 4p tax on householders using the front door in the 11th century and they still had the habit of going in the back entrance. When I visited that part of Scarborough, a car repair building opposite the Nicholsons' house had been replaced by 10 very smart detached houses and a notice on the wall said: 'Nicholson Estate Agents' (no relation).

Jack Tresadern, a small, dapper man from Leytonstone, was appointed manager of Tottenham from Crystal Palace and he hardly spoke to Bill in the two-and-a-bit seasons that he was in charge. Tresadern always wore a black Trilby and he didn't look like a manager. He was famed for being West Ham's skipper in the 1923 FA Cup Final, known as the 'White Horse Final', when he complained of being trapped by spectators – 200,000 got into Wembley, twice the number permitted – following David Jack's first goal. Tresadern told how he was unable to get back on to the field when the game resumed, but it made little difference to the result. In those days managers had little contact with the players – the trainer was the key man and he did the training, which mainly consisted of running round the track. The heavy leather balls were rarely seen until kick-off. Danny Blanchflower always joked about it when he first joined Barnsley before transferring to Tottenham: 'They kept the ball away from us because they thought we would be eager to get after it.'

Tresadern was unpopular with the fans and directors alike and left Spurs at the end of the 1937/8 season. The man who took over was Peter McWilliam from Inveravon, Banffshire, who managed the club between 1913 and 1927, and he helped to win the FA Cup Final in 1921 on a rain-soaked Stamford Bridge. For the first time, two kings – George V and his son, George VI – attended. Both were saturated and neither of them really liked football. McWilliam never gave tactical talks, preferring to leave the players to work things out for themselves. Instead, his strength lay in boosting their confidence.

Spurs were always renowned for their meanness and in 1927, Middlesbrough offered McWilliam £1,500 to become their manager. When Spurs refused to give him a rise, off he went. It took 11 years for them to get him back. He wasn't so successful that time around and retired to live in Redcar in 1942. Soon after Bill arrived in 1936, the new grandstand opened and there were more girders for him to paint. The cost of the stand, mainly of wood, cost £60,000. Financed by Barclays Bank, it equalled the club's profits since World War I.

Bill's shyness soon evaporated and he made friends with the other boys. One in particular was W.A.R. Burgess, who joined the club on the same day. Known as Ronnie, he was a thoroughly nice young man and the two became lifelong friends. Born in Cwm, south Wales in 1917, he learned his football by kicking balls on slagheaps above the river Ebbw and had just signed up as a coalminer when Tottenham called him up to White Hart Lane for a year's trial.

When his trial ended, Tresadern and his trainer thought he wasn't up to standard and so they gave him his rail fare back to Wales. Before Burgess headed off home, he went to watch the 'A' team. Finding they were one short, he volunteered to play and proved himself the most influential player in the team. He was promptly re-signed. In 1939, he was capped by Wales before joining the RAF. After the War, he captained Spurs for eight seasons, leading them to success in the Second Division and in the First in successive seasons, alongside Bill in the midfield. Burgess was one of the chief instigators of Arthur Rowe's push-and-run style of play, his stamina almost inexhaustible and probably derived from his running up and down on coal deposits as a boy.

When I interviewed Bill for his book in 1983 and 1984, I asked him who was the best player at Tottenham had produced in his time. There were plenty of candidates among those that he had worked with, including Greaves, Blanchflower, Mackay and White, but without hesitation, he told me: 'Ronnie Burgess. I liked him very much. He was genuine and honest, and although he later became captain, he was never afraid to seek advice. He was too nice a person to order people about and make decisions affecting their livelihoods, which was the main reason he was less successful as a manager than as a player. He was my favourite player. He had everything: good feet, ability in the air, strength in the tackle and was a beautiful passer of the ball. In some ways he resembled Bryan Robson, but I believe he was a better player than Robson.'

Was he better than Dave Mackay, I asked? He laughed. 'I'm not going into that,' he told me. 'I'm sticking with Ronnie!'

In 2004, the same year as Bill died, Burgess passed away at the age of 87. He was two years older. The two pals had testing lives but as a testament to their superb fitness and self-discipline, both lived to a grand age and kept close to their original playing weights throughout their lives.

Bill confessed to me that in his first months in London he wondered whether he might have a future in the professional game. He had no tricks – unlike his manager Peter McWilliam, who brought in the 'wiggle' when he played for Newcastle – but he made the best of his considerable assets: strength, stamina, the simplicity of his passing game and determination in the tackle. Some people thought he wasn't first team quality at the time and he was of the same view.

Bill was 19 and raw when he made his debut in the 1938/9 season: however, the first team left back Billy Whatley was injured and so he was forced to play out of position against Blackburn Rovers at Ewood Park. Rovers won 3-1, during which he strained a thigh muscle and had to play outside right in the final minutes because substitutions were still decades ahead. 'I cannot really remember anything about the game,' he said.

At the time he was the tenth-youngest player ever to have appeared in the first team.

CHAPTER FOUR:
'THE BEST THING I EVER DID'

In October 1939, Bill Nicholson was called up for military service and joined the Durham Light Infantry at Brancepeth Barracks. Brancepeth is a village five miles south west of Durham, no more than 65 miles from Scarborough. 'It was tiring work,' he recalled. 'When we first arrived, we had to drill with wooden rifles because the real thing was in such limited supply. I worked hard to pass the Cadre course and became a lance corporal and then a sergeant. Most of my six years in the Army were spent in Britain as an instructor, first in infantry training, which I knew little about, and then in physical education at Brancepeth.'

In World War I, hundreds of footballers were slaughtered, many of them with 'Unknown Soldier' on their gravestones because of the carnage and confusion on the battlefields. But in World War II, senior officers were intent on using footballers as trainers and role models. Few sportsmen fought at the front line. One exception was Captain Hedley Verity, the Yorkshire and England bowler, who died in a prisoner-of-war camp in Italy after being shot at Caserto in 1943. Eleven years older, Verity was a hero to Bill Nicholson while he was growing up and collecting cigarette cards of cricketers. In the winter months, each barrack room at Brancepeth was rationed to just one bucket of coal a day and soldiers often stole coal from any source they could find. To keep warm, they had to keep on moving and Bill was at the forefront, teaching large groups of men on 16-week courses.

Between 1939 and 1946, the Football League was suspended and the local professional clubs were not allowed to play in competitive matches, but friendlies were permitted and he made 15 appearances as a guest with Newcastle, Darlington, Hartlepool United, Middlesbrough, Sunderland and Fulham. Fan John Noble first saw him play when he was representing Darlington: 'He helped Darlington to be one of the best teams in England and one of the other quality guest players was Jimmy Mullen of Wolves. As kids we used to hang around outside the changing rooms, kicking a ball about, waiting for the players to come out, hoping they would join in. Bill Nick always did for a short time and that made our day. He was always smart in his uniform, ready to get the bus back to camp.'

In 1939, a quiet and reserved young Bill left north London but within weeks he was on his way to becoming a confident, authoritative lecturer, used to addressing huge numbers. It was no surprise that so many ex-Army people became football coaches when the Football League resumed in 1946. 'My experience proved invaluable because one of the prime requisites in coaching was being able to put your ideas over,' he said. His Army spell was extended when he was sent to the headquarters of the Central Mediterranean Forces in Udini, Italy. There he was fortunate to meet Geoff Dyson, the dynamic athletic coach, who later became the AAA coach. Bill recalled: 'Geoff was a fantastic organiser and lecturer and probably had more to do with my becoming a coach than anyone.'

The other person he met at that time who proved a strong influence was his first and only girlfriend, Grace Lillian Power, who lived at 17 Farningham Road, a few hundred yards from White Hart Lane. When he was first billeted out at Tottenham, he lodged at 23 Farningham Road, four houses up, and started taking her out. He came round almost every night and she later recalled: 'My father had a billiards table and he often used to come and play.'

Mr and Mrs Power had three daughters: twins Grace and Ivy and elder daughter Winnie, of whom Bill once admitted: 'I fancied her originally, but soon changed.' The family nicknamed the twins 'Darkie' and 'Fairy' because Grace was dark-haired and Ivy was fair. 'I detested the name Grace and I preferred Darkie,' explained Grace. Throughout her life, Grace's nickname continued despite the arrival of New Labour and political correctness. She died on 30 July 2007 at the age of 87 – in fact, all three sisters died within six months of each other. Daughter Jean said: 'She was a wonderful mother and everyone loved her. She always looked on the good side of life and never complained. Even after a particularly difficult visit to hospital, she thanked me for taking her and said she'd had a lovely day.'

Darkie called Bill 'Willie' and was the only person to use that name. Their daughter Linda described their relationship: 'I can see why she caught his eye when he lodged just up the road. You could tell they really loved each other and I think they were lucky to have each other.' The marriage took place at St Mary's Church, Lambsdown Road, Tottenham on 1 March 1942 during the groom's short leave from his regiment, with no time for a proper honeymoon. He was 23 and she was 21. Tony McKenzie, one of Bill's nephews, said: 'Darkie was always laughing and joking. She idolised him and she was always there for him – a perfect wife for a football man. Years later I sometimes stayed with them and she did all the cooking and Bill did all the washing up. They were happy days.'

The Nicholsons rented two attic rooms in Farningham Road for a while before moving to Commonwealth Road just around the corner. Living next door was Ted Ditchburn, the Tottenham goalkeeper who was born in Gillingham and played 418 appearances between 1946 and 1958. He was two years older than Bill and was able to buy a swanky American car, which he nicknamed 'the Dillinger'. The vehicle had running boards just like in the American gangster movies and, as Bill said, 'It needed some handling.' At the time Ditchburn had yet to pass his driving test.

It was eight years before Bill could afford his first car, a Morris series E. He didn't really need one: he could walk to work each day. In the early days of their marriage, the Nicholsons would cycle to Epping Forest on Sundays. It was a regular ritual. Commonwealth Road was hardly more than a Ditchburn drop-kick from White Hart Lane and Linda said: 'It was on the other side of the playing field behind the East Stand. Good job we grew up so close to the ground because we were able to see Dad at lunchtimes when we were in Coleraine Park Elementary School and later, when Tottenham County Grammar School was built. Sometimes fans knocked at the door and Dad was always very nice to them. Mostly I think they respected his privacy, though. We used to have budgerigars when we lived in Commonwealth Road and they spent a lot of time out of the cage. Later we adopted a stray cat. At first Dad didn't want to bring her into the house, but he ended up fussing over the cat more than anyone else.'

Most football managers take new jobs and moving around the country is often a trial for wives and children alike. Bryan Hamilton, the former Northern Ireland manager who played and managed at Ipswich, Everton, Millwall, Swindon, Tranmere, Wigan, Leicester and Norwich, once said he moved house on 18 different occasions. Bill Nicholson was the exception. He lived at Farningham Road and Commonwealth Road between 1936 and 1958 before first renting and then purchasing his detached three-bedroom in Creighton Road, two years later. Bill and Darkie lived in an area just under a mile from White Hart Lane for their happy marriage of 62 years, and in their final two years, they lived in nearby Potters Bar – an incredible record.

Darkie was an expert seamstress and was proud of her achievement in passing the City and Guilds exam, which enabled her to teach Home Furnishings and Upholstery at Tottenham Technical College. With new clothes in short supply – clothing coupons were needed to obtain them – she customised garments with other bits of material, very make do and mend. Linda recalled: 'In the War most people had to be strong characters because they never knew what was going to happen when they woke up the next day so they tried to make the best of everything and enjoy a simple life. I think that is a lesson for today's generation.'

Interviewed by Hunter Davies for his highly praised work, *The Glory Game*, Darkie was quoted as saying: 'We didn't have much of a social life together but I am not moaning. I accept it all. I understand why he has got so much to do. He knows that he's missed things. He would love to have been more of a family man because he loved his own family. Even though they didn't have much, they were very happy. Who would have thought when he arrived as a boy from Yorkshire in 1936 that he would be lord of it all at Tottenham? He's said many a time that there is only one job in football and that's playing. When you finish playing, the enjoyment ceases. He says it is a bastard of a job, being manager. That's the word he uses. All he watches for is mistakes, jotting them in his little pad. I'm for it if I don't get refills in time. It's his job to watch for mistakes and he doesn't enjoy it.'

Frank McLintock, Arsenal's driving captain in their 1971 Double, told a wonderful story about Darkie. 'She was an amazing lady, so highly regarded by everyone she met, and I often went to watch Tottenham's matches. One day I said to her: "It's a terrible job to park around White Hart Lane. You haven't got any ideas about it?" She said: "You know where I live, come and park at the back. Bill's got a couple of spaces. You can use one." So Arsenal's former captain, the hated figure, parked at the house of Tottenham's manager!'

Linda remembered: 'When Dad left the house he always had to

look immaculate. Darkie made sure his shirts were nicely ironed, but he always shined his shoes every morning; he loved shining all of our shoes. She did all the cooking and always had a cooked lunch ready for him because he was not often there for dinner. But he was always the one who had to time his boiled egg to perfection. Mum definitely played a big part in his success and I told her on many occasions how proud I was for her and Dad as well, keeping the household going and making sure the right things happened at the right time. When things went wrong, she generally had to fix them. I learned at a very early age how to put a plug on a new appliance and things like that!'

Darkie would stay up at night, waiting for Bill to return home from one of his scouting trips, and he would sound the horn of his car to let her know when he had arrived.

Joe Hulme, the famed England and Arsenal right-winger and Middlesex cricketer, was manager of Tottenham when Bill was demobbed in 1946. Joe was renowned for being one of the fastest wingers in the history of the game and in the 1932/3 season he scored 33 goals for Arsenal, a record for a winger in one season, and over his career he played in five FA Cup finals. Cristiano Ronaldo, who may be a shade quicker, has upped that scoring record considerably.

Joe was born in Stafford and starred with Blackburn, Arsenal and Huddersfield; he also scored 8,013 runs with 12 centuries for Middlesex (1929–39). He was appointed Tottenham's assistant secretary in 1944 and two years later took over from manager Arthur Turner, the accountant who became secretary and worked at White Hart Lane for more than 40 years. I knew Joe well – he worked for the *People* for many years and was very popular, always joking with the players.

When Bill reported back, Joe asked him: 'Do you fancy playing against Chelsea on Saturday?' He was enthusiastic and Joe said: 'You'll be up against Tommy Lawton.' He might have thought it was one of Joe's jokes: though Lawton was only 5ft 10in tall, he was the finest header of the ball in the game at that time, possibly ever. A year or two before, the two faced each other in an Army game and Bill, who was 5ft 9in, thought he had a good game against him. 'Don't worry,' said Lawton this time, 'you'll be okay.' Again, Bill used his expertise to nullify Lawton's powerful headers.

During the 1945/6 season, he played 11 League matches and joined a summer coaching course organised by Walter Winterbottom in Birmingham. Sir Stanley Rous, the 6ft 4in tall FA secretary who had been headmaster of Watford Grammar School and refereed the 1934 FA Cup Final, was the first person to think of starting coaching courses in the late thirties. Born in Oldham in 1913, Winterbottom played several matches as an amateur for Manchester United before a back injury ended his brief career. During World War II, he was head of PT at the Air Ministry and reached the rank of Wing Commander. After leaving the RAF, he was about to apply for the post of principal at Carnegie College (where he had worked earlier) when Rous offered him the job of England manager in 1946. Members of the FA Council knew little of Rous's surprise plan and shared the view of most managers and players that coaching was unnecessary. But Rous was a dominant figure and talked his colleagues round: eventually Winterbottom became the national manager and also, the national director of coaching. He held his jobs for 16 years, the same term as Bill's managerial career.

Bill soon signed up for the course and passed his Full Badge at the first attempt alongside Joe Mercer, Alan Brown, George Smith and George Ainsley. He recalled: 'Walter was an exceptional man. He had more influence over the game in England than anyone and he worked prodigiously hard. He travelled the country on his own, lecturing non-stop. He persuaded dozens and dozens of players to take up coaching and he was like a Messiah, spreading the word.'

Winterbottom observed: 'There were managers who didn't manage, they just signed cheques. It was player power, with the older players deciding the tactics. The game was nearly all long balls and there was a loosely created midfield. Nobody worked out even simple things.'

Winterbottom and his disciples, Bill among them, met considerable opposition. Because of his lack of top-class experience as a player, Winterbottom was branded a man who didn't understand the game. Journalists mocked him, but those who believed in him knew that he expanded their knowledge and made them better players and managers. Each year they would gather at their summer coaching conference to discuss the game and learn from each other. They didn't claim expenses for travelling: they paid their own.

In the next three seasons under Hulme, Tottenham finished sixth, eighth and fifth in the Second Division and Bill Nicholson missed just five matches out of 126. He was possibly the most consistent player of that time. Although he rarely made the headlines, his teammates realised he wouldn't let them down. Mostly he played on the right as a defensive wing half, but his supreme fitness enabled him to do plenty of attacking as well. It was a happy time and his daughters were born at home: Linda on 26 February 1947 and Jean on 1 October 1948.

'I was born in the middle of the Deep Freeze in 1947,' remembered Linda, who has now lived in the USA for more than 30 years. 'The country was covered with ice and snow for three months and there weren't many matches played. There was a snowstorm on the day and the midwife had problems getting to us. I'm certain that Dad wasn't present at both births – men didn't do that in those days. And I'm not sure he changed a nappy!'

There were some influential players under Joe Hulme and one of them, Vic Buckingham, who graduated from Northfleet in Kent – the same nursery club as Bill – had many interesting, educational talks with his teammate. He was a humorous, debonair man, who had also obtained his FA Badge at a young age and was always available to pass on his knowledge. Four years older, he went on to become an innovative coach with a worldwide reputation. He started out by coaching Oxford University and the amateur side Pegasus, who won the FA Amateur Cup under his direction (Pegasus was run by Professor Sir Harold Thompson, a powerful and destructive influence at the FA). Buckingham shared similarities with Danny Blanchflower – a wing half who created good things. He went on to manage Bradford, WBA, Ajax, Sheffield Wednesday, Fulham, Ethnikos, Barcelona and Seville. It was an impressive CV.

But another pioneering coach was about to enter Bill's life – Arthur Sydney Rowe was born in Tottenham, a 10-minute walk from White Hart Lane. He had a season with Northfleet before signing as a professional with Tottenham; between 1929 and 1939, he made 182 appearances when he retired because of a knee injury. Not many footballers of that time went through their careers without having a cartilage or two removed, leaving them with permanent limps. Thirty-three, he was a qualified coach and coached the Army team. He was successful with non-League Chelmsford City and they won both the Southern League and the Southern Cup in the same season. Six months before World War II broke out, he coached in Budapest and soon won the respect of board officials and players alike: 'I was enjoying it, but I was lucky to have got back to England before someone blew the whistle on me.'

Jimmy Hogan, a tiny winger from Burnley, was one of the earliest coaching pioneers when he coached the Dutch side in 1912, moved on to train the Austrian side two years later and coached the Hungarian and German sides in the 1930s. They liked his unorthodox style of coaching and he was revered in Hungary. His work contributed to the emergence of the Hungarian players after World War II, who went on to become the first country to beat England, 6-3 at Wembley, in 1953 and forced English football to look outwards, inside of inwards, finally ending their decades of insularity.

Arthur Rowe was offered a three-year contract from the Hungarian FA in late 1939, probably inspired by Hogan's reputation, but it was too late: the war had begun. With Tottenham finishing fifth in 1948/9, Joe Hulme was sacked and the directors made a surprise appointment – the Chelmsford City manager Arthur Rowe, one of their own.

Walter Winterbottom, Joe Mercer, Ron Greenwood, Bill Nicholson, Arthur Rowe, Vic Buckingham and Jimmy Hogan loved football with a passion and wanted to improve it, to make it more entertaining. These coaches weren't in it for the money or material goods: they never besmirched the game and they upheld the old, true Corinthian creed of fair play. Bill Nicholson typified that approach.

On 5 May 1949, the signing of Alf Ramsey was complete and Rowe, who had been appointed on 4 May, now had another strong voice in his dressing room. But there was one essential difference: Ramsey didn't go in for coaching and had his own opinions about how the game was played.

CHAPTER FIVE:
ARTHUR ROWE'S ELECTRIC SHOCKS

B etween 1949 and 1955, Arthur Rowe introduced a way of playing the game that transformed Tottenham into a championship side and was also copied by clubs around the world. It was called 'push and run'. Peter Barnes, secretary of Tottenham between 1982 and 2000, observed: 'Arsenal play that way today. They are the only club who use it and I still think they are the best footballing side in the Premiership. I love watching them.'

It came from the streets. Rowe learned his football kicking small balls against walls and kerbs and Bill Nicholson did the same, as did Alf Ramsey. Using a wall to collect a 'pass' became an essential part of coaching under Walter Winterbottom, although these days the tactic is rarely used, but it is a difficult art to defend against because of the speed with which it is executed. In 1949, when Ramsey was introduced to the players by his new manager Rowe gave him number 12 locker, next to Bill.

The award-winning writer Leo McKinstry, author of *Sir Alf*, claimed the two men had an awkward relationship and in his autobiography, Bill said: 'He would have been a fine player in any era. As a person, he was not an outward going type. He had a history in the East End, we were led to believe, and no one asked him about it. He was eager to acquire knowledge and you had the impression he was storing it up for when he became a manager. He wasn't the type to share it.'

Ramsey's 'history' concerned the rumour – which he always strenuously denied – that he came from gypsy stock and was ashamed of his background, so he took elocution lessons.

One of the last 'tennis ball players' famous for his wall passing was Trevor Brooking and in his autobiography, he said: 'I used to run along the pavement kicking a tennis ball against the garden fences, controlling the rebound. Time and time I would repeat this and I think this early training may account for why I was looked on as a fairly skilful player. I also worked on kicking with both feet.'

No one knows for sure who first used the 'wall' pass, which has since gone into football manuals as part of the game, but Arthur Rowe took it to a higher level. He didn't like the phrase 'push and run': 'That was the label they came to pin on our style although, quite honestly, I was never fond of it. You often saw something like our style happening in a match, a side suddenly stringing together short, quick passes and players moving intelligently to give and take them. It is as if the game suddenly got an electric shock. The thing about the Tottenham side I had was that we tried to make it happen all the time. I never told anybody how to play. I just made suggestions on playing patterns, put up ideas. I'd ask players if they had ever tried a certain move, talk it over with them, get them to talk about it themselves, then we would try it out.'

Ramsey was encouraged not to over-use his longer passes down the right and fit in with the team pattern, with Bill Nicholson covering in front of him. The longer the pass, the more likely the ball would go astray, said Rowe. Short passes tend to be more accurate. Eddie Baily, chief joker of the team, recalled: 'Arthur had arrived at a club of natural footballers. He didn't come in with some great system and tell us exactly what to do. He encouraged us in certain directions, got us thinking, trying things and then, when it all came together, he would say, "That's it, that's the way to play." Rowe was always using phrases like "make it simple, make it quick". He would leave notes in the dressing room about his team and how they should get maximum results from these tactics.'

Later, when Bill became manager, he copied these mini-slogans to show them to his players. 'You have to keep reminding players what they should be doing because few of them are capable of acting instinctively,' he said, rather critically. Another weakness of the professional player is that often they will forget their instructions in the tense minutes before kick-off. A short, snappy phrase is much more useful than a speech.

According to Bill, Eddie Baily was Alf Ramsey's closest friend, despite being opposites. 'They shared a room on away trips and got on well,' he recalled. 'Eddie was the best first-time passer of a ball I ever saw. He was a quick-witted character and I remember one match against Huddersfield in the 1951/2 season, he drove the ball against the referee from a corner, collected the rebound and chipped to the near post, where Len Duquemin headed in a goal which condemned Huddersfield to the Second Division.

'The referee allowed the goal but Huddersfield claimed, quite rightly, that Law 17 says a player cannot touch the ball after taking a corner kick until another player has touched it. I said to our players: "There's nothing we can do. It's the ref's decision, not ours." In professional football you don't own up as a fielder does when he admits that a "catch" hit the ground before it was completed. One day you can be on the receiving end.'

Rowe considered Eddie Baily one of the finest one-touch players he had ever seen. 'I never saw a man who could play the moving ball either way and with either foot as quickly or as accurately,' he said. 'One-touch play is like hitting the highest notes in music: it cuts out the marker and enables the receiver to have extra time for his next move.'

Playing push and run meant that Tottenham nearly always had the ball more than their opponents, and seeing it zipping everywhere in tight triangles tired their opponents more than themselves. 'It demanded maximum fitness because it was not possible to play that way unless all ten of the outfield players were 100 per cent,' explained Bill. 'In the 1949/50 season, when we were promoted with 61 points, we only used 13 players and we were lucky as regards injuries. I believe good players are injured far less than average or poor players. If they are playing in a good side, there is a continuity about the play and they are supported to the hilt by their colleagues – they are not left to struggle on their own. There is always someone to pass to and Liverpool used to play like that in their title championship seasons.'

Ted Ditchburn had to change his way of distributing the ball. Asked why he kept throwing the ball out (which was unusual in that era) instead of kicking it, he admitted: 'It suits me because I'm such an awful kicker of it.'

Phil Soar, in his admirable history of Tottenham, *And The Spurs Go Marching On*, wrote: 'Rowe's push and run swept Spurs to the top and they stayed there almost the rest of the season. Nobody could have bargained for such a dramatic impact in the new manager's first season. Ronnie Burgess and his boys powered away on an unstoppable run from the 2-0 defeat at Plymouth on August 31 until Leeds halted them on January 14, an unbeaten sequence of 22 League matches. It meant from the beginning of September until the season closed on May 6, they stood astride the Second Division.'

Indeed, they won 27 games, eight more than any other club and ended with nine points ahead of Sheffield Wednesday.

Ditchburn and centre half Harry Clarke didn't miss a game and at the end of one victory, Harry complained to Bill: 'I only touched the ball nine times – I didn't get a kick or a header. You're mopping everything up on one side and Ron Burgess on the other.' When he was manager, Bill always wanted a very tall defender – Clarke was 6ft 3in – and Maurice Norman was his first and later, Mike

England. 'It is imperative to have one like that,' he observed. 'Some critics complain when they see the ball chipped into the box and say it is boring, repetitive and unproductive. I think we don't see enough of it. An accurate chipped pass is the most effective means of finding a way through a crowded area and one of the faults in the game is that there are few wingers. We had Sonny Walters on the right and Les Medley, who only played 150 games in six years before he went to Canada, on the left. He could beat opponents in great style and put over inch-perfect crosses. He was much quicker than he looked and his specialty was to appear suddenly in the inside right position, shout for the ball and thunder it into the back of the net. Few players can do it. In post-war football there was no one capable of surpassing the pinpoint accuracy of John White.'

Born in Edmonton, Medley was the top scorer, converting 18 of the 81 goals Tottenham scored. When he shot, it was with bullet-like ferocity – 'Cec Poynton, our trainer, used to say, "I never saw him. Where did he come from?"' The amateur George Robb took over, but he wasn't as quick and he too had knee trouble. Bill considered his inside forward Les Bennett to be the exception to the rule about push and run: 'He liked to hold the ball and run with it. He shaped to pass and then dummy his opponent, and he had what all midfield players need: stamina. Though he gave the impression of not tearing about, he was always on the move.'

Unlike some of their successors, few of Burgess's players were heavy drinkers. 'They drank a pint or a lager, but weren't big drinkers,' said Bill. 'But some of them were heavy smokers – Les Bennett, Arthur Willis, Ted Ditchburn, Sonny Walters, among others. Later, there was hardly a single smoker left in the squad. They were more health conscious.' In that period, Bill was earning £8 a week. 'We didn't worry about money,' he continued. 'You were in the team: that was enough. Like most of groups of young men, we liked a laugh and a joke and practical jokes were common.' Good-quality winning football attracts spectators and Tottenham averaged 54,405 in the 1949/50 season: 3,024 more than Arsenal. They topped 50,000 in 15 matches and on 25 February, 70,305 watched the match against Southampton, which they won 4-0. The crowd was tightly packed, almost crushed in some parts, with most of them standing. Segregation hadn't been heard of and boys, accompanied by their fathers, were handed over the heads of men ahead so they could see down at the front. It was rare to see any women.

'Hooliganism, tribal fights and exchange of insults were practically non-existent. There was no thuggery in our game,' recalled Rowe. 'We did it in style, no jealousies, all pals together. The roar of the crowd keyed the players on and it was stimulating, enthralling entertainment.' Around 1.5 million spectators turned up that season and that record has never been beaten.

The 1950/1 season started with a 1-4 defeat by Blackpool, but six successive wins put them on the way to winning their first championship of the First Division. There was an unusual happening on 9 November when half of the first team beat Cambridge University, coached by Bill Nicholson, 2-1; on the same day the other half drew 0-0 with Oxford University, whose coach was Vic Buckingham. The impression to be drawn was that University football was of a much higher standard then.

Nine days later, a full-strength Tottenham beat Newcastle, that season's FA Cup winners, 7-0, with Medley and Baily scoring hat tricks. Rowe admitted: 'When it was flowing like that, I would sit there transfixed. I was jealous for them, anxious that they should do justice to themselves. That was the only pressure, the rest was sheer pleasure.'

Seven of the players came from a short radius to White Hart Lane, a tribute to the excellence of the work of chief scout Ben Ives. The win bonus was just £2 and only two of the players, Ditchburn and Burgess, had cars. Rowe lived in Clapton and he was 34 before he owned a car. Often he caught a bus to Tottenham High Road and most times he had to stand. Fans would ask him about the prospects for another victory; also the likelihood of a Double. But there was no chance of a Double because they lost 2-0 to their bogey side, Huddersfield, in the third round of the FA Cup. Bill Nicholson played 41 out of the 42 matches, scoring one goal.

In those days Christmas was a busy time for footballers. On 23 December Rowe's side beat Arsenal 1-0, then drew 1-1 at Derby on Christmas Day and on Boxing Day beat Derby 2-1. The championship was won in their 41st League match: a hard-earned 1-0 victory over Sheffield Wednesday who were relegated. Matt Busby's Manchester side were runners-up, for the fourth time in five seasons.

In those days the players' gear was much more conservative – no advertising, only a simple, small motif of the cockerel on a plain white shirt, long sleeves (usually rolled up), medium-length black shorts and the distinctive socks, almost half-white and the rest black. The tough leather boots and hard toecaps gave much more protection than modern footwear and all the players used white laces. There were rather small baths to wash in, hardly bigger than today's Jacuzzis, and up to eight players squeezed into them. Arthur Rowe made some money from designing a new football boot – 'The Arthur Rowe' – and everyone was buying them.

Eddie Baily recalled how they trained in those days: 'We hardly ever saw a football, but plenty of medicine balls to build our stomach muscles. We wore old sweaters to make us sweat and we did 18 or so laps, two laps running and two walking in succession, punched the punch balls and finished up skipping. Often we brought a ball ourselves and played 18-a-side matches by a pub. Bill was the first manager to use the football nearly all the time when he took over.'

Bill missed five League matches in the 1951/2 season and scored his usual one as Tottenham were pipped by Manchester United for the championship. He said it was a wet season and the White Hart Lane pitch resembled a morass for much of the winter. The directors decided to put in a new pitch and 3,500 tons of earth was taken away and dumped on Hackney Marshes. In its place 2,000 tons of new topsoil was put in, with 25,000 turfs laid on top.

But the pitch was never a good one until recent years, mainly because of the lack of circulating air through the absence of gaps in the corners. As the season ended, the club started a series of 12 friendlies, the first one held in Paris on 3 May and the final one on 18 June in Quebec. During the voyage, most of the players were seasick but Denis Uphill, one of the reserve players, recalled: 'We travelled across the country by train and usually stayed in big log cabins. Canada was terrific, very different to post-war Britain, much more open.'

Despite the amount of travel, Bill thought the series was well worth it, but Rowe's artists were losing their bloom: Bill made just 31 League appearances and failed to score his usual goal in the following season when the club finished tenth. At 33, he was thinking about a career as a manager.

In 1953/4, Tottenham ended sixteenth and Rowe brought in new players, some of them unable to play the type of football he required. He was harshly criticised for being too loyal to his older players, the strain was affecting his health and his doctor advised rest: he was heading for a breakdown. Jimmy Anderson, a former groundstaff boy who joined the club in 1908, but never made a senior appearance, became stand-in manager. He had filled most jobs, including secretary. Now 65, he celebrated 50 years with Tottenham. Bill explained: 'I was asked to take over the coaching because Jimmy was more of a desk manager.'

Earlier in the season, Bill had told Rowe: 'I'm not as fit as I used to be. Perhaps it is time you put someone else in my place.' It was a remarkable thing to say. Hardly any player would volunteer to drop out – they all want to play as long as they can. 'I felt it was an honest way of going about it,' he revealed. 'By speaking up, I was making it easier for him. As a manager later on, I had to leave many players out and it was not a pleasant task.'

In fact, Rowe was such a nervous man by this time that he didn't like confronting players with bad news. Nicholson had helped him out and he was grateful.

At the end of the season Bill saw the club doctor about a sore knee and was referred to a specialist, who recommended 'to remove some floating bodies', as the dreaded phrase goes. Today's specialists still say the same thing, except they have the equipment to do the work without cutting open the skin and leaving a scar.

Often the operations of 50 years ago went wrong, but Bill was lucky – although he had a scare in the close season while walking in Bridlington during his two-week summer holiday in North Yorkshire. 'The knee suddenly seized up and I couldn't move,' he recalled. 'I was taken to Scarborough Hospital, but the tests could find nothing wrong and I spent a month in hospital before discharging myself. Back at White Hart Lane, I walked on sticks for a while before full movement was restored.'

In all, he missed more than half the season and made just 10 appearances. Tottenham were still struggling, finishing in sixteenth place again. Burgess departed to Swansea, leaving a gap which couldn't be filled.

Rowe once said that outstanding teams only stay on top for three years before they decline. That might well be true about Nicholson's Double side too, which followed the same pattern. But with Rupert Murdoch's billions poured into the bigger clubs since 1992, Manchester United, Liverpool and Chelsea are all set to stay ahead unless the banks foreclose on them.

With coaching taking up so much time, Bill retired as a player in the 1954/5 season: he had a record of 306 Football League appearances and just six goals. He would have passed 550 appearances and maybe he might have reached double figures with goals, but for six years serving his country. Eddie Baily said: 'He was a very reliable player and when he started putting his boots on, we didn't have any worries about him. We knew he wouldn't let us down. I asked him, "Who was the player who gave you most trouble?" and he said, "Jimmy Logie of Arsenal. He used to turn me inside and out."'

After months of recuperation, Rowe declared himself fit and resumed his managerial duties. He consulted Bill about buying a creative midfield player and was keen to sign Danny Blanchflower as his replacement. 'Get him,' advised Bill. 'He's a highly intelligent and skilful footballer.'

Though he had played his last senior game, Bill volunteered to play in the reserves and 'A' team to help the younger players – another unselfish act – and missed the FA Cup defeat at York at Bootham Crescent on 19 February when Spurs were humiliated 3-1 on a pitch covered in snow and ice. Blanchflower described it as the worst atmosphere he had experienced at a football club. The defeat affected Arthur Rowe so badly that he was sent home, suffering another breakdown. Jimmy Anderson, who always wore plus-fours (a way of tucking the trouser into the sock), was appointed manager.

I became a good contact of Arthur Rowe in his later life with Crystal Palace and he was a very kindly, cheery but sensitive man who loved talking about the game, encouraging young players and infusing them with his passion. He recovered and went on to become coach at West Bromwich Albion, and between 1958 and 1971 he took a number of posts at Crystal Palace, from manager to secretary. He had yet another breakdown in the 1962/3 season and briefly returned as manager in 1966. Well into his seventies, he was still acting as a consultant with Millwall.

During his last years he was showing signs of Alzheimer's, the disease that seems to particularly affect ex-footballers after years of heading the heavy leather balls used in previous decades. Olaf Dixon, assistant chief executive of the League Managers' Association, told a very sad story about him: 'Chris Hassall, who was Crystal Palace's secretary for many years, told me once that a police officer was crossing one of the bridges over the Thames in the middle of winter and saw an old man in a short-sleeved shirt and no jacket, and he asked, "Are you all right, sir? Can I help?" The old man said, "My old club is in trouble and I've got to see them and sort them out." He was Arthur Roswe and he was talking about Tottenham.

'The policeman made the arrangements to take him back to his residential home. Arthur's wife couldn't look after him and she lived some miles away and found it difficult to visit him by bus. The League Managers' Association don't have large reserves, but they have a fund to help out in these circumstances and we paid for her taxi visits until Arthur died at the age of 87.'

CHAPTER SIX:
AN EARLY GOAL

Bill Nicholson scored a goal with his first kick on his England debut, at Goodison Park on 19 May 1951... and was never picked again. But he was chosen on 22 occasions as a reserve on the bench. Most footballers would have been resentful, but not him. 'I accepted the situation because I was in competition with Billy Wright, who was a better player,' he explained. 'Billy was a versatile player, like me, and could play in midfield or centre back. He was not a particularly classy player but was very consistent and hardly ever had a bad game. He was short in height, as I was [Wright was an inch shorter than Bill, who was 5ft 9in], and both of us were able to jump well. I liked him. He was similar to me in many ways, with no pretensions. He was a down-to-earth person, who was respected by everyone. Walter Winterbottom insisted on high standards and he was the ideal choice as captain because he upheld those standards. I was just pleased to be involved.'

Born on 6 February 1924, Billy Ambrose Wright was also a one-club man and both men were never sent off or suspended. Both were awarded the OBE, while Billy won 105 caps to Bill's single cap; had Billy incurred a serious injury, the figures might well have been different, but he maintained a high standard of fitness until the end of his career. Billy was not quite 100 per cent for the Goodison Park game but he was fit for the next match in October and never lost his place until he retired in 1959. By that time he had switched from the No. 4 to the No. 5 shirt and played at centre half, not wing half.

After World War II, English footballers were among the best in the world and other wing halves such as Ronnie Clayton of Blackburn (who took over from Wright as captain), Bill McGarry, Len Phillips, Ken Armstrong, Ron Flowers and Jimmy Dickinson were chosen over Bill.

At the time of writing, Bill still holds the England record for scoring the fastest goal on a debut, just 19 seconds. He said: 'The ball came to me and I lobbed it forward. Stan Pearson nodded it back and I ran on to let go a first-time shot which, from the moment I hit it, I knew was going in.' He wasn't swamped by his colleagues, or patted or embraced. Several players congratulated him verbally and they got on with the game. England won 5-2 with Jackie Milburn, who scored two goals, and Sir Tom Finney, whose club name of Preston North End should be inscribed on his heart; Harold Hassall of Huddersfield and Bolton were the other scorers. The previous record holder was John Cock of Huddersfield and Chelsea, who scored his goal in 30 seconds, in 1920. John, who was also known as Jack, scored again in his second game, though not so quickly, and was never picked again. Tommy Lawton claimed the overall record, but not on debut, scoring after 17 seconds.

Harold Hassall, now 80, played for England only five times and is one of the survivors of the Portugal victory. 'Everyone was delighted when Bill put that one into the net because he was well liked,' he recalled. 'But it wasn't enough for him to be selected again. In those days there were a lot of good players around and

Walter Winterbottom had a lot to choose from. Dear old Walter, as we called him, liked being the boss. One player gave him a chit for his rail fare and he looked at it and said to him, "You've overcharged us and that won't happen again." He never chose him again.

'Bill had a wonderful team in the sixties, and Arsenal play a similar style today, but it's all about speed and money today and you can't compare teams from different eras. I start watching these games on TV and often I switch off before half time because you rarely see a shot at goal.'

These past heroes should really be known as the 'Titanium Men' because of the metal in their joints. Harold, who still plays golf, has had two hip replacements and one knee replacement.

According to Hunter Davies when he interviewed her in 1972, Darkie was present when Bill made his England debut. 'That was one of the very few matches she ever saw him play,' he revealed. 'She'd like to go and watched every match avidly on television and read the sports pages, but he considers her a Jonah.' He quoted her saying: 'Basically, he doesn't think women have any place in football. I feel an outsider really, as if I was a member of the opposition. Bill was picked for the next match after the game at Goodison Park, but he was injured and called off. He said he wanted to get fit for Spurs rather than England. Spurs paid his wages and it was his duty to get fit for them. Not that I ever tried to persuade him – I've never been involved in any of his decisions. I see it all from the wings. I don't know what his salary is today; he never tells me and I wouldn't ask. I don't know what he's saved either. I think he's got money in a building society because I've seen the letters, but I really don't know much about anything like that.'

Bill had to wait three years for his debut and at the age of 32, he was well aware that he wouldn't have a long international career. He was first included in the England squad in 1948 for the friendly against Italy on 16 May 1948. Italy were world champions in 1934 and 1938, while England were yet to enter the World Cup but were looked on as the second-best side in the world, mainly within their own borders. George Hardwick was England's captain, but he was injured and Frank Swift was appointed in his place, a popular decision made by Winterbottom.

When the aircraft landed at Milan Airport, the England players were astonished to see a huge crowd – newspapers reported that 10,000 or more fans had turned out to welcome them. 'We were treated like liberators,' Bill said. 'Never had I encountered such enthusiasm and hospitality.' England won 4-0: Tom Finney starred with two goals and Stan Mortensen and Tommy Lawton scored the remainder. Bill recalled: 'To win by such a convincing margin was unparalleled. If there was a peak in the history of the England football team, that was possibly it, surpassing even the home win over West Germany in the 1966 World Cup. The only player who didn't receive acclamation was Wilf Mannion, but I never knew why he should have been singled out.

'Our team that day must rate as one of the best we've sent abroad – Frank Swift, as fine a keeper as this country has ever produced and a great character; full backs Laurie Scott of Arsenal and Jack Howe of Derby, both dependable players; Neil Franklin, the centre half with Billy Wright and Henry Cockburn the wing halves, and the forward line consisted of Stan Matthews, Stan Mortensen, Tommy Lawton, Wilf Mannion and Tom Finney. I don't think there has been a better England forward line than that and Geoffrey Green, the doyen of the soccer writers, said: "What a string of jewelled names! They caress the palate like a smooth wine."'

Three hours before the kick-off, the ground was filled with 75,000 noisy, jabbering Italians. Bill recalled that it was impossible to have a conversation because of the hubbub. Matthews laid on the first goal for Mortensen after four minutes, while Spanish referee Escartin disallowed two 'goals' for offside; the Italians struck the crossbar and Swift made two wonderful saves from Carapellese. Bill always thought Finney was the better, all-round player than Matthews: 'They were both great footballers, but I shared the view of Bill Shankly that Finney was the more complete player. Tom could play in all five forward positions and was very strong for his size and could withstand the roughest of treatment from defenders. He could score with either foot and was useful in the air, too. Stan concentrated on his primary task of creating goals and he must have laid on many hundreds of goals in his long career.

'When I took over at Tottenham, I asked Cliff Jones (or whoever was playing on the left) to drop back and cover Stan, giving him two opponents to beat and he never liked that. Both Tom and Stan had long and distinguished careers without being injured too often which bore out my point that the good players are rarely hurt.' Thirteen cameras recorded the match and next day it was shown in the city's cinemas. There were queues for that, too. Shop windows showed pictures of the England team saying: 'Made in Britain'.

A year later, most of the Turin players who took part in that match died in Italy's most tragic air disaster. 31 people died, including 18 players, when their plane flew into a thunderstorm and crashed into the hill of Superga, near Turin.

In the next season, Bill was a reserve and watched England's 2-0 win against a newly created Italian side at White Hart Lane. The previous international was at Stockholm and he watched incredulously as skipper Billy Wright decided to kick into the sun in the first half. His friend Ted Ditchburn was chosen and though he wore a cap, to shield his eyes from the sun, he couldn't see the ball properly and conceded three goals in a 3-1 defeat. Ditchburn was at fault for two of them, but Bill said: 'I thought Billy Wright was more at fault by kicking the wrong way.'

Ditchburn took four years to regain his place and his six appearances spread over seven years. Bill had a common sense approach to the game and he didn't need a coaching manual to tell him about the problems of the sun. His professionalism never wavered, whereas Billy Wright sometimes made casual errors that later brought an abrupt end to his managerial career at Arsenal.

Bill was there at Belo Horizonte, in Brazil, on 29 June 1950 – England's Pearl Harbor day of infamy when the USA won 1-0 in the biggest upset in the history of the World Cup. He was shocked at the amateurish way in which the FA dealt with England's introduction to World Cup football. Temperatures were expected to reach the eighties with high humidity but instead of acclimatising themselves to the heat in Brazil, they trained at a non-League ground at Dulwich Hamlet FC at Dog Kennel Hill (the FA had decided that it was too costly to go earlier).

Stan Matthews had been overlooked and was playing for an FA XI in Toronto when FA secretary Sir Stanley Rous told Arthur Drewry, the leader of the England squad, that Matthews should be switched to Rio. The press was clamouring for Matthews to be called up and so Drewry relented. A week before the start of the tournament in Rio de Janeiro, the party arrived and stayed at the Luxor Hotel on the noise-filled Copacabana Beach.

'When I inspected the kitchens, I was almost sick,' said Winterbottom. 'Nearly all the players went down with tummy upsets at one time or another.' Prankster of the squad Stan Mortensen (with Eddie Baily) joked: 'Even the dustbins had ulcers!' The players were upset to learn that no doctor had been called out.

Jimmy Dickinson, the svelte midfield player from Portsmouth, was named ahead of Bill in the first England side to take part in a World Cup tie and an unimpressed crowd at the Maracana Stadium saw them beat a Chile team 2-0 consisting of ten amateurs and one professional: Newcastle United's George Robledo. Matthews wasn't selected after Arthur Drewry insisted, 'We should keep an unchanged side.' Finney was moved to the right and Jimmy Mullen of Wolves was on the left.

The squad travelled by bus to the British-owned Morro Velho goldmine, 16 miles away, for the second match and stayed in primitive, wooden chalets normally used by miners. Even so, this was a big improvement on the Luxor Hotel. Arriving at the ground, they noticed the narrow pitch had coarse, uneven grass and was covered in small stones. Winterbottom was so upset at the state of the newly built dressing rooms that he took the players off to change at a local athletic club, ten minutes away. Back at the ground they were greeted by 20,000 unfriendly fans kept behind concrete walls surrounding the pitch.

The US team were all born in the USA except for three: skipper Glasgow-born Eddie McIlvenny, who had been given a free transfer by Wrexham three years previously and who signed up with Philadelphia Nats to qualify, rather mysteriously, for his new adopted country; full back Joe Maca (born in Belgium) and the Haitian Joe 'Larry' Gaertjens, who scored the only goal. Alf Ramsey described the goal as a million-to-one shot and his antipathy towards Scots may well have started then when he learned that a Scotsman named Billy Jeffrey of Penn State assembled and coached the team to their unexpected success.

Bill watched from the back of the stand, which he had to reach from a ladder. 'I was close to the press corps, who couldn't believe what was happening any more than we could,' he recalled. 'The match should have ended 10-0 for England, but instead a deflected goal earned the victory for the unrated USA. Most of the big names took part – Wright, Mannion, Mortensen, Finney, Jimmy Mullen and Dickinson, who was a consistent player who never let anyone down. You couldn't say England played badly – it was simply that the ball wouldn't go into the net. The players afterwards sat in the dressing room almost in a state of shock, not saying a word. We were looked on as one of the favourites to win and we'd lost to the 1,000:1 outsiders.'

The goal in the 37th minute was a fluke. A hard shot was going straight to Bert Williams, the Wolves goalkeeper standing on the goal line, until the ball hit Gaertjens (who was only three yards out and unmarked) on the back of the neck and changed direction, leaving Williams stranded. Gaertjens was carried off at the end by a moustachioed man dressed in white and another wearing a tie and a black suit. A yard or two ahead a man in white trousers lay face down on the ground and kissed the spot where Gaertjens scored.

Some time later the unfortunate Gaertjens died in prison after joining an attempted coup to remove Papa Doc Duvalier in Haiti. Meanwhile, Finney described it as the darkest day in his life and Mannion declared, 'Bloody ridiculous! Can't we play them again tomorrow?'

Three days later, England kicked off against Spain in front of 74,462 spectators, less than half the capacity of the Maracana Stadium in a temperature of 105 degrees. Again there was no place for Bill. Another Bill, Eckersley, Milburn, Baily and Matthews came in for John Aston, Mannion, Roy Bentley and Mullen; though England played well in the first half when a 'goal' was disallowed by Italian referee Giovanni Galeati for offside, they failed to score. Zarra headed in the only goal in the 49th minute and Spain played defensively for the rest of the game. The Brazilians booed them off: England were out at the first stage.

Afterwards, the football writers wrote scathingly of Winterbottom and his players but most of their venom was directed at the amateur officials of the FA. Drewry, a fishmonger from Grimsby, stayed on the FA Council and five years later, he was appointed chairman. Until the appointment of Ramsey as Winterbottom's successor in 1962, the FA councillors still picked the England team, which accounted for so many changes over the years. They always voted for their favourites in their own clubs and Winterbottom couldn't do anything about it. It was sabotage from within.

Bill said: 'The councillors tended to press for the inclusion of their own players, which partly explained why players from Portsmouth, Sunderland, Birmingham and a few other unfashionable clubs won caps. When Alf took over, he insisted on picking the team himself and the FA let him do it. Only one person can pick a team – the man who coaches and works with it. He knows the players and their moods.'

Bill liked to go on pre-season or summer tours and learned a lot from players all around Europe. In 1951, a newspaper arranged a challenge match in Brussels between Tottenham (reckoned to be the leading club in England at the time) against FC Austria, the best club in Austria. The match ended 2-2 – penalty shootouts hadn't been thought of – and the captains had to toss to decide which club should receive the trophy. The referee showed Ron Burgess a coin and not knowing much about it, Ron mumbled something in his Welsh accent. As the coin landed, he said: 'That's it, we've won!' The captain of FC Austria didn't argue and so Tottenham took the trophy home; it is probably still there in the club's trophy room.

Bill observed: 'Our experience against the Austrians proved invaluable a few months later when the Austrian national side visited Wembley to take on England and Alf Ramsey and Eddie Baily were in the England squad. I had been selected, but had to withdraw due to injury. We were able to give Walter Winterbottom some useful advice. However, the Austrians proved difficult opponents and the match ended 2-2.'

Led by their attacking centre half Ernst Ocwirk, the Austrians led 1-0 with 25 minutes to go until Baily was brought down inside the penalty area and the referee awarded a penalty. The responsibility of keeping England's proud record of never losing at Wembley fell to Ramsey and as he placed the ball with the laces facing the goalkeeper, he was about to make contact with his right boot when he noticed the keeper moving to his right, so he side-footed the ball to the other corner.

Alf was renowned for the accuracy of his crosses and soon afterwards, he put another free kick over and former coalminer Nat Lofthouse rose to head in. Near the end, the talented Austrians equalised from the penalty spot. The *Daily Mail* described it as 'a glorious fighting display that completely rehabilitated the reputation of English football, threadbare since Belo Horizonte. The author was Roy Peskett, the man who slaughtered England's players the year before.

Arthur Milton made his debut in that match, putting his name on the shortlist of all-round sportsmen who played both cricket and football for their country. 'To be honest, I got lost a bit in the game, not having had much experience at that level, but I got no passes from Billy Wright,' he admitted. 'I always felt Bill Nicholson was a much better wing half than Billy Wright.'

The return match took place in Vienna's Prater Stadium and hundreds of British soldiers came on to the pitch to celebrate at the end when England won 3-2 from a courageous, solo goal scored by Nat Lofthouse, which has gone down in the history of England football as one of the all-time greatest. After his two goals he was dubbed 'Lion of Vienna' by an English writer.

Bill (who was left on the bench) said: 'Nat took a lot of punishment as he went through to score that goal single-handed. He was strong and well built, the typical English centre forward of the day.' In contrast, Bill's time with England was like a long apprenticeship and it helped him to take the next step towards management.

George Cohen, England's World Cup winning right back, recalls the only occasion when he played under Bill's management: 'I was picked for an FA XI against the RAF and I remember that he trained us hard. He never let up – the sweat was pouring off us!'

CHAPTER SEVEN:
PIPPING RAMSEY TO THE POST

As Bill began his first season as a coach under the tactically naive Jimmy Anderson in 1954, the Tottenham directors wondered whether he was the right man to be manager. Though popular, Anderson was a late starter – too late, really, to lead the club on to more glory. Still recovering from illness, Arthur Rowe talked of a comeback and returned to work in 1957/8 until his health suffered again. Although he had wanted to stay on at the club, the stricken manager was currently out of action. Bill, meanwhile, had all the qualifications to do the job and the only other candidate in-house was Alf Ramsey. But it was too soon for Bill to go straight into management. Had the board approached him, Ramsey would have been overjoyed – it would have meant a great start to his managerial career.

Goalkeeper Ron Reynolds told award-winning writer Les McKinstry: 'There was a very strong rivalry between Alf and Bill because I think they both had come to the conclusion that they were going to stay in the game after they finished playing and both of them had designs on Tottenham.' Anderson was a supporter of the better-qualified Nicholson, who was an FA Staff Coach and one of the trusted disciples of Winterbottom. Ramsey, however, had never sat a football exam in his life. He wasn't interested in studying the methods of Winterbottom and others whom he thought had a more amateur approach to the game. Instead, he learned a lot from the push-and-run way of playing, observed the other styles of play and assimilated the best features. He squirrelled away nuggets of information, ready to launch his new career in his own way and not Winterbottom's nor anyone else's.

Just before Christmas, while driving his Ford Anglia to training, Ramsey told Ed Speight, one of the reserves: 'I don't know what's going to happen because I think I am finished. They are about to sign Blanchflower.' At the time, Blanchflower was 29, while Alf was 35 and slowing up appreciably. The two players wouldn't have gelled in the same team and, realising that his future no longer lay at White Hart Lane, Ramsey started looking for a new club. Anderson was now running the club full-time and although Alf was club captain, he dropped him from the team and left him out of the off-season tour to Hungary without any warning. Instead Ramsey travelled to Southern Rhodesia (now Zimbabwe) and did some coaching. His wife Victoria (who he called 'Vic', while she called him 'Alfred') and her daughter Tanaya accompanied him. On his return, Anderson rang to tell him that Great Yarmouth wanted to sign him as player-manager.

Ramsey wrote to them saying: 'I am flattered by your offer, but I want to stay in League football.' Nat Shaw, a longstanding director of Ipswich who owned seaside fairs and had a love for greyhound racing – Alf had a penchant for it as well – was told that Ramsey was available and tipped off his chairman, Alistair Cobbold. Scott Duncan, Ipswich Town's veteran manager, then 67, wanted to retire and the directors had heard of Ramsey's reputation and agreed to contact him. Old Etonian John Cobbold, a nephew of Alistair and one of football's great jokers, recalled: 'We got permission to speak to him and after a bit of humming and hawing, he decided to accept the post of manager. It wasn't a lot of money because we didn't have much.'

'Mr John', as he was known in Ipswich, was the youngest director to join a Football League club when he was 21 and also lost in three Parliamentary elections as a Conservative. His uncle, Harold Macmillan – Prime Minister between 1957 and 63 and variously called 'Supermac,' 'Mac the Knife' and 'The Unflappable' – came to speak at some of his meetings, but it made no difference. It didn't stop him from making a highly critical speech about Churchill's best friend from the other side of the Atlantic, President Dwight D. Eisenhower.

His father, Captain John 'Ivan' (nicknamed 'the Terrible' as a family joke) Cobbold of the Scots Guards, was also an Old Etonian who went shooting with King George VI and Winston Churchill on his Glemhall Hall estate. 'Ivan' was promoted to Lt-Colonel but he was among the 120 fatalities when a doodlebug, an unpiloted flying bomb, landed on the Guards Chapel near Buckingham Palace in 1944. During the War he had worked with General Alanbrooke, often attending meetings in Churchill's War Rooms off The Mall.

'Mr John' had a brief and unsuccessful time with the Welsh Guards – his father wanted him to join his regiment, the Scots, and John joked: 'I did it to upset him!' His brother Patrick, also a director and chairman of Ipswich, was invalided out of the Scots regiment when he was accidentally shot in the leg during training.

On his arrival at Portman Road, Ramsey was escorted to the boardroom, where Cobbold poured two glasses of whisky and handed one to him. 'This will be the first and last time I ever offer you a drink in the boardroom,' he told him as he threw the key to the drinks cabinet towards him. 'From now on, Alf, feel free to come in and help yourself!'

Ramsey was taken aback. He rarely went to the boardroom except to say hello and goodbye, and never poured himself a drink.

An alcoholic, Cobbold was widely believed to be homosexual although he never admitted it. Asked about his sex life, he once said: 'Well, I suppose it could be the donkeys.' He kept two donkeys on his Capel Hall estate near Felixstowe.

Not knowing much about football, Cobbold let Ramsey get on with it and during the next seven seasons, he took the small, almost broke club from the Third Division to the greatest of heights, outwitting Bill Nicholson when he became manager of Spurs and beating him to the Championship in 1961/2. Cobbold called Ramsey 'Stoneface' to his face and pulled his leg mercilessly, but the two odd men got on extremely well. 'My only job is to fill the glasses in the boardroom,' said Cobbold, while Ramsey realised that he had struck a goldmine. The directors left everything to him and didn't interfere. But if Arthur Rowe had been fit and able to persuade his directors to appoint Ramsey, not Nicholson, as manager of Tottenham then the history of English football might have been so different. Alf could have taken Spurs to the Double with Bill, backed by Winterbottom and Sir Stanley Rous, ending up as manager of England. We will never know – but one thing is for sure: England would have played more attractive football using wingers.

Bill became good friends with John Cobbold through the Under-18 South East Counties competition, which started in 1954 and was subsequently scrapped by the FA in 1999. Alan Leather, who was also on the committee, recalled: 'Bill loved going to the meetings and also the annual dinner. It was all voluntary, but it meant quite a lot of work, marking reports from clubs and handing out punishments to players who were sent off, and things like that.' Cobbold was president for a time and Lawrie McMenemy remembered: 'At one dinner, John obviously had a lot to drink and when he rose to speak, he slowly collapsed head-first onto the table, knocking everything onto the floor. When we pulled him up, we realised he couldn't speak and he always said: "That was the finest speech I ever made!"'

Anderson did his best to revive Tottenham, signing two exceptional players in Maurice Norman from Norwich and Chelsea's Bobby Smith, but he fell out with Eddie Baily, who surprisingly quit to join lowly Port Vale. But Eddie knew he had made a mistake and after one season he left, going on to play two seasons at Nottingham Forest and one with Leyton Orient before retiring in 1959. He was a big loss to Tottenham and they could have three or four more seasons from him.

Tottenham wanted to sign Danny Blanchflower to add some style to their midfield, but their efforts were continually thwarted by his dispute with Aston Villa. The articulate, argumentative Blanchflower was one of the first footballers to fight against the Football League's iniquitous transfer system, saying: 'I held no truck with the League regulations that allowed the clubs to play about with such sums of money and yet was so restrictive on the players. My club Aston Villa were not guilty of the whole affair – they didn't produce the system on their own account, they were merely following the system and if they were guilty of slave trading, then so was every club guilty.' Blanchflower's mother had a lot to do with his strident attitude: she was a footballing suffragette and actually played the game as a centre forward.

After prolonged negotiations Blanchflower's transfer to Tottenham for a fee of £30,000 finally went through in December 1954. Villa had wanted £40,000 – £6,000 more than the record fee paid by Sheffield Wednesday to Notts County for Jackie Sewell. Arsenal were first in the bidding but wouldn't go higher than £28,500. Danny was staying in London with the Northern Ireland squad when there was a telephone call for him and a voice said: 'Eric here [Eric Houghton, the Villa manager], you've been transferred to Spurs.' Danny's brother Jackie happened to be the one who picked up the phone and he said: 'I'm not the right Blanchflower, but I'll tell him.' Once that was sorted out, Arthur Rowe called soon afterwards and told him that he would pick him up by taxi: 'I loitered near the hotel doorway and when I saw his taxi arrive, I nipped into it,' he remembered. 'I felt like a secret agent who is being shadowed – they wanted to shake off the journalists who wanted to see me.'

Bill soon built up a good relationship with the controversial and outspoken new signing. 'The directors soon discovered that he was no ordinary footballer,' he said. 'He had written a weekly column in the *Birmingham Argus* and agreed to sign up for a similar column with the *Evening News*. The FA reminded the club that players were forbidden to write in newspapers and the directors asked him to stop, but he refused. He was a very independent person. Eventually a compromise was worked out whereby we agreed to have his articles vetted but as far as I knew, no one at the club ever saw them before they went into print. Danny was a good writer and he had a feel for words and a love of the game.' Blanchflower had contempt for the members of the Football League Management Committee and often lampooned them in his writings. If he was alive today, he would probably have tried to expose the shady people who are now running too many clubs and exploiting their loyal supporters.

One of Bill's steadiest and most reliable players was Peter Baker, his right back and a one-club man, who was born in Enfield. Blanchflower's arrival literally changed his life. He recalled: 'Bill called me in and said to me, "Your days as an overlapping full back are over. Danny isn't going get behind the ball so you'll have to cover him." I didn't mind – I was in my thirties and I knew my place. I had a great respect for Bill and all the players felt the same way. He had total discipline over them and no one stepped out of line and his ideas were excellent; I don't think he made many mistakes.

'Bill was careful in talking with the journalists but I just thought he was shy. Danny was all mouth, just the opposite. When Danny eventually packed up, he wanted a young right back to take over from me and he chose Cyril Knowles and my time was up. I got an offer to play in Durban and I lived there for many years.'
Peter was stuck on 299 appearances, but he didn't complain. He was the type of player Bill relished: completely honest.

When he was captain of the Northern Ireland side, Blanchflower was given licence to change things on the field by the manager, Peter Doherty. Arriving at White Hart Lane, however, he soon managed to upset Anderson and the directors by making switches in three key matches of the 1955/6 season. Bill thought it might cause trouble and he was right. The first time was against West Ham in the Sixth Round of the FA Cup when Tottenham were 1-3 down, with 20 minutes to go. Blanchflower told Maurice Norman, playing at right back, to go up to the front and it worked: the team earned a replay, which they won 2-1.

Anderson also upset both Bill and Blanchflower by leaving Tommy Harmer out for the semi-final against Manchester City on St. Patrick's Day. Said Bill: 'Jimmy Anderson was going to decide between Alfie Stokes, who I always thought didn't work hard enough on his fitness, and Dave Dunmore for the outside right position. Tommy had been playing in that role. He was one of the most popular players at the club – he was a small, waif-like figure and everyone liked him. He had immense skill, tremendous vision, and could play balls around with great accuracy. He also had that rare quality of seeing the next move before it happened. He had an unusual way of taking deadball kicks: he approached the ball from sideways on, and would turn and screw it back across the keeper. The crowd loved it until one day he slipped in the mud and missed a penalty.

'He played 205 League games and scored 47 goals, and no doubt he would have played many more matches, had he been physically bigger. Being small is no handicap to a footballer: some of the greatest players have been below-average height, but Tommy was skinny with it. He was a player opponents thought they could intimidate. He was very highly strung and would chain-smoke most of the time – he even lit up at half time. The club rule was no smoking in the dressing room so he used to go to the toilet and smoke.'

Dunmore, a centre forward, was picked to take on Manchester

City and Bill recalled: 'We already three centre forwards in the team that day – Dunmore, Smith, Duquemin – and Danny had told Maurice Norman to be the fourth. It was rather crowded up there.'

City's 1-0 win destabilised Tottenham's season of 1955/6 and Blanchflower said: 'As I was peeling off my football strip, Jimmy Anderson rushed through the door and said: "You shouldn't have done that. My directors are up there, asking me what you are doing and who gave you the authority to change the team?" I said I tried to win by taking a gamble – it's better doing that than doing nothing.

'We left it there but nobody had any heart for the train back to London. One of the saddest sights in football is to see the defeated semi-finalists on their way home. The press climbed all over me and they ganged up on me. Later I realised that this was prejudice: the pressmen in the South like to have a southern team in the Cup Final.'

Relegation looming, Blanchflower defied his manager again, agreeing to let Tony Marchi go up front with 15 minutes against Huddersfield. Again, the gamble failed and Anderson lost his temper with his defiant captain.

On the Monday, Anderson left Blanchflower out of the squad for the trip to Cardiff before he dashed off to Swansea to sign Terry Medwin, another player Bill had approved of, after going to see him in action. Anderson told the press that Blanchflower was injured, but when his player phoned Jack Orange, the sports editor of the *Evening News*, to discuss his column, Orange asked: 'How's your injury?' Blanchflower told him: 'I'm not injured, I've been left out.' The newspaper splashed the story across the front page.

Three days later, Anderson called his captain in and said: 'That was a dirty trick you played on me, phoning up the newspaper to tell them you weren't injured!' But Blanchflower explained his position and insisted that he should be given powers to make changes, saying: 'If not, I'll hand over the captaincy to someone else.' Anderson held firm and Harry Clarke was given the responsibility. 'Harry didn't fancy it,' recalled Bill, 'and we had a succession of captains – the inexperienced John Ryden, a centre half of ordinary ability who came from Accrington Stanley and for a while, Bobby Smith was captain but he wasn't a leader, either.'

Bill learned an important lesson: the manager has to make the changes, not the captain. Also, he preferred captains who were midfielders and so in contact with the back and front of the team. In his view, centre forwards ought not to be captain. When he took over as manager, he encouraged his players to speak up and try to correct errors, but he insisted on having the last word. He had some strong characters in his dressing room, but that was one of the reasons why he had such an effective side.

Tottenham managed to avoid relegation, finishing 18th position that season, two points ahead of the relegated Huddersfield. The easy-going Tony Marchi, Blanchflower's roommate, was given the captaincy in 1956/7 and the players seemed more relaxed. They were responding to Bill's coaching and until 16 February were hotly challenging Manchester United for the title. Third Division Bournemouth were their opponents in the Fifth Round of the FA Cup at Dean Court and Tottenham's players found themselves confronted by a new tactic which upset them immensely: whenever they took a throw-in, Ollie Norris jumped up and down, almost eyeball-to-eyeball with the thrower, to distract him.

Bill was livid and said: 'Our players didn't show any intelligence. The referee let him get away with it, but today he would have been cautioned for ungentlemanly conduct. All they had to do to combat Norris was to step back a yard or two when they took the throw, but none of them did.' Eventually Bournemouth won 3-1 and their manager, former Arsenal winger Freddie Cox, was a national figure for the rest of the season.

It was a month before Tottenham won again but they ended the season with a flourish, scoring 104 goals, one more goal than champions Manchester United and claiming the runners-up spot, eight points behind Sir Matt Busby's team. Six players all scored double figures – midfielders Johnny Brooks, 11, Tommy Harmer, 17, wingers Terry Medwin, 14, and George Robb, 14, plus strikers Alfie Stokes, 18, and Bobby Smith, 18. Stokes must have heeded Bill's advice about his fitness because his 18 goals came from only 21 matches.

Tony Marchi never missed a League game that season but Gigi Peronace, the Italian scout who lived half the year in a luxurious flat round the corner from Harrods, negotiated a deal to take Marchi to Juventus for £42,000. The lure of a signing fee of £7,000 was too much to keep the Edmonton-born player at home. Peronace took 10 per cent and it was an odd deal because Juventus already two permissible foreign players so Marchi, who had an Italian parent, was loaned out to Lanerossi and Torino. Two years later, when Bill was manager, he bought him back for £20,000 and Peronace pocketed a further £2,000.

Before the start of the 1957/8 season Anderson told Blanchflower: 'It's a bit difficult now with Tony off in Italy. What am I to do for a captain?' But Blanchflower turned him down. Later, he said: 'It would have been embarrassing for him to give it to me on my terms. He implied a compromise, but I felt that the conflict might easily arise again without clear statement and understanding of the responsibility.'

The ineffectual Ryden carried on as captain and it was no surprise that the club won just one match in their first seven League matches. A 0-3 defeat in the FA Cup at home to Sheffield United appeared to herald another relegation fight, but Bobby Smith's goals spurted out like an oil-well and his 36 in 38 League matches hoisted Tottenham to third position, 13 points behind Stan Cullis's championship-winning Wolves.

Bill said: 'Smithy was an old-fashioned centre forward, who took all the knocks and kept going. I like that type of battling centre forward.' Born in Langdale End, eight miles from Scarborough, in 1950 he was signed as a professional for Chelsea at the age of 17 and looked to be the next Lofthouse until he started putting on weight. Five years later, Tottenham signed him for £18,000. Bill was always geeing up him about his physique and it worked until 1963 when he was sold to Brighton, where he was less successful. Soon he was washed up and unwanted – except by Hastings, where he had a brief spell in the Southern League.

Bobby Smith had a phenomenal scoring record at White Hart Lane: 176 League goals in 271 League games. Few players have bettered his ratio per game of 1:5. Sadly, he is now one of the aforementioned 'Titanium Men'. These past heroes paid a high price and none of them made fortunes from their fame. Gerry Williams of the *Daily Mail* and I went to see him to report on one of Bobby's matches for Hastings, when he was taken off early in the second half. We knocked at the door and came into the tiny dressing room and there was Smith sitting alone on a bench, holding his head. Gerry, being bold, said to him: 'Are you ashamed of yourself playing in this type of football? Not so long ago you scored two goals against Spain at Wembley!' We were about to turn and run until he looked up, hesitated and admitted: 'Well, yes I am.' Bill had trained him well – at least he was honest about it.

That season Danny Blanchflower was voted Footballer of the Year by the Football Writers' Association, and four years later, he repeated that feat. Only four other players have won the accolade twice: Tom Finney, Stanley Matthews, Cristiano Ronaldo and Kenny Dalglish. Thierry Henry has won it three times. The writers usually get it right – that list certainly contains the all-time greats. Blanchflower had an outstanding World Cup in Sweden in the summer of 1958 when he played in all four matches, but he was mentally exhausted afterwards. He skippered Peter Doherty's side to a 1-0 game against the Czechs and three days later they were beaten 3-1 by Argentina. To go through to the next round, they needed to see off West Germany, but drew 2-2 in another creditable performance. Now they had to beat the Czechs in the group play-off, but weakened by the absence of their inspirational goalkeeper Harry Gregg, they went down 2-1.

In the England camp, Bill Nicholson was appointed alongside Jimmy Anderson, the Burnley captain, and from the outset, Walter Winterbottom ran into unexpected problems. Three weeks before the tournament started, England were routed 5-0 by Yugoslavia in Belgrade and Bill told Winterbottom that the players were unfit. The squad trained at the Bank of England ground in Roehampton for a week and Bill recalled: 'After the first session, some of them were sick. You expect that at the start of a pre-season, not when the players have been training all season and were about to go off for the biggest competition of their lives. Some were late getting up and went straight out after eating a large English breakfast. Walter cancelled the afternoon session and lectured them about their responsibilities. I told them they had their reputations to protect and suggested an 11 o'clock curfew in Gothenburg. They stuck to it. Relaxing later, we had a laugh about a note on the official FA card issued to the players. It read: "No one is allowed to take out more than £10 with them. It is not permissible to spend this amount while abroad."'

Don Howe, the right back who later became England's longest-serving coach, recalled: 'Walter Winterbottom was always asking questions of the players. He'd make friends, get them on his side. He was years ahead of his time, like working on the mental side and getting his players in the right frame of mind. He never fell out with anyone. There were no awkward customers in those days – he did all the bookings, the travel, the food, everything. Bill and Jimmy had Harold Shepherdson of Middlesbrough as the trainer, and that was all. These days England go abroad with a huge number.'

Three of England's finest players – Duncan Edwards, Roger Byrne and Tommy Taylor – had died in the Munich air crash four months before the tournament and this surely contributed to England's early exit. Strangely, Stan Matthews and Nat Lofthouse were left behind and Bobby Charlton, who was chosen for the squad, wasn't picked for any of England's games. England drew

The Nicholson family – Bill is being held by his father, Joe.

Above: Bill *(second row, centre)* with the Scarborough High School Under-14 team.

Below: 15 Vine Street, Scarborough, where Bill was born and brought up. The entrance to the Nicholson family home can be seen on the right.

Above: Bill (*second row, third from the left*) at the British Army PT Centre in Udine, Italy, in 1945.

Below left: Bill as a PT trainer at Aldershot.

Below right: Sergeant Bill Nicholson.

Above: Bill's wedding to Grace 'Darkie' Power, in 1947.

Below left and right: The happy couple in the early years of their marriage.

Darkie with Bill's mother, Edith Nicholson.

Darkie on her famous bike – she regularly had bicycles stolen from around White Hart Lane.

Above: Bill (five rows back, on the left) with the 1950 England World Cup squad.

Bill photographed in 1950.

their three group matches – 2-2 in the opening match against the USSR, 0-0 against winners Brazil and 2-2 with Austria – before going out 1-0 to the USSR in the group play-off.

Winterbottom's odd decision to prefer West Bromwich Albion's Derek Kevan to Bobby Smith may well have been crucial. Bill observed: 'I didn't think Kevan was up to international standard, but as I didn't have a say in the selection I kept my opinions to myself. He played fourteen times for England, one less than Bobby who, in my view, was a much better all-round centre forward.' He thought Howe was just as good as George Cohen and that Bobby Robson 'was a great enthusiast, but not tremendously skilful with the ball.'

Winterbottom was always enthusing about the skill and excellent preparation of the Brazilians and he sent Bill to spy on them. 'I found it impossible to do my usual job,' said Bill, 'because the names in the team sheet rarely corresponded with the names of the players taking part!' That might explain the way England were surprised at the sudden emergence of 17-year-old Edison Arantes do Nascimento, otherwise known as Pelé, who scored two goals in Brazil's 5-2 win over Sweden in the final.

Before the match against Brazil, Bill worked out a defensive system to prevent the Brazilians from scoring. Howe was moved to centre half to partner Billy Wright and midfielder Eddie Clamp took over as an attacking right back. Winterbottom was delighted, but unfortunately, England's attack failed to function. Bill Slater, one of the reserves, still has an immense affection for Bill. 'He was a very nice man,' he said. 'We all liked him and he was a very good coach.'

Just before the team flew back to London, Bill met with Eric Taylor, the secretary-manager of Sheffield Wednesday, and he was offered the job as manager at Hillsborough. 'I told him I was happy at Tottenham and did not want to leave,' he said.

Blanchflower admitted he lacked enthusiasm for the start of the 1958/9 season and it certainly showed on the field. Tottenham lost four of the first five matches, with Jim Anderson suffering the same depression that had dragged down Arthur Rowe. Jesse Carver, the former butcher's assistant who became one of the most renowned foreign coaches in Italy, was brought in to help but he couldn't stem the flow of goals scored by the opponents.

Carver had taken Juventus to the Championship and coached five other Italian clubs with varied results. Blanchflower and Harmer were both dropped and in the first week of October, Anderson called Bill to his office and told him that vice chairman Fred Wale wanted to see him at his company, Brown's of Tottenham. Bill said: 'What's it all about, Jim?' Anderson told him: 'You go down there, you'll soon find out.'

During their meeting, Wale told Bill: 'Jimmy Anderson isn't going to carry on as manager. Would you like the job?' Bill accepted straightaway: 'I've been coaching now for four years and I feel I could do it.' 'Fine,' said Wale. The vice chairman never mentioned a pay rise, nor indeed a contract. Bill said later: 'I didn't raise the subject either. I never had a contract in my life as a manager – I reasoned that if I was good enough to do the job, they would keep me. If I wasn't good enough, they would sack me. A contract wouldn't make any difference.'

Tottenham were sixteenth, with nine points after 11 matches. Their next opponents, Everton, were in the bottom three. At lunchtime, Bill was asked to attend the boardroom to be told by the directors that he had been confirmed as manager. Tottenham had a tradition of appointing within – Billy Minter, Rowe, Anderson and Keith Burkinshaw were other examples – but in recent years they have departed from this, appointing foreigners with little knowledge of the club and its traditions.

Harmer was mightily relieved to be recalled and was the magician who laid on most of the goals in one of the most extraordinary matches ever played – Tottenham 10, Everton 4, equalling the previous highest aggregate in a First Division game, when Aston Villa beat Accrington 12-2 in 1892. One critic wrote:

'Tommy Harmer scored one and made nine' – a slight exaggeration. As they came off, Tommy told Bill: 'We don't score 10 goals every week, you know.' Bill replied: 'I've been in this game long enough to know you can be in the clouds one minute and down-to-earth the next.' Bobby Smith scored a hat trick and Jimmy Harris scored one for Everton.

In his book *The Glory Game*, Hunter Davies revealed that Bill never told Darkie that he had been appointed manager. She said: 'It was on a Saturday and he went in as usual in the morning. It was apparently on the radio, but I was rushing around all day with the girls and didn't have it on. He didn't mention it when he came home till my mother arrived and said to him: "Congratulations." I thought she was saying it because the team had beaten Everton 10-4, but she kept on about it and then it all came out. I said, "Why didn't you tell me, ring up or something?" He said he hadn't had time – he'd been rushing all day. Yet he'd known about it from twelve o'clock when they'd had a special directors' meeting before the match. But that's the sort of person he is.'

Alan Leather, the newly appointed assistant secretary, recalled: 'At the time BBC put on an American series about crime and the police department had its call sign 10-4 and we saw that as a good omen.' Rather prophetically, Danny Blanchflower declared: 'It can only get worse.' And it did: up to Christmas, the new manager presided over six defeats in seven matches and made the decision which won the respect of his playing staff – he left out Blanchflower. He called Danny in and told him: 'You are taking too many liberties. When the ball is played into our box, you are often on your way out, looking for a throw from the keeper. You should be in that box marking someone and doing your defensive job.' Blanchflower said: 'I took it with as much humour as I could and approached my new experience – playing for the stiffs – with the intention of doing my best and enjoying it. I was visiting places I had never even heard of.'

Cliff Jones recalled: 'Bill brought in a young player named Bill

Dodge to replace Danny and I think he played one game and was never heard of again.' In fact, young Bill from Eton Manor played in six matches, and the first four of those were won, before he was transferred to Crystal Palace.

Blanchflower said: 'I was 33 and I still thought I was capable of first-team football for some years, so I asked for a transfer. Bill was a young manager making his way and I wondered what he thought of me. He wasn't very pleased when I asked to go, but he took it well. He told me the directors wouldn't let me go. I respected him for his comments and a week later, the board rejected my request. I forgot about the idea – I felt I could get along with Bill.'

The rapprochement took place in a hotel in Wolverhampton at 6pm on 2 March, the day Tottenham were due to play the prospective champions, Wolves. Bill read out the team and Blanchflower was named in his usual position. 'And you're the captain,' he said. The union between manager and captain was later blessed by a meaningful result under the Molineux lights. Said Danny: 'We played well for our 1-1 draw and the following Saturday, we beat Leicester 6-0 and that took away any thoughts of relegation from our minds.'

The foundations for a new and exciting team to take over the mantle of the push-and-run side of the previous generation were now firmly laid. Bill signed Dave Mackay, Cliff Jones and Bill Brown and brought Marchi back from Italy. Cliff Jones commented wryly: 'He wanted us to call him Bill, which we did, but he was the governor all right. Like Alex Ferguson now at Manchester United.'

CHAPTER EIGHT:

ASSEMBLING HIS GREATEST TEAM

Today's managers buy their star players through the services of agents, often with more than one agent involved in the deal. They study videos of the players and rarely meet the signed performer until the negotiations are at an advanced stage. Most of their purchases come from abroad. In Bill Nicholson's day it was very difficult to buy foreign players – they had to have a work permit and the Ministry of Employment were very strict about it. But Bill scoured the home countries for new stars and though he had players from Wales, Scotland and Northern Ireland, all signed before he was manager, he only bought three Scottish players, Dave Mackay, Bill Brown and John White in that period. It was almost a Great Britain XI.

Each week, he drove hundreds of miles to watch the players, often standing on the terraces and buying his own programme. He flew frequently to Glasgow to watch a game and took a late flight back to London. Eddie Baily often went with him: 'We came back on those Vanguard aircraft and often we were the only passengers.'

Bill said: 'If you let everyone know that a certain player is available, other clubs will be chasing them so you have to keep it to yourself.' To ensure secrecy, many of the deals were completed in his car and rarely met players in hotels. Cliff Jones, one of his best buys, commented: 'I knew he had me watched and I was serving in the King's Royal Horse Troop in the Regent's Park Barracks in St John's Wood, near Lord's cricket ground, when I signed in February 1958. I was a gunner or private and I can still remember my number – 3306136. I worked mucking out in the stables and helping to look after the horses.'

Bill Nicholson did the same when he was a boy, but whereas Cliff rode the horses, Bill was reluctant to mount them. 'I played in the British Army and we had a great side,' said Cliff. 'Duncan Edwards, what a player he was, Bobby Charlton, Dave Mackay, Maurice Setters and other big names. We played the French Army and the Belgian Army, and they were good matches. I had a crew cut and Bill liked that – he liked a short haircut. My first match was at Highbury and I came by underground and the commissionaire wouldn't let me in. "We've heard that story before," he said. "I've never heard of you." It was some time before I managed to get in and Bill's first words were "You're late!" It was a 4-4 draw, and I slipped as I tried to get round Jim Fotheringham and fell. Bill told me off for not having the right type of stud – he was a stickler for things like that, he was so professional.'

Five men called Bryn Jones have played League football, the most famous being the one who joined Arsenal in 1938 for a then record fee of £14,000. He took some time to settle in. Cliff Jones, his nephew and son of Welsh international Ivor Jones, experienced the same problem. The transfer fee paid to Swansea was £35,000, a daunting sum for any 22-year-old, and the crowd wanted to see a superstar. Cliff said: 'I wasn't really fit and I'd played a lot of football. In a pre-season club game Peter Baker caught me with a 50-50 tackle and I had a hairline fracture in a leg, but it turned out to be a good thing because being out for four months enabled me to get fully fit. When I started out as an inside forward at Swansea Ivor Allchurch was the golden boy of that time and I had no chance of taking over from him. Joe Sykes, one of the staff, suggested I should play on the left wing despite being right-footed. Terry Medwin was on the right, but I didn't mind. It meant I could cut inside the full back onto my stronger foot.'

Bill had another slant on the story about his recruitment: 'Jimmy Anderson and I were given permission by Swansea to talk to him and we arrived at the barracks to discover he was missing. No one knew where he was and the suspicion was that he was absent without leave. "We've got him into trouble," said Jimmy. But things were sorted out next day and he duly signed.'

Years later, Cliff explained: 'Chelsea wanted me and I saw Ted Drake, but I preferred Tottenham. It wasn't about money – we hardly talked about money. With the maximum wage, you knew the most you could earn and I only got a small amount as accrued benefit.' Bill said: 'Cliff took some time to settle down. Despite his pace and ability to score, the crowd didn't accept him for a time. That injury enabled him to have a gradual introduction. He had the Stan Matthews trick of being able to lift the ball over the stretched leg of an opponent. He got through more tackles that way than any player I knew. He was enormously brave and would go flying in at the far posts for headers like a centre forward. That first year he spent most of the time in the treatment room, but in the following season he scored 20 goals from 38 games, a great record for a winger.'

Jones was 5ft 7in tall and Jimmy Greaves once said of him: 'He used to rise like a salmon to knock in those far post headers.' He was just over 10 stone – now in his seventies and only a half stone more, Cliff declared: 'I've always been active and it's probably down to my metabolism, like a grand old Welsh lightweight!'

Just a year after his arrival, Bill made what Jones believed was the most vital signing of all: Dave Mackay from Hearts. Mackay was the original footballing braveheart and when he went onto the field, he intimidated opponents as if to say: 'There is only one winner out there'. 'He was a winner,' said Cliff, 'and that spread to everyone in the side. None of us were going to lose when he was in the side.'

Bill was a good friend of Tommy Walker, the manager of Hearts, who was a Christian renowned for his honesty. Over the years, they had spoken of possible transfer targets and Walker always insisted that he would never sell Mackay. Bill had a strong link with Swansea because Ron Burgess was manager and when Burgess left, Trevor Morris took over. Morris surprised Bill by saying that he was willing to sell Mel Charles, brother of that all-time great, John Charles of Leeds and Juventus. Bill could be cutting about players – sometimes he was a victim of his own truthfulness – and he once said of Mel Charles: 'I wasn't excited about him. His best position was centre half and we already had Maurice Norman.'

In fact, Charles was capable of playing in several positions, like his brother. When Bill asked him which were his best positions, Charles didn't reply – something that didn't inspire confidence in his prospective manager. Managers like all-rounders, such as Paul Madeley, the England and Leeds defender that Bill wanted to buy before Don Revie changed his mind about him and realised that he couldn't release such a key player to another club. A day later, Charles rang Bill to tell him that he was going to join Arsenal. 'I was relieved,' said Bill. He was right: at Highbury, Charles never made the grade.

A day before the transfer deadline, Bill phoned Walker about Mackay. To his astonishment, Tommy indicated that Hearts would accept £30,000 for a player who had won medals in Scottish football and was looked on as someone who would never leave Scotland. On the Sunday, Tommy rang Mackay at his home in Edinburgh and said to him: 'Tottenham want to buy you and I can tell you that Bill Nicholson is an honourable man. Come to my office at 10am tomorrow and let me know your decision. Bill is travelling up to Edinburgh tomorrow as well and you have the opportunity to meet him.'

Mackay was shocked. 'I was born and bred a Hearts fan,' he admitted. 'When I was a kid, I crawled in under a fence to watch their matches. I dreamed about playing for them and when I did, I wanted it to be forever.' Scotland's captain, he was a hero north of the border. Secretly he suspected that his career might be cut short because he had already suffered three bone fractures in a foot: as he saw it, Hearts could cash in while the money was good. He said: 'Yes, I had a few broken bones but never a broken heart. I was very upset at the way Walker treated me, but I suppose Hearts needed the cash.'

Just before the midnight deadline, the two managers shook hands on it. Bill told the story of how he caught the London train the next day. 'The platform was virtually deserted except for the station master wearing a top hat,' he remembered. 'He recognised Tommy, who introduced me as the manager of Tottenham. The stationmaster enquired, "Oh, and what might you be doing here?" I said, "Hearts have just sold Dave Mackay to us."'

The stationmaster looked stunned, and when the news came out, football fans in half of Edinburgh felt the same way.

Isobel, Dave's pragmatic wife, helped him to make up his mind about moving to north London. 'You have to go where your work is,' she said. He was still on the £20-a-week maximum wage, but Spurs gave him handsome expenses to move house. Next day, he donned an overcoat and took the *Flying Scot* train to St Pancras. Bill said: 'I can't promise trophies, but I know you will be playing in an exciting, entertaining and rewarding football.' He said he would be given a clubhouse and the deal was completed in time to meet the season's transfer deadline.

For the first few weeks in London, he stayed in small hotel near White Hart Lane. He played for Scotland against England at Wembley and teammate Tommy Docherty asked: 'Where you living?' When he said a hotel, Docherty told him: 'We can't have you living in a bloody hotel! You're moving in with Agnes and me, and I won't hear of anything else.' So he became a lodger at the Dochertys'.

When they eventually moved into the rented house laid on by the club, Isobel didn't like it. She said: 'One day I told Dave I was going to do something about it because he wasn't too bothered. I rang Bill Nicholson, and introduced myself and explained the problem. He was taken aback. I don't think he'd ever been rung by a wife of a player. He stuttered a bit and said, "I'll have to do something about it – I'll come back to you." He was very apologetic and polite.

'He rang again and he said he had someone to pick us up and show a new house, a bungalow in Enfield. We saw it and I fell in love with it. It was much more costly than the other one, almost double in price, but Bill said they would keep the same rent. I got very friendly with Darkie and she often told me she'd had another bike stolen. She was a lovely lady.' Most days, Darkie would ride her bike to White Hart Lane – she chained it to a fence but that didn't stop the thieves and souvenir hunters.

Alan Leather, the then Tottenham secretary, found Isobel's dream home from an estate agent and though the club had a limit of £4,250 limit for players' houses, it cost £7,250, with the club covering the extra expense. Tottenham weren't always tight with their money.

In the close season of 1959, Bill told his staff that he wasn't happy about his two goalkeepers, Ron Reynolds and John Hollowbread. A Scots journalist Jim Rodger became one of his chief suppliers of information and suggested that he should buy Bill Brown from Dundee: 'He's a bonny keeper and he's at his peak at the age of 27.'

Brown made his debut in that England versus Scotland match and Bill said: 'I wanted to sign an international-class goalkeeper, who was going to help us win the championship. I fancied him and went to watch him at Wembley. I didn't like the way he brought the ball down, but he was agile and a good stopper of shots. Once I agreed the fee of £16,500, I caught the overnight train to Dundee and put the necessary forms in front of him early next morning. He signed straightaway and I was heading back for London by lunchtime. Brown was to prove one of my best signings.'

Today no transfer would be conducted at such speed. Danny Blanchflower considered both Reynolds and Hollowbread unlucky to be ousted. He wrote: 'Ron had proved himself over the years, but at critical times he suffered bad injuries. A few kicks around the head hadn't helped his eyes and he had to wear special contact lenses. It must have been a disadvantage. Hollowbread had shown that he was a very capable deputy. He kept almost the whole of one season and some people thought he had been unfortunate to lose his place. Bill was determined to take the club to the top and wanted another keeper – he thought three would be safer than two.'

Bill's recruitment from Scotland continued in October, when he signed John White from Falkirk for £20,000. John was born in Musselburgh, Mackay's birthplace, and played for some exotically named clubs, including Prestonpans YMCA, the Musselburgh Union Juveniles, Bonnyrigg Rose and Alloa, before joining Falkirk for just £3,500. Mackay called him 'the last piece in the jigsaw' and labelled him 'The Ghost' a year or two before Martin Peters earned the sobriquet.

'He was a great player, who shared Danny's ability to find space and could read the game better than most forwards of the day,' said Dave. 'Although his goal ratio was one goal every five games, he made many more for others. We became great friends and I warmed to his modesty and his quiet sense of humour. I wouldn't say he was the fittest player at White Hart Lane, but he was the hardest trainer.'

For weeks, the ubiquitous Jim Rodger was on the case and Bill flew up to Scotland to see White in action: 'I was excited with the prospect of landing him. He didn't make a single bad pass. Falkirk were short of money, and Leicester and Chelsea had made offers. Leicester's bid was £13,000 and they were close to reaching agreement.'

Many years later, Colin Appleton, Leicester's captain, revealed: 'Matt Gillies, our manager, changed his mind when one of his scouts told him: "He can't play in wet conditions." That was a laugh. He could play equally well in rain, snow or sun.'

Danny Blanchflower played an international against Scotland in Belfast and was suitably enthused about White. When he returned to Tottenham on the Monday, Bill asked: 'What do you think of John White?' 'I liked him very much. Seems to have a wonderful sense of position and good control of the ball in a quiet, smooth way. He would suit us,' was Danny's reply. Bill said: 'I like him, too and I can get him for £20,000.' Danny responded: 'Fly up there right away and don't waste time!'

Bill had one reservation: White was slight in physique and he worried about his stamina. Could he be another Harmer? Dave Mackay soon disabused him of that idea, saying, 'He's a champion cross-country runner.' White was serving in the Army at the time and so Bill rang the sports officer at his unit to check. 'That's right,' said the officer. 'He's so good that he won't be playing football this coming Saturday because he'll be running for the Scottish Command.' And so the matter was settled, or very nearly: when the Falkirk manager Tommy Younger brought him to London, he said: 'John was a bit worried because he felt he wouldn't be good enough to play with the Tottenham players.' Both he and Bill convinced him that he would be a rising star.

Harry Evans, the popular assistant manager under Bill, lived nearby and White became the Evans' lodger. Soon he fell in love with Sandra, their daughter, and they were married and started a family in their own home. The once-shy White entertained his colleagues with his partying antics, including the odd practice of eating chrysanthemums in pubs, and was blissfully happy.

The next piece of the jigsaw was the signing of Les Allen from Chelsea reserves in December in exchange for the erratic Johnny Brooks, who had plenty of skill but not too much physical strength. 'Some of our supporters were surprised, but I thought Les was a vastly underrated player,' said Bill. 'He was good at sniffing out scoring positions and was a sound finisher. One of the saddest things was that I had to replace him two years later when Jimmy Greaves became available. I felt sorry for him – he had done nothing to deserve being replaced, but a manager can't afford sentiment. Greaves was the best goalscorer of his day and I had to get him.'

Allen came from Dagenham, the place where Alf Ramsey, Terry Venables and a host of players learned their football. In his two seasons with Tottenham, he scored 47 goals in 119 matches. Soon after he arrived, Les scored five goals in Tottenham's record score, 13-2 against Crewe in an FA Cup replay at White Hart Lane. His son Clive, who made an even greater impression later, recalled: 'Dad was pretty pleased, and Bill came up to him and said, "It should have been six!" That was typical – he always wanted the best. But he did congratulate players on other occasions.'

Dave Mackay was also a victim after the Crewe game: 'He said to me, "Dave, I don't expect to see you going in on tackles like that, risking injury to yourself and others, and getting booked or sent off. Anyone would have thought we were 10 goals behind, not 10 goals up." He had a point.'

When Jimmy Greaves arrived in December 1961, Allen lost his place but stayed on for four years before joining QPR as player-manager under Alec Stock, who became general manager. He recalled: 'I was still scoring goals and after a game against Spurs, Bill came up to me and said, "I made a big mistake to let you go when I did. We needed some cover and I didn't have it." I thought that was good of him to say it. I got on well with him; he was always pointing to your mistakes and how to correct them and didn't smile a lot, but that was him: he wanted the best from every player. When I became a manager, he always came over for a chat and he had time to help younger managers.'

Dave Mackay was injured before the next round at Blackburn and Tottenham lost, ruining their chance of the Double. At the time, they were top of the table and finished third, two points behind Burnley. Phil Soar wrote:

Spurs had two unaccountable home beatings in 48 hours – 0-1 to Manchester City on Easter Saturday and another 0-1 to Chelsea on Easter Monday. They lost the championship by two points and they should have had both against Manchester City. Cliff Jones' penalty at the end of the first half was well saved by Bert Trautmann, but the Welshman, following up, tapped home the rebound. Unfortunately for Spurs, the referee had added time on for the penalty to be taken and the goal didn't stand. Had it done so, it might have approached the second half differently and not conceded City's vital single goal. Having said that no team which loses its last two home matches deserves to win anything very much.

When football teams are struggling, humour is usually in short supply. But when the Russian FA invited Tottenham for an end-of-season tour in 1959, Bill told the directors that it would be a good move – not to make money, but to use the trip to work on training routines for the next season and it would also help relationships between players. 'We trained every morning, just as though we were still playing matches,' he remembered. 'I think it helped create the spirit that was needed. The food was awful and the facilities were rudimentary, but in those circumstances there was more to laugh about, especially when ordering our meals. Most of my time was spent working out menus with the managers of the hotels and it was like negotiating a wage deal with a trade union. One day I asked for rice pudding and it came in cold slabs and the players couldn't eat it. We appointed Alan Leather as the food taster.'

The multi-talented Leather said: 'One day the players wanted boiled eggs and when they brought the eggs, the water was tepid and it was obvious the eggs hadn't been boiled, so Bill went into the kitchen to show them how to boil them. It was a memorable trip. It was my first flight and even now it was my worse. We wondered how the Aeroflot aircraft got into the air. It was shuddering and banging as though they loaded it up with every gallon of fuel.

When he landed, we were surprised to see thousands of excited Russians at the airport and Roy Peskett of the *Daily Mail*, the only journalist with us, put over a story to his newspaper about this amazing reception.

'Later we learned that thousands had turned up to welcome Comrade Sergey Ilyushin, the inventor of 38 different types of aircraft. We stayed in the 6,000-room hotel close to the Kremlin and we were invited to look at Lenin's tomb. The floors were highly polished and we were told to put soft pads under our shoes to avoid making marks. The players were slipping and sliding everywhere and they thought it was hilarious. We were asked to go and see the Bolshoi Ballet, but most of the players said they didn't want to go. Bill told them they had to go. When they saw how good it was, and its relevance to body and leg movement, they realised how wrong they were.

'One player, I can't remember who it was, had a smart set of clothing and an expensive pair of shoes, and a Russian went up to him and asked if he could buy them. The locals were poorly dressed and he saw it was a chance to improve his lot. He pulled out a wad of roubles, and the player thought it was a good piece of business and they did a deal. When he realised he couldn't take roubles home, the player was mortified. I think one or two of them were caught over changing money, despite Bill warning them not to do it.

'We played three matches and won the first two – beating Moscow Torpedo in the Lenin Stadium in Moscow 1-0 and defeating Dinamo Kiev 2-1 – and we lost 3-1 in Leningrad against a Select XI. A total of 210,000 people watched the games and they were delighted to see such a good footballing team from England. We had no chance in the final match: the officials made sure of that.'

Ron Henry, probably the most loyal of the Tottenham squad in that era, believed those matches convinced the players that they were on the way to glory. In Keith Palmer's book, *White*

Lane Legends, he said: 'I knew that somebody up there put that team together.'

John White was 'arrested' for clapping loudly and scaring away pigeons in Red Square. Ron recalled: 'He was messing about, but a group of Russian police officers hauled him off to a police station. It was nip and tuck at one time before they let him go.' Bill was convinced that his 'training' trip to the USSR proved a key factor in improving the side and getting them ready to challenge for trophies.

Alan said: 'After the Double year, we were invited to tour South America and these days big clubs would have jumped at it, but Bill said no: "It would take too much out of the players," he said. I was at the meeting and I thought the directors might object, but Fred Bearman said, "All right, Bill – I accept your decision." Bill was a fledgling manager, but they respected him from the start.'

CHAPTER NINE:
THE DOUBLE

In 1953, Sir Edmund Hillary and his Sherpa guide Tenzing Norgay reached the summit of Mount Everest in the Himalayas, named after the Surveyor-General of India, Sir George Everest. A year later, Sir Roger Bannister was the first man to run a mile inside four minutes. Both were knighted, as you might expect, but the other person responsible for the last of the trio of great feats of that era, Bill Nicholson, was never knighted despite a petition being presented to 10 Downing Street in his later years. Perhaps there was a reason why Bill Nicholson, OBE, never made it: he wasn't a money man and Tony Blair seemed more interested in giving knighthoods to obscure, rich people who could back New Labour.

Danny Blanchflower, the Sherpa to Bill Nicholson, wrote in his book *The Double Before*: 'When we reported for pre-season training in July 1960, I was convinced that the season ahead was to be one of destiny for us. "We'll win the Double for you this year – League AND the Cup," I said to Fred Bearman, our aged and respected chairman, when he visited us at training and asked me, as his custom at the start of the season, as to how I thought we would do. I answered him instinctively without much thought of what I was saying. I said it quietly and confidently; I wasn't timid and I wasn't boasting. "All right, my boy," he said, "I'll believe you."

'At practice I was impressed with the team: its individual ability, its teamwork and its whole personality. Even the fates held promise; Tottenham had won the FA Cup in 1901 and again in 1921. There was no competition in 1941 and it was easy to figure that we were favourites in 1961. Spurs had won the Championship in 1951. Why not the Championship again in 1961? I am not blindly superstitious but these things can influence the thoughts of a neighbourhood and when people think it's likely to happen, they are liable to help make it happen, particularly when the team is good enough.'

Bill described Danny's confident prophecy as 'fanciful', saying: 'He was a bit of a romancer.' He also commented: 'I know that I made no such confident predictions. Bad luck plays such a large part in football. We could be drawn away in the Third Round of the FA Cup on a wet and windy day in early January and find ourselves out at the first hurdle. Over 42 matches the best side usually comes out on top, but the Cup is the one that lets you down. But I can foresee the day [he said this in 1984] when one of the big city clubs does the Treble. Before the maximum was lifted in 1961, no club was able to pay higher wages than any other so the talent was spread around the clubs. Even Manchester United, with all its wealth, did not have a monopoly of good players. It started the decline of the Lancashire clubs like Blackpool, Preston, Bolton, Blackburn and Burnley, and the rapid rise in wages nearly forced many clubs out of business.'

Maurice Norman, the tall centre half from Mulbarton in rural Norfolk, believes the master plan was created when the players sat in front of the easel which Bill used to make his points in training and later, before matches: 'It was like in a school,' he recalled. 'He went through all the points, telling each player what he wanted from them, what his immediate opponent would do, and spelt out the routines for corners and free kicks.

'One day he came up with a new one, especially for the next team, and it wasn't used again. His knowledge of the opposing players was fantastic. He would watch teams and make notes, and he also had scouts at matches as well bringing back detailed reports. He did an immense amount of travel to accumulate all that knowledge. It would take a half an hour or more and it was a lot to take in. He liked sitting next to you as well and telling you what he wanted from you. Sometimes a player would forget something and he would tick him off, but he rarely lost his temper.

'He was a great coach and Danny was always there to give his views. He was the liaison man. I played one or two matches against him when I arrived from Norwich in 1952 and he was a very useful player, but rather slow. Later, he would fault me for lack of speed and I would say, "And you weren't very quick either." Bill had a great way of handling the players: if he thought someone needed to do more work he would scold him, but he would pass messages on to me from Peter Baker or Ron Henry, our full backs, so he wouldn't have a go at me in person.'

One player who couldn't be faulted on his work rate was Terry Dyson, the 5ft 3in winger from Malton, eight miles from Scarborough. He was the son of the famous jockey 'Ginger' Dyson. 'If I had to name a player who had the attitude I wanted, it was Terry,' declared Bill. 'He needed no motivation.' One day when Bill was giving his team talk, he moved the subject to Bobby Charlton. 'Have you noticed the way he tracks back when United lose the ball?' he asked. 'Well, you ought to follow his example. That will help us.'

'I was in awe of him,' said Dyson. 'What he said had to go, but he mellowed a bit over the years. He dedicated his whole life to Tottenham and he was so proud of the club that he almost thought we should play for nothing.'

Years later, Keith Burkinshaw made a very telling point: 'Bill was such a great bloke – he was my mentor – so I'm reluctant to criticise him, but his one weakness was that he was very protective about the club's finances. He always wanted the club to be in the black and not pay too high salaries. Some of the stars were earning less than they should and members of the staff were on very low wages, ridiculous really. One of the coaches was on £2,000 a year when I started. It helped to create an image of a club being mean, and it was.'

Pat Jennings told a story that confirmed this when he was released after playing in 480 matches over 12 years. 'I didn't want to go,' he admitted. 'I had a testimonial coming up and Sidney Wale said to me, "We wanted to restore the club's homely atmosphere and the directors would be ready to help players, if they need assistance. I asked him if the club could give a loan of £10,000 to bridge the gap between the house I was selling and the new one. I thought it would be a formality, but they said the club had already budgeted for that year and couldn't do it. I was shocked.'

Bill introduced many innovative ideas in that summer of 1960, when Tottenham did their pre-season training at Cheshunt. He organised lopsided training games and all day long, except for a light lunch, the players went through various routines related to the game. 'Statistics show that a third of goals is scored by a team from re-starts so we spent hours rehearsing our tactics,' explained Bill. 'I believe we were the first club to put a marker on the opponent who takes a throw-in. The season was well advanced before many worked this one out. We had five to six free-kick routines, with each player knowing precisely his role, and we were one of the first clubs to send our centre backs into the other team's penalty area for corners. Often the opposing strikers didn't spot this and we scored many goals this way. At corners I insisted on having a full back on either post, not standing next to the post, but two yards inside the field so that the keeper could see the ball if it was coming straight at him. And I had wingers switching sides to upset defenders.'

One of Bill's ideas was to recruit Bill Watson, a famous

weightlifter, to build up the players' muscles. Dave Mackay described this in his autobiography, *The Real Mackay*: 'In short but effective sessions, he built us up physically. Each morning, we focused on something different, whether it was ball work, running or set pieces. On Fridays, we were allowed to do what we wanted. Not go off to the pub or golf, but to decide which element of the training programme was felt we needed to work on the most. It was an enlightening regime.'

In the following season Benfica coach Bela Guttmann was told about Tottenham's weight-training programmes and he came up with a perfect knockdown – 'Winning matches is about skill, not muscles,' he insisted.

Some of the players, led by Mackay, volunteered to play five-a-side games in the indoor gym. 'It wasn't big and there was no way out,' he recalled. 'I truly believe that five-a-side is the best training method. I took no prisoners and fights would break out. I'd love to get one of my colleagues with the ball in a corner and not allow him out. Sometimes this would lead to an elbow in the guts, with tempers fraying, but once it was over, it was finished. Nobody bore grudges.'

Before the ball court, or gym, was built the five-a-side mini games were played outside on the hard surface. One day, seeing the placid Ron Henry making a run with the ball, Mackay slid into a low tackle and won the ball but caused a nasty burn on his leg. 'Are you f****** mad?' asked Henry. Peter Shreeves, later the youth coach and then manager, defended the ball-court policy. 'Certainly,' he said. 'It's all right playing silky stuff on a Friday morning, but next day you are going to take on some tough characters who can kick a bit. You've got to get used to it and give it back. I think that hardened up the players and that was borne out by the results. We won a lot of matches in the North, where it's tougher. Players born in the North are hardier, Bill used to say.'

Danny Blanchflower described players like Mackay, Jones, White, Dyson and Harmer as being obsessed with football for football's sake. They loved trying to perform tricks to outdo each other: 'One was to throw up small coins into the air, catching them on their foot, flicking them up again on their forehead and then nodding the coin back into their pocket. They could do a similar trick with oranges.'

Cliff Jones would challenge Danny, who always replied: 'When you can do that with a coin and a ball at the same time, then come and see the old pro.' He meant himself.

Peter Shreeve told a lovely story about Tommy Harmer, who tended to rely on Bill for advice on all sorts of matters. 'One day Tommy had driven to the ground in a new Ford car, which he'd bought,' said Peter, 'and he was showing it off to the players. When he left, he turned left to go down the High Road and stopped at the pedestrian crossing. Unfortunately a bus ran into the back of his car. Tommy went straight back into Bill's office, a few yards away and told him what had happened. "Did you get the number?" asked Bill. "I think it was 283," said Tommy.'

In the week before the start of the season the team experienced a setback and it gave Bill the chance to give his players a rollicking: 'We staged a public trial match watched by 11,000 fans and it was a dismal failure. The reserves drew 4-4 and I had no hesitation in saying it was the worst trial match I had ever seen. If there had been no crowd, we would have stopped it, I said. It was dreadful, despite the hard work we had put in on the training pitch. But once the League programme started on August 20, we settled down and played some impressive football.'

Indeed, Tottenham won three matches in the opening eight days and the next two games at home: victories over Blackpool, 3-1, and Manchester United, 4-1. The first 11 matches were won, beating the League record of nine wins held by Hull City in 1948/9. Blanchflower said: 'We started off, as Robb Wilton [a comedian of the day] used to say – like a house on fire. After those 11 wins, we dropped a point at home against Manchester City and won the next four. Sixteen games, one point lost – all entertaining, exciting affairs, in which we maintained a very consistent and high degree of skilful football. It was a fantastic run and I could hardly believe it.'

One commentator was so enthused that he said: 'Danny Blanchflower is telepathic and Dave Mackay is psychopathic.'

Two clubs – Preston, known as 'The Invincibles' in 1889 and Aston Villa in 1897 – won the Double, but professionalism had just been legalised and there were only 12 clubs in the championship, all drawn from Lancashire and the Midlands and the number of entrants to the FA Cup was small compared to today's figure. The Doubles of Preston North End and Villa lacked authenticity; Tottenham's was the real one. The Double, the first of the 20th century, was on its way.

On 12 November, the visitors were second-place Sheffield Wednesday, managed by Harry Catterick, who was about to make his reputation as one of the greatest managers of all time at Everton. Ten months older than Bill, the two men had many similarities. Catterick was a tough disciplinarian who insisted his players should be first to the ball. A student of tactics and an avid reader, he shunned publicity. Bill was wary about this fixture and he was proved right: 'They were a hard, dour side with defenders of the class of Peter Swan and the ginger-haired Tony Kay [both men were found guilty of the bribes scandal in 1963] and I knew it would be a difficult to win. It was the most physical encounter we had experienced up to then and we lost 2-1, our first defeat.

'I did not complain. As I left, I shook my fist in jest at Harry and said: "When you come to us, we'll give you more of this!" We were old rivals. When we went to Everton, chairman John Moores used to hold Tottenham up as the example he wanted to see copied at Goodison Park.'

After suffering a mild heart attack in 1972, Catterick went back to work for five more years. Like Jock Stein, he died watching a football match. While cheering Everton on against Ipswich Town in an exciting FA Cup tie in March 1985, he collapsed and never recovered. He was 65.

Les Allen had a triple heart bypass operation in the spring of 2009. He was one of four players who took part in all 42 First Division matches – the others were Ron Henry, Blanchflower and John White – and four others: Bill Brown, Peter Baker, Maurice Norman and Terry Dyson played 40 or more. This meant that Bill could almost put out an unchanged side. 'We were pretty fit because we did some heavy work in pre-season,' revealed Les. 'He wanted us to play flat out in practice games and we were thrashing the reserves 6-0 or worse. It all came together. He spent a lot of time talking about tactics and if anyone didn't follow the instructions, he would be out. But no one did. His organisation was brilliant. He wanted one touch right the way through the team. Knocking it off first time makes it very difficult to defend against "give it and go," he would say.'

Eight weeks after surgery Les was recuperating in bed when he watched Barcelona's humbling defeat of Manchester United on TV. He told his wife Pat: 'That was the way we played at Tottenham – United's couldn't get the ball from them.'

There was a lot of kicking, shoving and fouling during Tottenham's defeat at Hillsborough, but in his report in the *Sunday Pictorial* Edgar Turner wrote: 'Spurs never surrendered their dignity. At the final whistle Blanchflower ran to congratulate Alan Finney, the Wednesday captain and the two teams walked off, arm in arm.' Blanchflower was a Corinthian, as was Bill Nicholson. If only one of today's leading managers – say Sir Alex Ferguson – could copy their lead! Phil Soar wrote: 'It was a surprisingly cheerful team coach which left Hillsborough that evening and some of the players were singing on the way to the station. Long before that defeat they earned a glowing tribute from that stern taskmaster Stan Cullis, manager of Wolves, after Spurs had buried them again, this time 4-0 at Molineux – 'They are the finest club I've ever seen in the Football League, even better than the great Spurs of ten years previously.'

During Tottenham's Double season of glory some fine writing by

Ian Wooldridge, Professor Freddie Ayer, Karl Miller, John Arlott and others was published. A report on Spurs 4, Burnley 4 on 3 December 1960 was possibly the most stirring encounter of the lot and Wooldridge, then writing for the *Sunday Dispatch*, gave it his best:

A century of bitter North-South sporting partisanship was interrupted yesterday for an historic two-minute truce as 58,000 true soccer fans stood shoulder to shoulder in pouring rain to cheer off 22 men of London and Lancashire – men who had combined to make this the most thrilling match I have seen since Stanley Matthews turned a Cup Final into a one-man mutiny against fate. The flat accents of Burnley's few followers and the Cockney cheers of Spurs' thousands soared in one chorus of adulation, which told the whole story. It would have been tragedy, had either team lost. They produced football of immense majesty on a pitch that looked like Passenchendale. When Dave Mackay made it 4-0 after 36 minutes we knew the game was dead. Spurs had done it again in insolent style. But this was Burnley – a Burnley team fighting to show the South that British football extends further than the length of White Hart Lane. They did just that. Three goals came from mistakes and with 13 minutes left, Burnley pulled away from a desperate crisis in their own penalty area. An immense hush descended over the ground at the majestic sight of John Connelly streaking downfield towards a decimated Spurs defence. He swept the ball out to Jimmy Robson, picked up the return pass without a moment's falter in his fabulous run, and slammed in the goal that turned a massacre into an epic.

Bill was very upset after his team had conceded four goals, observing wryly: 'We scored all eight goals.'

Eric Todd of the *Guardian* was one of the outstanding writers in the North and this was his introduction in his Manchester City 0,

Tottenham 1 report: 'City's home Football League game against Tottenham at Moss Side took ill around 3 pm, rallied strongly for half an hour, had a relapse at 3.35 and expired at 4.10. At the inquest, a verdict of "accidental death" was recorded.'

Bill believed he had a squad of responsible players with no egos, who supported each other: 'I had a sensible bunch, who liked each other and wanted to play. There was no odd man out, no maverick in the camp. They were wholehearted enthusiasts and were a team in every sense of the word, and a happy team with it. There were plenty of laughs and jokes in training.'

Each season, today's England team play up to 12 matches or more, but in the 1960s the international programme was much smaller and there was less demand for the Tottenham players. When they were picked, they rarely made eight-hour flights to places like Almaty in Kazakhstan, close to the Chinese border. By Christmas the pitch was almost grassless and whenever it rained, it was churned up so badly that it was difficult to play one-touch passes along the ground. Tottenham were so far ahead of their rivals that only a major disaster could stop them. Manchester United inflicted a second League defeat at Old Trafford on 16 January, and 19 days later Leicester added a third loss: 2-3 at Filbert Street.

Tommy Harmer played 37 League games the previous season, but had to make way for John White, who played every match. A fragile personality, Harmer took it badly as he stepped up his use of Woodbines, the popular cigarette of the day. In October, Bill sold him to Watford, who soon let him to go to Chelsea. He retired at the age of 35 and should have had more recognition – one appearance for England B didn't reflect his ability.

On 17 April Tottenham duly won the title and their opponents were Sheffield Wednesday. Eerily, Tottenham won the championship in 1951 by beating the same team 1-0 on 18 April, a day later. 'That was appropriate and the score was the same – 2-1,' said Bill. 'Once again it was a rugged game. Ron Springett, the

Wednesday keeper, was charged into a post by Bobby Smith and was carried off, but managed to return a few minutes later. Our reserves came second to Chelsea in the Football Combination and the third team won the Eastern Counties League. Two out of three in the Leagues and now the FA Cup to come!'

Peter Lorenzo of the *Daily Herald* wrote: 'It was 90 minutes of tension accompanied by some terrifying tackling.' Laurie Pignon, one of the most expressive writers of his time, wrote: 'Five thousand crazy fans, drunk with success, brushed police aside and rushed to join the gigantic chorus in front of the directors' box calling for Danny, Danny, until I felt my ears would split.' Many of the 60,000 crowd came onto the pitch at the end; somehow the players managed to reach the tunnel and made their way up to the directors' box to acknowledge the roars of delight.

'Danny seemed faintly embarrassed,' said Mackay, 'and someone placed a hand on his shoulder and squeezed it, saying, "Come on, Danny boy, the pipes are calling." I looked at Danny and great gobs of tears came from nowhere and clouded his eyes.' Danny took the mike and said a few words, mostly drowned by the noise.

There was just one record they missed: Arsenal's 66 points in 1930/1. They equalled, but didn't beat it. Winning 31 matches was a record, though, and so was their tally of 16 victories on opposing grounds. They drew only four matches, one of the lowest number of draws in a season ever (the record for the highest is 18), and it emphasised the attacking way the team played. Bill was rarely happy with a draw. The total of 115 goals was a club record and the leading scorers were the two strikers: Bobby Smith with 28 and Les Allen with 23. Wingers Cliff Jones with 15, and Terry Dyson, 12, were next, with John White on 13. A total of 2,054,306 spectators watched their 42 League matches: an average of 48,912, with 474,011 at the seven FA Cup matches, average 67,715 – more than any other English club of that time.

Blanchflower was the celebrity figure in the club – not that he would accept that, though – and his face was seen everywhere: in his newspaper column, an advertisement for a breakfast cereal, which started with the words, 'Hello there!' and in February, the BBC began preparations to get him on *This Is Your Life*.

Eamonn Andrews, a fellow Irishman, was the presenter and he and his team made arrangements to bring the guests to the studio. The idea was to invite the subject to attend an interview at the BBC and when he came in to the studio, he would be surprised by Eamonn approaching him with the familiar red book marked *This Is Your Life*. But Danny refused to come in and took a taxi back home instead. The programme ran for several years and he was the only invited subject not to take part. Around 40 of his friends and footballing colleagues were there and Dave Mackay said: 'We had a party anyway. I felt like an idiot because I told some people to tune in to see it on TV. Instead of Danny, the programme was about an old man, who fostered scores of children.'

Asked later, Danny explained: 'I did it for personal reasons. If I told you what they were, they wouldn't be personal anymore, would they?' One of the players told me: 'Danny had a few secrets and he didn't want them to come out. His marriage with Betty was in trouble and he had someone else.' In fact, Danny was a womaniser with a tangled love life and he eventually married three times. He turned Eamonn Andrews down because didn't want to face an embarrassing inquisition. One of his friends said: 'Danny didn't smoke or drink, but he was very keen on the other.'

Bill's fear of losing in the early stages of the FA Cup wasn't realised. They scraped through 3-2 in the Third Round against Charlton at White Hart Lane, overwhelmed Crewe 5-1 at White Hart Lane in the Fourth Round, and won 2-0 against Blanchflower's old club Aston Villa in the Fifth Round. A visit to Sunderland's intimidating Roker Park ended in a rough and tough quarter-final tie on 1-1. The crowd came onto the pitch and according to Bill, it was the first major pitch invasion in English football – until then, fans didn't climb over the barriers.

Back at White Hart Lane, in front of 64,797 fans, Tottenham

waltzed through 5-0. Luck went their way before the semi-final because their opponents – champions Burnley – had lost 1-4 in Hamburg in the European Cup three days earlier. 'The wind blew and the pitch was hard,' recalled Bill. 'It wasn't a good game and we won 3-0.' Leicester City, one of the seven sides to beat Tottenham that season, went through to the final and were second favourites.

There was a feeling of anti-climax around the Tottenham club about the final. Danny Blanchflower, still unfit after being scythed down in the final League match and left with a swollen knee, and also worried about the state of his ailing father, summed it up: 'I didn't feel the same emotion that I had done before some of the previous rounds in the Cup. The press were pressuring us, the ticket spivs wanted our tickets and though we all wanted a great Cup Final, it didn't happen.' Bill observed: 'It didn't live up to the pre-match publicity – Cup Finals rarely do. I believe it is because the players are loath to take chances. Even experienced players are affected by the tension and do not play as well as they usually do.'

Most players and the occasional manager used to make large sums from selling their ticket allocation at the time, but Bill never got involved although he knew the gang of ticket operatives personally: Johnny the Stick, One-Arm Lou, 'Ginger', Stan Flashman and others. He even failed to recoup on his allocation. 'I had to buy mine like everyone else and not everyone paid for his ticket,' he recounted. 'So many relatives wanted tickets that I was unable to satisfy them and Darkie had a party round at the house to watch the game on TV.'

Alan Leather said: 'Organising tickets was a nightmare. I think our allocation was 12,000 out of 100,000 and we could have sold the 100,000.' Bill booked the team into the nearby Hendon Hall Hotel – the place where the England World Cup winners stayed in 1966 – and took the players to watch the late-night showing of *The Guns of Navarone* at the local Odeon. 'It was midnight before we got back,' remembered Blanchflower. In the morning the players watched *Grandstand* and heard Wally Barnes, the former Arsenal and Wales left back, talking about the time when he severely twisted his knee in the 1952 Cup Final and wondering whether another such accident might ruin the match. Matt Gillies, the amiable Leicester manager, had dropped his centre forward Ken Leek and replaced him with teenager Hugh McIlmoyle. Maurice Norman was relieved: 'Ken always gave me problems – he was very good in the air and always scored against us.'

As the teams lined up, HRH The Duchess of Kent was introduced to Blanchflower and she observed: 'The other team have their names on their shirts.' Danny quipped: 'Yes, but *we* know each other!'

When the match started, both sides played with extreme caution, as though copying the movements of history's first man on the moon. But in the 19th minute, Les Allen – who started out his career at White Hart Lane before joining Chelsea – tackled Len Chalmers, the Leicester right back. Chalmers needed prolonged treatment before he was carried off. The spot where it happened was almost the same position where Barnes had fallen nine years earlier. Bill considered the tackle fair and Dave Mackay commented: 'It really hurt Len – it was an accident, but it may have looked like it wasn't.'

Chalmers returned and stood on the left wing, not able to play a proper part in the match. Substitutes weren't introduced until 1965, with Charlton's Keith Peacock being the first, so Leicester had to play 10 against 11 and it meant that their players tried that much harder. Colin Appleton, Leicester's captain, said: 'We were still in the game and I was proud of the way we kept at it. Sometimes teams find it hard to play against 10 men and that's what happened. Len couldn't do much – just knock the ball back to a colleague.' Despite their best efforts, however, Tottenham won 2-0.

Appleton recalled: 'After the game, we were in the bath, feeling quite chuffed and not too disappointed about the result, when Bill came in with the FA Cup filled with champagne. "Well played," he said, "have some of this!" I don't think a manager had done that before, but that was the kind of man he was. I rated him in the top five of managers, right up with Matt Busby, Jock Stein, Bill Shankly and Alex Ferguson. I know Liverpool had some outstanding managers, but the ones who followed Shankly had something to work on. Bill built a great side, which played some wonderful attacking football.'

Frank McLintock, the best player on his side, said: 'We weren't disgraced, losing against one of greatest sides of all time.'

The day before, Bobby Smith had been given a painkilling injection, and he wanted another to ensure his painful knee was still numb. Bill called him one of the gutsiest players he had under him. Once again he opened the scoring with a feint and a crashing shot past Gordon Banks in the 67th minute before Terry Dyson, the outstanding Man of the Match, headed the second 10 minutes later. Up until then, Tottenham had been short of adventure and Maurice Norman, who often came up for his side's corners, never went up for the entire game.

Said Appleton: 'Terry came from Malton and I knew his family well. He was a tenacious player, who never stopped working. When he played junior football in North Yorkshire his team used to travel in a converted ambulance to their matches.' Terry should have brought that ambulance to Wembley: it might have taken Len to hospital.

After the insipid 2-0 victory, Bill showed little emotion: 'If I won £1m on the pools or in a newspaper competition, I wouldn't jump for joy. If something has been your ambition and you have achieved it, then that's fine. I wanted us to show how good we were, but the match wasn't particularly entertaining. In those days you were not mobbed by TV and press. There were no press conferences and I do not remember giving a press interview, although I did speak informally to some reporters later. In those days the game didn't need to sell itself – grounds were full at clubs which were successful.'

The banquet was held at the Lancaster Room in The Savoy and it turned out to be a raucous night. Leslie Grade of the Grade brothers organised the entertainment and Harry Secombe was the first on. With the players making a lot of boisterous noise, Shirley Bassey declined to sing, claiming she had a sore throat. Blanchflower said: 'So I finished the day looking down Shirley Bassey's throat.' Alan Leather recalled: 'It was rather embarrassing – a disaster, really.'

Early in the evening Les Allen was glum. Some of the players were upset that none of the Leicester players had accepted his apology for the tackle, but after dinner some telegrams were read out and one was from Chalmers, saying: 'Forget it – congratulations!'

Next day there were few signs around White Hart Lane of decorations on nearby buildings to celebrate Tottenham's success and Alan Leather admitted: 'Bill was worried that hardly anyone would turn up. We had this open-top bus – I think it came from Brighton – and we were thinking that it might be a big let-down. When we got to Edmonton Town Hall, we were surprised to see that thousands of people were there. I've never seen such a gathering. The police thought it was as much as 500,000 all along the route. When we passed by blocks of flats, people were thronging the balconies. And when we passed the Palais, the dance hall, they had a full orchestra playing "Glory, glory."'

At the time Bill's annual salary was £1,500 – about twice the national average wage – and he received a modest bonus for achieving the Double. He had kept an unchanged side for 29 of the 42 games, an incredible record. Seven players appeared in 40 or more matches, confirming his view that good players are less prone to injury. Brave ones, like Mackay, Blanchflower and Smith, just played through the pain. Bill said of Mackay: 'If he had served in a war, he would have been the first man into action and he would have won the Victoria Cross.' Recently, Harry Redknapp asked a football writer: 'Did you ever see Mackay play? It would need three players to take his place.'

Bill had a small group of first team players, much fewer than today's top clubs, and he was always trying to buy better ones. His prime objective in challenging for a Treble in the following season was to bring Jimmy Greaves to White Hart Lane – and he soon succeeded.

Ken Jones, the former *Daily Mirror* sports writer, told a remarkable tale of Bill's interest in trying to sign George Eastham during the Double season: 'I had a call from Harry Evans and he wanted me to come over to see Bill to discuss the Eastham affair. Bill knew that I was involved with getting George a job with Ernie Clay when he went on strike from Newcastle, just before the maximum wage was going to be removed.

'When I arrived in Bill's office, he took out the *News of the World Annual* and said, "I've just noticed that George scored 29 goals in 124 matches with Newcastle and that's not a bad scoring rate for a midfield player." He was keen to buy him, but when he realised that he would have to break one of the Football League rules to do it, he changed his mind. He was that kind of man, so straight and honest. Arsenal bought him, a short time later.'

Was his Double better than Arsenal's, 10 years later? Bill was certain his was the better one: 'I think we would have edged it. My team had more variety, more style. The players were encouraged to express themselves, though not at the expense of teamwork. With Arsenal, you always felt that the team was working to a plan and did not allow the same degree of licence. Arsenal's was based on discipline and determination. It was a good side, with excellent players, but we scored more goals – 115 in our year to Arsenal's 71 in 1971.' Few would disagree with that.

'There was no single secret about our success,' he continued. 'Just as there is no school for managers where you can go and be told how to win things. The players didn't get the rewards they should have, though that wasn't clear at the time. I am sorry about that, and I was always too busy to appreciate the small things about people and about our success, which is a great pity.'

CHAPTER TEN:

KNOCKED OUT BY ALF RAMSEY'S HAYMAKERS

Bill Nicholson started pre-season training for the 1961/2 season with the aim of becoming the first manager to win all three major trophies. 'I want to win the championship, the FA Cup *and* the European Cup,' he told his startled players. But for his old adversary, Alf Ramsey – now in his first managerial job as boss of Ipswich Town – and a referee whose decisions cost his side victory over Benfica in the European Cup, he would have done it.

Nicholson versus Ramsey should have resulted in an easy win for Bill. He had more managerial experience than the unqualified Ramsey and better players, a bigger, noisier crowd and far more money. It was the suave Spurs against the country rustics of Town. But, without any international players, Ramsey matched Tottenham's performance in winning the Second and First Divisions in 1949/50 and 1950/1, taking his ageing team from the Second Division in 1960/1 and – against all the odds – capturing the Championship the following season.

The fate of the Championship was decided by just two matches, both won by Ipswich, and had Tottenham taken four points off Ramsey's side – as they should have done – Bill would have been the victor. Bill admitted that it had been a disaster on two counts: 'At a team meeting before our first match against Ipswich on October 21, I suggested that our midfield players should mark their wingers, Roy Stephenson and Jimmy Leadbetter, leaving our full backs to move inside to help take care of Ray Crawford and Ted Phillips, their central strikers. Ipswich had an effective system. Stephenson and Leadbetter were withdrawn into midfield and Crawford and Phillips were played up front.

'Blanchflower agreed with me, but Mackay didn't. He said he had just won three matches playing the way he wanted to play. "Why change to suit them?" he said. "We're good enough to beat them playing our normal style." It was one of the few times I bowed to the players' wishes and we lost 3-2 at Portman Road.'

On 14 March the teams met at White Hart Lane and Bill, with his men still in favour of playing it their way, decided to employ the same tactics and that turned out to be another calamitous mistake. Ipswich won 3-1: for the second time all the goals were scored by Crawford (73 in two seasons) and Phillips (58 in the same period). Known as 'Sticks' because of his thin legs, Leadbetter passed like a wizard from his withdrawn position, giving plenty of service to the former National Serviceman Crawford and Phillips – known as 'Cannonball' because of his ferocious shooting. Ted's shooting was once timed at 87 mph, well ahead of Ronaldo and today's stars.

Some of the Ipswich players were heavy drinkers and the right-winger, Roy Stephenson, became so drunk on a flight back from Europe that he tried to unlock a door and jump out of the aircraft. He had to be restrained.

Ramsey shared Bill's view that the best way to be successful in football is to keep possession of the ball as much as possible, but he also used the long ball to his strikers and this simple tactic worked, if only for a short time. Once the other managers got used to the Ipswich method, the team started to collapse and Ramsey moved on to England, where he came up with another simple tactic: replacing orthodox wingers with hardworking wide midfield players. That worked too, but it didn't last.

Bill correctly observed: 'When we played Ipswich next time, in the Charity Shield at the start of the next season, I made sure we played my way and we won 5-1 at Portman Road. Not every side had a coach in those days and Ramsey was one of the first to insist on a certain way of playing and sticking to it, whatever happened. It was a marvellous feat, guiding an average side to the title and one that may well not be repeated.'

Tottenham finished third behind Ipswich and Burnley, and with their strikers Bobby Smith and Les Allen reduced to scoring just 6 and 9 goals respectively, Bill started to make efforts to sign Jimmy Greaves from his miserable incarceration with AC Milan. Arthur Rowe had been courting Greaves's father while Jimmy was still at secondary school and everyone at White Hart Lane thought he would sign for the club. The reason why they failed, however, was because of the rule forbidding payments to parents of young apprentices about to join League clubs. 'We never paid inducements to parents,' explained Bill. 'Spurs never did when I was manager and I am certain they didn't before I took over. But it was an open secret that fees or presents, or both, were handed over by most clubs. I think the League should sanction these payments because they were out of date. The reason why the League forbids it is they have to be given evidence but no one complains, certainly not the club which signs the youngsters and the parents.'

The man who took Greaves to Chelsea was the legendary scout named Jimmy Thompson. Small in stature, Thompson nearly always wore a brown bowler, but on some of his expeditions to school matches he wore a disguise, such as a wide-brimmed hat, and often hid behind bushes or trees to avoid being spotted by rival scouts. Greaves was born in east London's Manor Park in the Blitz of 1940. After their house was demolished by a bombing raid the family moved to Dagenham. His father worked for the London

Underground and was treasurer of Fanshaw Old Boys, a local club that derives its name from a school boasting Les Allen, Terry Venables and Martin Peters as former pupils.

At 15, Greaves was chosen for the London Schoolboys and he admitted: 'I had a pretty quiet game and I was due to have an interview for a job at *The Times*.' Thompson stopped his chances of working in the print and instead took him to Ted Drake, where he soon did a deal – £50 in Irish fivers to Mr Greaves, which he had won betting on horses in Ireland the day before.

The footballing prodigy quickly fulfilled every promise, scoring 124 goals in 157 League games for Chelsea, but the club was close to bankruptcy and with the Italian League lifting their ban on signing foreign players, they were willing to sell him. Greaves was 20 and married to his childhood sweetheart Irene with one daughter, having lost a four-month-old son; it seemed a good idea to make money abroad in a new environment. He accepted a signing-on fee of £15,000 and a weekly salary of £130, while Chelsea received £80,000. But he soon changed his mind, only for Chelsea to remind him of his responsibilities. After four months, during which he scored nine goals in 14 matches – 'I was the top scorer' – AC Milan agreed to sell him and Tottenham was the first to call.

In the previous May, Bill had bumped into Greaves in the bathroom at the Cafe Royal in Piccadilly and told him: 'You went to the wrong club – you ought to be here with us.' 'I think I will, next time,' conceded Greaves, who had found it impossible to work under the fearsome Nereo Rocco, the AC Milan coach. Now his directors wanted to sell him for £100,000. Bill insisted on £99,999 and explained: 'I refused to make him the first £100,000 footballer because I didn't want a millstone round his neck and I didn't want that reputation, either. Some of our rivals were criticising us for bumping up fees already and in a way I felt they had a point.'

Arriving at the door of the couple's flat, he asked Irene: 'Do you know I am?' 'Yes,' she replied, 'Our saviour!' Chelsea said they wanted Greaves back, but this was a dodge to placate their fans – they had no chance of outbidding Tottenham. The discussions between clubs soon became fraught, with an irate Bill telling Andrea Rizzoli, the AC Milan President: 'This is becoming like a scene from *The Merchant of Venice*.' 'You are impertinent,' was Rizzoli's reply. As the talks dragged on, Tottenham and Chelsea were asked to submit written bids. Learning that Chelsea's was £96,500, Bill bid the same. John Battersby, their secretary, was playing a game of bluff and Chelsea withdrew their supposed offer. Rizzoli stuck on £100,000 and finally caved in on £1 less.

'It was a lot of money, but the outlay was worth it,' said Bill. 'What I liked about him was his attitude – he was always friendly and interested. Nor did he bear any malice after rows we had about minor matters. He had the natural gift of timing and the accuracy of his shooting was uncanny and his reactions were fantastically quick. Some players complained about his work rate, but I would say, "He's in the team and he scores most of our goals."'

Greaves was happy with Bill's offer of £60 a week, three times the average of the maximum wage of £20 until the limit was removed, two years earlier. Few footballers could equal the impact Greaves had on his debut at White Hart Lane on 16 December 1961, when he scored a hat trick in Tottenham's 5-2 win. Though he played just half the season, he scored 30 goals, almost a goal a game. He surprised his colleagues by wearing rubbers, not studded boots, unless pitches were extremely muddy. Mackay shared the same penchant: he too preferred rubber. In his seven years at White Hart Lane he wore just four pairs of boots.

In the early weeks of his signing, Greaves felt resentment from some of the players. They thought that Les Allen had been badly treated and one said: 'We've just shown we are the best team in the country. Why make changes?' But the flood of goals from the newcomer soon brought about an acceptance.

He was to star in a show that transformed football into a new, dynamic era in English football. In 1954, Wolves pioneered the use of floodlighting by staging friendly matches against Spartak Moscow, Honved and Barcelona in a packed, throbbing Molineux; a year later, a Belgian journalist – Gabriel Hanot – came up with the idea to form a European League played under lights. It started in 1956 and Real Madrid, inspired by the Argentinian Alfredo di Stefano, won the first five tournaments before Portugal's Benfica took the next two. Sitting outside when the sun has gone down and the temperature drops might not appeal to some, but the well wrapped up majority appreciated that floodlit football appeared to be faster and more exciting than games played in daylight.

Greaves missed the first two rounds of the 1961/2 European Cup season but he realised that joining Tottenham had given him his best chance of winning it – with the help of one of the thunderously noisy supporting armies in world football, almost rivalling Boca Juniors in Buenos Aires. Most other competing clubs had large, sprawling grounds encircled by running tracks but at White Hart Lane, with its high elevation of enclosed stands only a few yards from the action, Tottenham's players found themselves propelled into a new strata of entertainment. The pace was frantic; the volume of noise never died. In fact it only lasted for two seasons, seven matches in all, in the European Cup and the European Cup Winners' Cup, but anyone who was there would never forget it.

Bill described it in his autobiography, *Glory, Glory – My Life at Spurs*: 'A new sound was heard in English football that year. It was the hymn "Glory, Glory Hallelujah" being sung by 60,000 fans. I didn't know how it started or who started it but it took over the ground like a religious feeling. No congregation of the biggest church assembly in the country could possibly match the noise that was to be heard off Tottenham High Road.' Danny Blanchflower said of the supporters: 'They were showing their faith and were not to be denied. I doubt whether any ground has ever echoed to a greater volume of noise in the South of our ground. It frightened the opposing sides from Europe – well, except Benfica. The noise came from everywhere, from everyone. A local vicar used to complain that the whole thing as like a substitute for religion and I suppose it was in a way.'

In the sardine-like press box, above the directors' box, the journalists who tried to pose a question such as 'Who passed it?' found themselves unable to hear the answer. Bill would be sitting in the back of the directors' box, scribbling notes on pieces of paper (he rarely used a proper notebook). If you were close enough, you could lean over and read what he wrote. It was usually something about who had failed to pick up an opponent, or who didn't get a tackle when he should; little reminders for when the players came in at half time or at the end of the match to try and eradicate more mistakes.

Tottenham was the fourth English club to play in the European Cup and their opening game took place at the Slaski Stadium at Katowice, a coal-mining town in the heart of Poland. Their opponents were Polish champions Gornik Zabrze and the date was 13 September 1961. A week before, Bill had gone on a reconnaissance trip and with no airport at Katowice, he caught an overnight train from Warsaw. He recalled: 'Gornik officials were there to meet me and it was a typical Eastern European railway station – badly lit, no platforms and an unwelcoming appearance. The officials led me along the track to a grubby-looking hotel. It was like a scene from *The Spy Who Came In from the Cold*. The place was filthy and I said I didn't want that. "Show me your best hotel," I asked them. "This is it," they said. I told them we would have to stay in another town. They took me to Chorzow and after being shown round their hotels, I realised that Katowice was the best one. When the team arrived, the following week, the hotel had been redecorated, but the players were still dissatisfied. They complained about bugs in their beds.'

While guards with machine guns looked on, prisoners were digging up cobblestones in the road. Meanwhile, at the ground, women on their hands and knees were cutting the grass with scissors. The playing pitch was better than Wembley.

There was a diplomatic row when two English journalists, Geoffrey Green of *The Times* and Laurie Pignon of the *Daily Sketch*, were arrested at Warsaw Airport and Tottenham officials contacted the British Embassy about releasing them. Laurie, now 90, said: 'Geoffrey Green pulled out a camera and took a picture of the sign "Warsaw" on the station, and suddenly we were arrested and whisked away to a police station and interrogated. I was terribly worried I would miss my deadlines, but Geoffrey was a wonderful man and made light of it with his jokes and tricks and an odd song, and eventually we were allowed to join the team.'

Arriving in Katowice brought back bad memories for Laurie: 'I spent almost five years down the coal mines there,' he continued. 'I was captured just before Dunkirk and no one told me that we were not to be evacuated. My mate "Porky" and I, and the rest of us, were transported across Europe and we spent a seven-day, ten-hour day without any respite, and a lot of them didn't make it. We existed on watery soup and a lump of horrible bread, and the worse thing was not having any soap, so we were like Black Minstrels most of the time. In the cruel winter of 1945 we were told to march to the West under escort from German soldiers and it took months.

'You could never keep your boots dry and I remembered speaking to a boxer some years previously about toughening your skin and he said, "Use vinegar." Of course we didn't have access to vinegar so I decided to pee on my bare feet every day and "Porky" and I were two of the survivors when we arrived in a place in Austria, where a factory built Messerschmitt 109s fighter aircraft. A lot of my friends didn't make it. Years later I met Dr Alan Bass, the Arsenal and England team doctor, and he said: "That was the best thing you did, peeing on yourself."'

Laurie was also the tennis writer of the *Sketch* and while football wasn't his first love, he got on extremely well with Bill. 'Lovely man and a loyal man,' he recounted. 'But in those days he was a bit introverted – he didn't crack jokes or go to nightclubs. But we respected him for his honesty and fairness. I remember one thing about the match, Dave Mackay kicking their best player and putting the guy out of the game.' Laurie, an inveterate pipe smoker, has had a remarkable life and he said: 'I'm still here because I didn't look after myself. All the friends of mine who looked after themselves are dead!'

After an hour against an average side Tottenham were 4-0 down, but Cliff Jones and Terry Dyson managed to make it 4-2 and avoid an early exit. 'I was bloody upset,' conceded Bill. 'We lacked discipline and determination.' The 'B' word was just about the limit of his swearing. He wasn't an 'F' man.

If ever there was a day when the Tottenham symphony reached its ultimate, it was the day of the return leg, 20 September, a week after the match in Poland. The roads were gridlocked for miles around and thousands who wanted to attend were denied. Well before kick-off, the noise began. There were no Polish supporters to support their players. The spectacle almost compared with the 50,000-capacity Coliseum in Rome, where 15,000 would be slaughtered within the first three years of its opening. Ernst Pohl, the Gornik skipper and much-capped international, scored the best goal, arguably, but there was no fear in the minds of Nicholson's players. Blanchflower converted a penalty and the floodgates opened, with Cliff Jones scoring a hat trick; two came from Bobby Smith and one apiece from Dyson and John White. Tottenham 8, Gornik 1, aggregate 10-5.

In the wood-lined dressing room the players were ecstatic, hugging each other and congratulating everyone including the trainer, Cec Poynton, who was pouring out tea from a huge enamel jug into small, plain cups. In those days they had duckboards, where the players sat down, making sure that their feet kept dry. Mackay said: 'They weren't a poor side, but we were irresistible on the night. We played the sort of game Bill would have liked us to have played against Leicester in the Cup Final, but didn't.'

John Bond, the former Bournemouth, Norwich, Manchester City, Burnley, Swansea, Birmingham and Shrewsbury manager, watched the game and said: 'I was playing for West Ham and I loved going to White Hart Lane to watch Bill's side. That game was the peak for me. Gornik was a tremendous side and they were knocked aside. It's difficult to compare teams from different eras, but I know this: if there is a better team than Bill's, it's going to be a really special one to beat it – Tottenham were different class.

'People talk about some of the foreign players today but I don't see a winger today who can do what Cliff Jones did. He could beat anyone at pace and though he wasn't tall, he could get up to head fantastic goals. We accept that Mackay and Blanchflower were exceptional players, but what about Bobby Smith? He'd be a star today. Fabio Capello would love a Bobby Smith in his team. Later, I got to know Bill quite well and I learned a lot from him. He always had time for people and he was a very humble man. I'd see him and Darkie at events and they looked like an ordinary couple, but he was a very great man.'

Tottenham had little trouble in overcoming Feyenoord in the next round. At that time, Dutch football hadn't emerged as a major force and Tottenham won 3-1 in Rotterdam, with 17-year-old Frank Saul scoring one of the goals. The return game ended 1-1 and it was a mundane event in complete contrast to the Gornik performance. Greaves was not eligible for the first two rounds, but he accompanied the party to Prague to take on the Czech Army side Dukla Prague in the quarter-final. He was relieved to be sitting in the stand because the pitch at the National Stadium was more like an ice-skating rink. Bill took no chances: he used Tony Marchi as a sweeper – the first time he had ever used a sweeper – and was satisfied to return home from a 1-0 defeat. Mackay showed his versatility in moving up to an attacking midfield role and scoring two goals in the 4-2 win in the return leg.

Bill was hoping that Real Madrid would be drawn against his team for the semi-final after seeing Madrid beat Juventus in the quarter-final, realising they had deteriorated and would be less of a threat to holders Benfica. At the draw the wrong ball came out: the Eagles of

Lisbon were first out. They were managed by a wily 62-year-old Hungarian, Bela Guttman, who spoke six languages and coached all around the world. During World War II, he survived a Nazi concentration camp. The Stadium of Light ground was filled with 86,000 Portuguese and a few hundred Tottenham supporters in a battle between two outstanding attacking sides. Aguas and Augusto scored early, and although Smith responded with a creditable goal, Augusto headed a second, leaving the first leg on 3-1.

Greaves felt Bill went into the game with a defensive approach, shifting Blanchflower from midfield into a back five. In his book, *Greavsie*, he wrote: 'I still felt we could win, but I didn't take account for diabolical decisions by the referee and some really shabby tactics from Benfica themselves.' He claimed the home side 'hacked and kicked' their opponents. 'The referee [a Swiss named Muellett] made a string of decisions that I not only found bewildering, but left me feeling downright suspicious,' he said. 'What aroused our suspicions was the fact that when Bobby Smith put the ball in the net, he blew his whistle and it was only then that his fellow linesman raised his flag to indicate that Bobby was offside. I had a clear view of the incident and Bobby wasn't offside. Minutes from the end I scored what I believed was a perfectly good goal only to have it disallowed, again for offside. I was too stupefied to protest, I simply stood hands on hips, staring in disbelief.'

In the early days of the European Cup, referees were given handsome gifts to commemorate their selection for major matches. Real Madrid, Benfica and the Italian clubs AC Milan and Juventus were renowned for this practice. Sometimes the presents were extremely valuable. Not a single game was investigated or replayed, however. It was impossible to assemble any proof, but as Greaves said, there is always an element of suspicion when highly trained, experienced referees suddenly start to make elementary mistakes. Terry Medwin shared the view that something wasn't quite right: 'Bill wasn't a man who moaned and would use the word cheat, but years later he said to me that those disallowed "goals" stopped us winning the European Cup.'

Before the return game, there was a debate about whether Bill should have man-marked Eusebio da Silva Ferreira, the explosive forward from Mozambique, who was the top scorer in the 1966 World Cup. 'I put Phil Beal on him in a tournament in Majorca, a few years later,' he said. 'Phil did such a good job that Eusebio was ineffective. It was the first time I had done that, but there was no question of doing that in either leg of the Benfica semi-final and I believe, but for some marginal refereeing decisions that went against us, we would have gone through.'

David Miller described the tie at White Hart Lane as 'the most electrifying 90 minutes of European football I have ever seen on an English ground.' An hour before kick-off, the gates were locked. Bela Guttmann worried that his players might be affected by the atmosphere and didn't allow them to go on to the ground to warm up. In his pre-match publicity, Bela kept urging the Danish referee Aage Poulsen to watch Dave Mackay and Bobby Smith closely and take the necessary action if they roughed up his players. Nicholson didn't think that was a factor but Guttmann conceded after his side's success, when they went through 4-3 on aggregate: 'Yes, we got many free kicks.'

Greaves had a 'goal' disallowed – the third in the two matches. He said: 'I was disgusted. The referee blew up for a goal, but his linesman had his flag up and the referee changed his mind. We had three perfectly good goals disallowed and that took some getting over. But for those questionable decisions I'm sure we would have gone on to win the European Cup.' In the end, Benfica retained the trophy, beating Real Madrid 5-3 in Amsterdam, to prove that they were the world's best club side at the time.

Bill said: 'I lost count of the near misses but credit to them, they were a very fine side.' Danny Blanchflower, as he often did, summed it up brilliantly: 'I think Bela was sharper than we thought.' Terry Medwin shared the general view that something wasn't quite right: 'Bill wasn't a man who moaned and would use the word "cheat" but years later, he said to me that those disallowed "goals" stopped us winning the European Cup. They were wonderful, magnificent battles, and I holiday in Portugal with my family and often meet people who still talk about them. Benfica had some marvellous players and one I respected was Germano, the centre half, who was a commanding defender. He was a keen book reader. Sadly, he has Alzheimer's.'

A month later Tottenham were back at Wembley to contest the FA Cup Final against Burnley, the League runners up. The dream of a Treble had ended and there was just one trophy left. Bill made a short speech, saying: 'You are the players who have been good enough to get us here – and you are good enough to win it. If each and every one of you does his job, we will win.' Hardly Nelsonian, but there was little more to say.

Greaves broke through to score within three minutes and at half time Bill wasn't happy. Terry Medwin recalled: 'He pointed to me and Cliff Jones, and said: "You two, you've got to get forward more."' Jimmy Robson soon equalised, Bobby Smith regained the lead not long after this and Blanchflower converted a late penalty. The result, 3-1, was a convincing win. The players thought it was magnificent contest, but their manager had a different view. He dismissed it, saying: 'It was another disappointing final, although no one was injured.'

The format of the celebratory banquet had changed: there were hardly any speeches, to give the players maximum time to chat and drink the champagne. Limbo dancing was the main entertainment and nearly everyone thought it a great choice. Bill abstained, but took to the floor with Darkie for a slow waltz.

Traditionally, a Cup Final dominated the thoughts of many of the populace during the first week of May. The BBC's *Match of the Day* had started and TV coverage on both channels began early in the morning and lasted until early evening. For all its coverage, though, this particular final seemed to slip by without drama. It might well have been the start of the downgrading of one of Britain's sporting protected jewels to what has now become a secondary event. Today, the Big Four clubs often put in their reserves, but Bill wouldn't have liked that – it's against the spirit of the game.

CHAPTER ELEVEN

'THE GREATEST GAME I'VE EVER PLAYED IN!'

Maybe we were harsh on Danny Blanchflower for calling him Bill Nicholson's Sherpa. On one of the key dates of Bill's career, 15 May 1963, he made a crucial mistake before the kick-off of the Final of the European Cup Winners' Cup at the Feyenoord Stadium in Rotterdam when he seized the initiative and took over. Blanchflower was by then in his final months as a Tottenham player and Bill gave him the job of assistant to the manager, as opposed to being assistant manager.

Instead of staying in the bustling city of Rotterdam, Bill plumped for a seaside hotel in Scheveningen, 40 minutes away. In his pre-match talk, Bill started off by saying that their opponents Atletico Madrid, holders of the ECWC Cup after beating Fiorentina in the previous final, were a cracking good side and he went through all the names. 'The keeper, Madinabeytia, is terrific,' he said. 'Bosses his area, great shot stopper. Right back Rivilla is quick and a good tackler, similar to the left back Ramiro. Both terrific. Then we've got Ramiro and we'll have to watch him – he's very good on the ball. Adelardo and Mendoza are a class act, great passers. Chuzo, their centre forward, very mobile, very skilful, great in the air. If we're not careful, he'll cause us problems.'

But Danny intervened and said: 'Hang on a minute, Bill. What is all this? Can you imagine their team talk next door? Their coach won't be saying how great Tottenham are. For heaven's sake, you are making them sound like world-beaters! They're not world-beaters, but we are. I say, forget them. Let's concentrate on our own strengths as a team, which, by the way, are far and away better than theirs. If their centre half is big and ugly, then ours is bigger and uglier. If this Chuzo fellow can cause problems in a penalty area, then Jimmy here can cause ten times as many problems for them. We are the team that's going to win it!'

In his autobiography *Greavsie*, Jimmy Greaves said: 'Bill could have felt that his position as manager was being compromised. It was then that Bill gave evidence of being the great manager we all knew him to be: he held up his hand and fell into line with what Danny said. Never again did I ever hear him pump up an opposing side. We were fired up when he went out on the pitch and produced one of the all-time great performances by a Tottenham team. Atletico were second behind Real Madrid and they were a very good team, but on the night they had no answer to us. To my mind, this game was the greatest game I ever played in. It had everything. Silky skills, precise passing and movement off the ball. It was passionate, entertaining, dramatic, colourful and, above all, peppered with goals.'

David Miller said that Bill gave 'a funereal team talk' and he quoted Greaves as saying: 'Nic's confidence seemed to have gone because Dave Mackay was injured and couldn't play. He always thought Dave was his key player.' Mackay was debating whether he ought to play: on many occasions he had a cortisone injection and played, but this time he couldn't take a chance. 'If it went, I'd be a passenger,' he conceded.

Tony Marchi, an underrated and versatile player, took over and hardly made a mistake. Blanchflower himself needed a cortisone injection before the game. Midway through the season his knee locked and the club's consultant recommended surgery. From January to mid-March, a big freeze settled in all over Britain which should have given Blanchflower time to regain fitness for the last stages of the ECWC tournament. At 37, he risked permanent damage after the remnants of a cartilage were removed.

Bill recalled: 'He made a phenomenally quick return and was back playing for the "A" team after a month. He was a very brave player. We both knew the Atletico game would probably be his last big game and I wanted him to play. When there is a doubt about a player's fitness, the manager prefers it if the player makes up his own mind. The man who is keen to carry on is going to make a more positive contribution to the team effort than one who is reluctant to play.'

Danny had told Bill: 'I want to play, but it's me on one leg or John Smith [a reserve] on two.'

'Okay,' said Bill, 'you're in.'

Terry Dyson, who turned out to be the hero of Tottenham's rousing 5-1 victory, the biggest margin ever in the competition, recalled: 'That finished Danny off – he came back too soon. The treatments in that time were ridiculous: they told you to put weights on your foot and keep lifting it, and run up and down stairs, and it took ages to get back to fitness. I had a cartilage once and being small, I didn't have the same trouble as the heavier, taller players.'

These days the experts warn that too much cortisone can ruin athletes in later life, but Bill, writing in 1984, said: 'Players knew the risk and some didn't like having them. Doctors warn that when the area of pain has been deadened it could cause more problems afterwards, but I can't think of any of my players who suffered in later life. Most of the Double side are still capable of playing as they proved in my testimonial in 1983. But Danny has needed operations to his feet in recent years and claims it was caused by football.'

One player whom Bill didn't select for the testimonial was

Tommy Harmer. When Tommy complained, Bill replied tersely: 'Well, you're 55 – it's a bit too late for you!'

Tottenham were the slickest and most determined of the two teams in Rotterdam: a fluke goal finished off the Spaniards. Early in the second half, Dyson beat Rivilla and sent a deep cross in from the byline. Goalkeeper Madinabeytia punched the ball into the net to make it 3-1. Dutch referee Van Leeuwen awarded the goal to Dyson. 'Aye, it was an odd one but they had to give it to me,' he conceded. Greaves scored from a Cliff Jones pass in the 16th minute while John White converted a cross from Dyson, which nearly went out of play before Collar converted a penalty.

Terry laid on the fourth goal – scored by Greaves – and crashed in the fifth from 25 yards. As the players came off, Bobby Smith told him: 'You'd better retire now – you'll never play better than that!' (In fact, Terry played on for six more years, ending his career at Colchester.) 'Bill was very pleased and it was probably the highlight of my career,' he recalled. 'We we had a great party afterwards at a nightclub in Amsterdam. Scores of our fans joined in. What a night that was!'

Greaves put an arm round Mackay to console him: 'I cried with delirium at our success and disappointment at having not been a part of the climax,' Mackay said. He suspected that the Double team had gone as far as they could and would soon be on the slide. He was quickly proved right.

On the way to the final in Amsterdam Tottenham's plans were disrupted by the Great Freeze of 1962/3 – week after week whole programmes of League matches were postponed, causing chaos. Between Boxing Day and late March, they played only two League matches, but managed to lose 3-0 to Burnley in the FA Cup on 16 January on a snow-covered pitch; their exit in the competition gave them a better chance of becoming the first British club to win a European trophy. Not that Bill thought so. After winning the FA Cup twice in succession, he wasn't pleased about losing his club's chances of making it a hat trick.

In 1956, UEFA started its three inter-country competitions with the European Cup, the Inter-Cities Fairs Cup in 1958 and the European Cup Winners' Cup in 1961; the ECWC tournament was rated second in status behind the European Cup. The 1962/3 tournament contained some strong clubs including Glasgow Rangers, Sparta Rotterdam, Napoli, Vitoria Setabul, Rapid Vienna, Borussia Mönchengladbach, Seville and holders Atletico Madrid. There were no duds from 'countries' such as Liechtenstein, Andorra, San Marino, Faroe Islands and none of the now-independent nations of the former USSR.

Tottenham's first opponents were Rangers, the two-legged round described as 'the Battle of Britain'. Unlike today's multi-national side, Rangers was packed with Scottish internationals, including 'Slim' Jim Baxter, then a modest 11-stone man with a huge thirst, Willie Henderson, Eric Caldow, Bobby Shearer, Ralph Brand and Davie Wilson. This was a time, fast disappearing, when Scotland could still take on England with a chance of winning. The hype was colossal, with the Scots commentators confidently predicting it would end in victory for the 'Gers.

Tottenham gave a reasonable percentage of tickets to the Rangers contingent and their fans were soon silenced at a full-house White Hart Lane as Maurice Norman, John White (2) and Les Allen scored four of the five goals in a 5-2 near rout. The other goal came from Shearer's boot. Bill said: 'I'd seen them a couple of times and I felt they were vulnerable to headers from corners. They had someone to mark Norman, but they didn't take care of John White, who headed both of his goals and wasn't renowned for his heading ability.' Greaves was piqued about not scoring, but on entering the dressing room he was surprised to be told by his manager: 'Well done, Jimmy! You set up all the five goals and you played a real team game.'

Only one club had a heated pitch in 1962, Arsenal, and it was six weeks before the second leg took place at Ibrox. Pre-match publicity was even more fanciful with most 'experts' north of the border saying their team would sneak it. The Rangers players had a £200-win bonus offered to them, but within five minutes Greaves scored to put his side four goals ahead and uncatchable. He recalled: 'It was as if somebody above had leaned forward, flicked a switch and turned off the sound of bedlam within Ibrox. It was eerie. There were 80,000 there, yet I could hear Bill Brown shout, "Yes!" and clapped his hands when the goal went in – it was that quiet.'

Tottenham won 3-2 with an 8-4 aggregate, but they paid a price. Blanchflower was brought down by two opponents both challenging from other side and needed a prolonged soak from Cec Poynton's sponge. Bill then showed his hard side: the match virtually over, he could have played on with 10 men but later he wrote: 'I wanted him to carry on and finish the match and he did so, playing out the remaining minutes at centre half – he was a brave player.'

A few days later, Blanchflower had his cartilage removed and missed the next 22 matches.

Like the weather, the competition went into a deep freeze because Tottenham's next opponents, Slovan Bratislava of the then Czechoslovakia, were frozen out for three months before the first leg took place in Bratislava. 'The river Danube was almost frozen over, with huge blocks of ice,' Bill remembered. 'But on the day of the match a thaw set in and the playing surface was wet and skiddy. Not surprisingly, it was not one of our better performances. We were lucky to scrape through with a 2-0 beating and we owed a lot to Bill Brown, who played with his nose plastered after a brave diving save at the foot of an opponent.'

He failed to mention the rough stuff that caused Dutch referee Leo Horn – an extremely tall man, rated one of the finest officials of the time – a host of problems. Horn could have sent several players off, but took the soft option. Greaves said it started when Bobby Smith charged into international goalkeeper Villiam Schroiff to send him crashing into a wall: 'From that moment on, it was all blood and thunder and as the players came off, they exchanged threats about what would happen in the second leg. Smith kept brandishing his fist in the face of centre half Jan Popluhar, shouting '*Londres, Londres*!'

By this time Greaves had started drinking alcohol at a faster rate, and he blamed it on his fear of flying. Before the flight from Heathrow, he had some drinks with Cliff Jones, another player who hated the idea of getting into an aircraft, but whereas Cliff stayed strictly within limits, Greaves went too far. Before too long, he was well on the way to becoming an alcoholic.

Schroiff was the goalkeeper who played in the losing final of the World Cup in 1962 and he wasn't used to being roughed up. In the second leg the match had just started when Jones crossed and Smith sent him crashing into the back of the net. A shoulder charge was permissible according to the laws but even in those days, this was an act of violence and Schroiff was very angry. Not long after, Smith caught him with an elbow, laying him out on the ground, and the Czechs realised they weren't up to the physicality of their opponents and went back to their usual clever passing game. The result was 6-0 and Schroiff admitted, 'I have never let in so many goals.'

If the previous two matches were rugged, the semi-final legs against OFK Belgrade were almost brutal. Jimmy Greaves, who was switched to outside right by Bill to keep him out of trouble, was sent off in the 55th minute in the Red Army Stadium for the first time in his career after taking a swing at Blagomir Krivokuca and missing. The Hungarian referee decided, rightly, that this constituted violent conduct. Minutes later, Smith and Krivokuca went up for a high ball and Smith caught his opponent with a blow to the stomach; he then collapsed. When he was revived, Krivokuca thought Greaves was his assailant, not Smith, and charged up to him, attempting to strike him in the face. Greaves ducked and tried a retaliatory swing – which Krivokuca avoided – and the referee sent Greaves for an early bath.

According to Jimmy, the referee also asked Krivokuca for his name and he replied, 'Blagomir Srdjan Krivoluca.' He claimed the referee changed his mind and let him off because he couldn't write his name down. As Greaves came off, a hail of missiles was thrown. Back in the dressing room Poynton told him: 'It's your fault, you ain't got no business being sent off! You shouldn't have reacted like that – you're a pro and you should act like one. You should be ashamed with yourself. You are the first Spurs player to be sent off since 1928. You've damaged the reputation of the club.'

'Who was the last Spurs player to go off?' asked Greaves.

'Me,' said Poynton.

There was more violence when defender Maric was guilty of a horrific tackle on Smith. In the next incident, Maric was left on the ground in a bad state with the finger pointed at the England centre forward. The referee was manhandled and decided not to send anyone else off. Tottenham won 2-1 and were cheered off with Dave Mackay hailed as the hero.

Was football of the sixties any dirtier or more aggressive than today's game? It seemed so.

A week later, OFK were in a more peaceful frame of mind and Tottenham won 3-1, with an aggregate of 5-2. Earlier in the day Blanchflower jarred his knee in the gym and asked the loquacious Irish club doctor Brian Curtin for another cortisone injection. Curtin, who liked his drink, readily obliged – he never minded giving an injection, but was less keen on stitching.

In the League, Tottenham raised hopes of lifting the Championship when they smashed Liverpool 7-2 at home four days after losing 5-2 at Anfield. However, they lost 1-0 to champions Everton in the next game and realised it was too late. Altogether, they scored 111 goals with Greaves claiming 37 of them from 41 appearances and ended runners up to Harry Catterick's side, 6 points behind. Smith played only 9 League matches – he was taking too much punishment and giving it. Still a feared opponent, he remained his side's greatest physical presence.

CHAPTER TWELVE:
STRUCK DOWN!

Was Bill Nicholson an unlucky manager? A case was building to support the idea. Because of questionable refereeing Benfica won the European Cup, not Tottenham. In the following season Bill's side should have won a second Double when he took the advice, ill-advisedly, of Dave Mackay and Danny Blanchflower not to change the tactics to counter Alf Ramsey's Ipswich Town's withdrawn winger's style of play. Had he followed his instincts, Ipswich would not have been champions.

But in the 1963/4 season dollops of ill fortune dropped on the frustrated manager. In quick succession Terry Medwin broke a leg and never played for the club again, Blanchflower retired through injury, John White was killed by a shaft of lightning and Dave Mackay also broke his leg. Cliff Jones was one of the first of his players to break a leg and Maurice Norman later experienced the same fate. Frantically Bill tried to recruit replacements of the same quality, but they were irreplaceable. He managed to sign Fulham's Alan Mullery and Jimmy Robertson from St Mirren, but needed a

Johnny Haynes (subject of a transfer hullabaloo in 1964 when Bill denied he had bid for him), a Bobby Moore, George Eastham or a budding George Best. Robertson (1963–8) was a combative Glaswegian who was a quality winger, but his record of 31 goals in 181 games didn't compare with Jones's 158 goals in 368 matches, Terry Medwin's 36 in 125 or indeed, Terry Dyson's 50 in 178.

Medwin, the son of a prison warder in Swansea, still had some mileage in his sturdy frame at the age of 30 and recalled: 'Just after the Atletico triumph we flew off to South Africa to play three matches against a South African XI and I broke a leg in the first game. It was a bad one and it finished me. I played for a while at Durban and was getting involved in coaching, so I wasn't too upset. I was paid £3,100 from my insurance and accrued benefit and worked as a coach at Fulham, Norwich and Swansea. Working with youngsters in the East End earlier was a real eye-opener and it taught me a lot about life and handling people. I think Bill tried to sign George Cohen from Fulham, but he went for Alan Mullery, a good, solid player whom he liked in preference to Charlton's Mike Bailey.'

Now 77, Terry is still sharp and alert, enjoying his 19 grandchildren. 'Bill never changed,' he said. 'He was out on his own as a manager and he didn't have an ounce of flashiness about him – he never made up anything and told it straight. He had a tough time that season, but never complained.'

Alan Mullery first met Nicholson when Bill was manager of the Under-23 squad. After seeing him play, he told him: 'You ought to play for England.' He was right – Mullery was capped 35 times, proving that he was well worthy to play for Tottenham. Fulham was paid a big sum for those days – £72,500 – on 14 March 1964, but there was a hold-up when Bill wanted to play him at right back and asked him to meet him in his car, parked close to Lord's, to finalise matters.

'I'm a midfield player, not a right back,' insisted Mullery.

'No, I'm sorry,' said Bill, who had to make way. 'Okay, you'll be in midfield then.'

Fulham was a jazz cap club with most of the decisions made by the senior players. At White Hart Lane, Mullery found himself in a far stricter routine. In his book, *Double Bill*, he recounted: 'Bill was a quiet, modest man of very few words until he got you into the dressing room. If he was in the mood to rip your performance to pieces, he would. He was very demanding and a very hard man to please.'

Mullery lived in Worcester Park but most of the players lived closer, mainly north of Edmonton. 'I don't mind the drive,' he said, and that impressed Nicholson. 'Once he made up his mind, he usually achieved what he set out to do,' said the manager. 'He was a forceful, influential player – different in many ways from Danny – but a commanding one, nonetheless.'

There are dates when some dramatic event occurs and people remember them, particularly in football: the Munich air crash, winning of the World Cup, when Bill Nicholson was there when England lost to the USA at Belo Horizonte, among others. Another was 21 July 1964: Bill was at home when the phone rang and a voice said: 'This is the Tottenham Police. I am afraid I have some sad news for you. John White has been killed by lightning.'

At first he thought it could be a take-off – twice in the previous two weeks he received hoax calls saying that Jimmy Greaves had been killed in a motor accident and his daughters Jean and Linda had received some obscene calls. He asked the officer to give him his number and rang it back. Bill was asked to attend the Prince of Wales Hospital morgue to identify the body. Sandra, John's wife, was so heartbroken that she was reluctant to undertake the task.

Cec Poynton accompanied Bill to the nearby hospital and together, they confirmed that the body was John's. As they went outside, Cec asked: 'Did you see that burn mark down his back?' Bill hadn't seen it. A massive bolt of lightning had struck White as he sheltered under a large oak, not far from the green of the first hole. Cliff Jones, his room mate and best friend, was about to join him on a round at Crews Hill Golf Club and he said: 'It was about

1.20 after training when I decided not to go because a storm was forecast. John was a very keen golfer and went on his own. Someone rang me and told the news and I couldn't believe it. He was such a lovely young man, always had a smile and a joke and a prank.'

Maurice Norman recalled that Jack Knight, his father-in-law, often played with John and he said: 'Earlier in the week Jack was going to play with him on that day, but the prospects weren't good and he didn't go.'

Dave Mackay was drinking at the Viking, his favourite restaurant in Edmonton, when his business colleague Jimmy Burton rang to tell him the news. He said: 'I walked out of the place in a trance and sat down in my car and switched on the radio. The music was Roy Orbison's "It's Over". I rested my forehead on the steering wheel and cried my eyes out.'

John's golf handicap was 14 and he played with Cliff several times a week. Had he not been sitting under the tree, he probably would have survived. The odds against being killed by lightning are around 4m to one. Bill shed a few tears at the morgue and also at the funeral at Enfield Crematorium – both chapels were packed, with hundreds outside. At the first match on 22 August, he joined players and officials at the centre circle for a minute's silence, which was strictly observed. Not a single person coughed or sneezed; there was hardly a dry eye in the stadium. At the inquest, the coroner recorded the inevitable verdict of 'misadventure'.

In his autobiography, Bill wrote: 'When I think about John White now, I feel uneasy because I don't think Tottenham did enough for his family. They started a fund and played a memorial game against a Scottish XI and the proceeds came, I believe, to £15,000. In his will, he left only £2,926.

'His daughter Sandra was the daughter of Harry Evans, who for a brief period was my assistant. I brought Harry to the club from Aldershot and he was an enormous help to me, particularly on the administrative side. Tragically, he died of cancer in his early forties.

If he had lived, I believed John would have played into his thirties, as Alan Ball had done.'

Laurie Pignon said of him: 'He could make good players great.' John was a unique player, never replaced by a similar talent. Glenn Hoddle was compared to him, but his style was much different – he liked to drag the ball away from defenders and aim for the long, killing pass into, or over the opposition ranks. John passed the ball on the run to support his colleagues and covered a vast amount of yards. Bill had just given him a pay rise and told him that he would rebuild his side around him. At 27, he had so much to give to the game.

Phil Beal said: 'John was such a lovely man. I came from Bletchingley in Surrey, and sometimes after a night game he would invite me to stay with him and his family because as a teenager, I didn't have a car at the start of my career.'

John Barnwell, who played for Arsenal between 1956 and 1963, and finished up as chief executive for the League Managers' Association, lived near to White in Winchmore Hill. Despite playing for rival clubs, the two became firm friends. 'Once a week we would meet at a gentlemen's club and we had a drink,' he said. 'Not that either of us were big drinkers, but we always had an enjoyable time. I met him first when we were picked for the Army side. I was in the Black Watch and he was in another Scottish regiment, and John was like Beckham: fair-haired, a great passer and played on the right until Bill Nic moved him into the centre. He was always practising and often he had no socks or boots and he reckoned, "If you time it perfectly, you don't cause any damage to your feet." He covered more ground than Beckham and if he'd lived on, he would have kept Tottenham on top for a long time. Around that time they were the best in the world.'

Danny Blanchflower played his last match in 16 November and for a while, stayed on as assistant to Bill. Meanwhile, he concentrated on his journalistic work and wrote some arresting pieces that drew a lot of attention, often critical because he was so frank. In 1967, he signed as a commentator for the CBS TV network broadcasts of the National Professional Soccer League matches in the US and was sacked within weeks. He kept telling the truth – that it wasn't proper football – and they didn't like to hear it. Then in 1978, he became manager of Northern Ireland but soon left and was appointed manager of Chelsea in the same year. He didn't last long at Stamford Bridge either, being dismissed within a year.

His exit – in 1979 – was done with decency and decorum. 'It's not a resignation, but a parting of friends,' he declared. 'I smelt things about the place. You are working with younger players who have grown up with greater financial rewards than we knew as players. Their values aren't my values, and I am not changing mine – a younger manager would be more flexible. I'm not a cheat. Because it is common to get round the rules, it is no longer looked on as cheating. You hear rumours of players who want £40,000 free of tax. I wouldn't get involved in that.'

He kept in touch with Bill, but had no more offers in the game. For a while, he worked as a PR for the National Sporting Club at the Cafe Royal but later it became evident that he was showing signs of Alzheimer's. Near the end of his life, I tried to call him several times but as with Arthur Rowe, one of his heroes, it was impossible to have a normal conversation by then.

His funeral took place at the Parish Church of St Jude in Englefield Green on 16 December 1993 and it ended with an extraordinary happening he would have loved. He had died at the early age of 67. After a simple service in the Chapel, around 80 people – a minute fraction of the number who watched him at White Hart Lane, including Bill, Cliff Jones, Bobby Smith and others – moved off to watch the committal at the far end of the cemetery.

It was a rainy, windy day with no sight of the sun when we walked through the mud towards the graveside. As we approached, the rain started to ease off and a gap suddenly appeared in the sullen clouds. The six, black-clad funeral staff were lowering the coffin into the grave when suddenly a blinding shaft of sunshine hit it. Tommy Harmer, the joker of the team, said: 'Crikey, I knew he was special but I didn't think he was *that* special!' It was as though Danny's soul was marching along in tune with the words of the American Civil War song 'Glory, Glory Hallelujah'. He was the shining star, with his own spotlight from above.

In recent years, more and more former footballers have gone down with Alzheimer's and Terry Medwin said: 'It was heading all those heavy leather balls. Fortunately, I didn't have to do much of that type of heading and I'm fine. It is a very sad thing that others can't enjoy their final years.'

In 2007, the House of Commons Public Accounts Committee was told that dementia costs the UK economy £17 billion a year – more than strokes, heart disease and cancer combined. Though the Professional Footballers' Association assists many victims, there is a lack of organisations to help out. Danny was one of the best and the brightest of his generation, his wit and vivacity sparkled in any company. Strong-minded and opinionated, he was a real leader. Bill was the genius who built the legendary Spurs side, but Danny often directed events on the field. Later in life, he could have spoken out about the wrongs in football.

As I stood alongside his grave I thought we should reinvent him. He could question the awful things which are occurring. You could imagine him saying, 'Why are they playing them £150,000 a week when others are only paid £5.73 an hour? Why are those money launderers being allowed to run clubs? Why should highly paid managers still qualify for bonuses when their players are transferred? Why are there only 60 players in the Premiership eligible to play for England? Why are referees allowing players to crowd round them and argue about their decisions and not book them for dissent?' His powerful advocacy could have started a campaign to help sweep away the injustices and crookedness. Peter Doherty, the former Northern Ireland manager, once said to one of his internationals: 'If one of their guys are causing trouble, don't hesitate to bring them down outside the box.' Danny is reputed to have replied: 'That's a sin, you have to play to the rules' – and he always did.

Tottenham's first match as the winners of the ECWC was against Manchester United, the current FA Cup holders, and an awful incident happened early in the return leg, which Tottenham won 2-0 at White Hart Lane. Eight minutes into the game, Mackay charged at the ball and coming the other way was the late Noel Cantwell, United's Irish defender. Noel's other Christian names were Eucharia Cornelius and he played with distinction for West Ham and Manchester United; also played cricket for Ireland and was once chairman of the Professional Footballers' Association. Bill considered it a 50:50 challenge, but years later Mackay revealed: 'I got to the ball and Cantwell got to my shin. I heard the crack and, if what people tell me to this day is true, so did half of the crowd. I didn't feel any immediate pain, but only panic when I looked down and my foot had twisted round by 90 degrees. I really believed that if Cec Poynton rolled down my sock and undid my laces, we would find that my leg was detached.'

Cantwell wasn't even cautioned. A shocked crowd watched Mackay as he was carefully placed on a stretcher and carried away by four sturdy St John's Ambulance men. The consultant was a Manchester United supporter and when he arrived at the hospital he took his transistor out and turned it on to listen to the match commentary. Having been given morphine, Mackay was drifting in and out of sleep and was just able to take in that the game had gone into extra time – United went on to win 4-1.

The consultant told him that it was a bad break in two places and could be the end of his career. After resetting the bones, he asked Mackay what he wanted to do: to stay in hospital or join the team at their hotel? Mackay opted for the hotel, where a reception was under way. By then the pain had got to him and he went straight to bed. One of his first visitors was Cantwell, who expressed his remorse. Mackay said: 'I was in no state to vent any anger.'

Later, he took the view that his leg was broken, not by an accident, but by Cantwell's tackle. 'I don't think Cant was anywhere near the ball,' he said. 'He may not have set out to break a bone, but that was the end result. I had a reputation as a hard man, but I was never a dirty player and wouldn't have been able to live with myself if the situation had been reversed.' Though he threatened retaliation, he never carried out his threat. A decent man, he was respected by almost everyone.

Mackay went back to London by train, with his leg propped up on a table. During the journey, he played cards with three of his teammates. He was forced to spend six weeks in hospital and the bones had to be reset a second time; altogether his leg stayed in plaster for 16 weeks, the muscles wasting away. Bill said: 'His leg was four inches thinner than his right and he sat for hours every day, lifting 15lb weights strapped onto his foot to strengthen the muscles. Not being active, I told him to diet and lose weight.'

Ultimately Mackay put on two stone and found it hard to get anywhere near his previous weight. Even sportsmen have that problem and the hundreds of thousands of people who have hip and knee replacements ought to have a Bill Nicholson handling their cases – too many of them rarely regain any kind of fitness.

Bill chose the loyal Henry as captain and he recalled, 'I remember lining up to go to the pitch for a game when Nick casually handed me the match ball. The full implications of what he'd done didn't hit home for a few seconds, but when it did, I was so proud.'

Henry was once asked: 'Who had the biggest influence on your career?' His reply was highly unusual: 'I am sure you are expecting me to trot out a number of names, maybe Bill, myself, or some obscure teacher from my past. The truth is, all of those helped me in no small way to become a better player, but the real hero in my life is Edna, my wife. She is an incredibly hard worker, who has backed me in everything I wanted to do. She had to contend with some extraordinarily long periods when I was travelling and playing, and always stuck by me despite the circumstances. Edna is simply the best wife I could have ever wished for and without her, my career would never have been so successful or enjoyable.'

Nine months later, Bill asked Mackay to play in the reserves against Shrewsbury at home to test his leg and a home player named Peter Colby tackled from him behind. His boot caught Mackay's left leg and broke it in the same place. He was in despair, but was able to say to one of the ambulance men: 'Don't tell Bill Nicholson, not yet. He's going to be mad about it.'

Next day, Bill drove to the hospital and told him: 'Well, Dave, you've done it again! There are lessons to be learned from the first time, aren't they?' This time Mackay stuck to a rigid diet and despite having a misshapen leg, he defied the medical experts and made his comeback on 25 August 1965 against Leicester, who were beaten 4-0 in a highly emotional game. Bill gave him the captaincy and congratulated him with a broad smile and a pat on the back.

In the 1963/4 season, with Mackay and Blanchflower missing most of it, Tottenham went down 2-0 against Chelsea in a third-round FA Cup replay and slipped to fourth position in the League. Still, they managed to be the top scorers: 97 goals, with just over a third (35) from Jimmy Greaves's 41 appearances. Bill was a worried man, especially after his defence let in 8 goals in two warm-up games against a Glasgow Select and Feyenoord in August. He decided to speed up the reconstruction of his side and his new young recruits – Cyril Knowles, Pat Jennings and Alan Gilzean – were all fine acquisitions. But there were failures as well and he made a mistake in signing two players from Arsenal: Laurie Brown, the utility player who could play at centre half or at centre forward, and winger David Jenkins.

No Tottenham supporter would welcome a Gooner and his directors made the same error when they came to replace Bill by another one, Terry Neill. Maurice Norman admitted: 'I was surprised that Bill bought him. You don't buy players from the enemy! He asked me to play right back, the position I used to play at when I first started and he wanted to try Laurie at centre half, but it didn't work.'

Jenkins was an even worse mistake. 'Perhaps he was my worst signing,' conceded Bill. 'He was never given a fair chance by the crowd and his confidence disappeared. As for Laurie, I told him I'd taken a gamble on him and it went wrong.' In addition, he might have been too cautious with two other juniors on his staff, Keith Weller and Derek Possee, whom he let go to Millwall because of their limited number of first-team chances.

One of Bill's greatest skills was his ability to pick out talent ahead of other managers and the Knowles' transfer in the close season of 1964 was a good example. He wanted a young replacement for Ron Henry at left back and started making trips to watch the tall, 19-year-old Knowles in Middlesbrough's matches. 'I liked him from the start,' he recalled. 'He was a hard man and all good sides need a hard man, a player who can win the ball. He had good pace, was a good tackler and had a determined attitude. We had a lot of work to do on him on the training pitch, but once we had him playing our way, his career advanced so much that he became of one of the best left backs of his day.'

Arriving at White Hart Lane, Knowles was greeted with a warm handshake from Bill. The new signing looked like a Beatle with an Elvis haircut, black suit with a pair of tight trousers and pointed, cherry-picker shoes. Bill's first words were: 'You look more like a pop singer than a footballer!'

Knowles spent 10 years there and was one of the club's most popular characters, enhanced by the song 'Nice One Cyril', which was 14th in the charts in 1973. Pat Jennings shared digs with him (they signed around the same time) and said of him: 'He was a cheerful fellow, always bubbling with the sheer joy of life, and he was good for a laugh.'

Knowles was driving home on a motorway one day when a stone

went through the windscreen of his car and struck the face of his young baby Jonathan in the back seat. The child died in the arms of his wife Betty. With so much support from the players, friends and relatives, including Bill and Darkie, he and Betty overcame that awful catastrophe but at the age of 30, he was forced to retire with knee trouble. He became a coach and manager, but died from a tumour of the brain in 1991.

Cyril Knowles appeared in 402 matches for the club, all of them played at high intensity and gritty determination, between 1964 and 1976, and Bill and almost the whole staff attended his funeral. Morris Keston organised a testimonial between the Tottenham and Arsenal Double-winning sides and it raised £140,000 tax-free for his family.

Bill had a strict rule about signing new players. He thought they were honoured to join Tottenham and he never offered higher wages and signing-on fees to newcomers if they were in demand and other clubs would outbid him. In the summer of 1964, he realised that Bill Brown wasn't so quick and agile as in previous years and so he looked for a replacement. The man he chose was 19-year-old Pat Jennings, who was from a Catholic family of seven with just one sister and born in Newry, County Down. He was playing for Third Division Watford. Jennings left school at 15 and worked for a fiver a week in a timber yard; the rugged work gave him a very strong physique, similar to Peter Shilton's.

Bill McGarry, the Watford manager, had the same approach to Bill in handling his players. He was strict and didn't waste any time on pleasantries. 'He rang me up and said that Bill Nicholson was waiting at Vicarage Road to see me,' recalled Pat. 'Bill was already a legend by then and when he met, he was carrying a small briefcase containing the transfer forms and he told me to call him "Bill" not "Mr Nicholson" and that put me at ease.'

Arsenal was the only club to have a goalkeeping coach then – they had Bob Wilson – and like the other keepers, Pat learned his trade watching the others and through his own mistakes. He had a stubborn streak and when Bill offered him £38 a week if he played in the first team, he told him that he was earning almost that amount already and expected more. 'Bill was polite but firm,' he recalled. 'There was nothing he could offer and he was disappointed because he had never been turned down before by any other player. We shook hands and I flew back to Belfast under the impression it was the end of the matter.'

Shortly afterwards McGarry rang him again and said Bill wanted to talk about terms. Pat rejected the idea and told him that he intended to continue his holiday at home before starting training early in July. Watford were in financial trouble – they have rarely been in the black – and McGarry told his awkward goalkeeper that if he didn't sign with Tottenham, he would stick him in the reserves. After long discussions, Pat signed for £40 a week, plus £5 for each first-team appearance and he also picked up £150 from Watford as his accrued share of benefit. Years later, he said in his autobiography, written by his friend Reg Drury, who tragically died when he was run over after his retirement from the *News of the World*, 'Sometimes I wonder what would have happened to my career if Bill had not been so persistent in pursuit of a raw kid. I'm glad he did. I would not have liked to miss my time at Tottenham or the chance to play under such a great, and straight, manager.

'He was in charge during my first 10 years at White Hart Lane and not all the players got on well with him but that there wasn't one who didn't have the greatest respect for him. Nobody ever cheated on him and though he was hard and even could be unintentionally hurtful in his approach, if he made a promise, it was always kept. Bill was Tottenham Hotspur. He kept the directors at a distance from us and seldom allowed them into the dressing room. If there was anything to be said, Bill was the man who said it. He rarely joined us at the bar, but after away matches, he would often slip a tenner to Dave Mackay and tell him to buy a round for the players. The money came out of his own pocket but he never made a fuss about it. He didn't go in for team meetings: his style was to sit next to a player and outline what he wanted from him. After the game, he would sit next to him again and tell him where he went wrong. He was seldom satisfied.'

In the end, Bill paid £27,000 for Jennings and considered it one of his successful deals: 'What I liked about him was his calm, steadying influence. Before a game he would be one of the most keyed-up players, but out on the field he gave the appearance of being the most controlled. I like players to show signs of tension before a game. It showed that total attention is being given to the task. In his first season he was too tense and hardly opened his mouth, and two seasons went by before he established himself in the side.

'When he had a bad game, I left him out, which didn't help his confidence. I had to appeal to the local press to stop pillorying him and give him a chance. A number of others, including Mullery and Venables, had similar problems about our crowd.'

Bill never explained in his book why he sold Bobby Smith so quickly after Bobby scored 13 goals in his 26 League appearances in 1963/4. Smith had gambling debts and part of the deal was that Brighton paid them up and the transfer fee they gave Tottenham was a meagre £5,000 in May 1964, six months after he played in his fifteenth and final international for England. He scored a goal in England's 8-3 demolition of Northern Ireland in the first evening international played under lights at Wembley. It was almost like seeing a switch going off in his career. He played just one season for Brighton, scoring 18 goals in 31 matches before joining non-League Hastings.

Smith's rapid descent from starring at Wembley Stadium to the Southern League grounds may be the swiftest of any top international player, but Bill was doubtless taking into account his physical state. He had taken a battering for some years. In his autobiography, Bill dismissed Smith's sale to Brighton in just a few words: 'I watched many strikers in the weeks leading up to

Christmas 1964 before deciding on Alan Gilzean ('Gilly'), a tall Scot who had scored some important goals for Dundee in their European Cup run in the previous season. From the moment I first asked Bob Shankly, the Dundee manager, for a price, the talks dragged on for three weeks and three times I had to raise my offer.'

Sunderland, Liverpool, Everton and Torino wanted him, and after talking to Denis Law, who had a short, unhappy spell with Torino, Gilzean ruled out a move to Italy. Sunderland made him the best offer, but Bill clinched it in his usual way, sitting with the new recruit in his car. Bill drove to Dundee on his own and parked beside the river Tay to discuss the deal. Gilzean was 26, and was a mature player who stood out among the rest of Britain's professionals at the time because he used his common sense. He realised that Tottenham had a good chance of winning more trophies, whereas Sunderland didn't and so he took Bill's lower offer. Sunderland were offering bonuses – £20 a win and £10 for a draw – but Bill told him it wasn't in the rulebook. The limit was £4 and £2, and he wouldn't go above that. 'Fine,' said Gilzean.

After the contract was drawn up, Bill met Alan Hardaker, the Football League secretary, and asked him about bonuses. Was there a limit? 'No,' said Hardaker. 'If it's written in the contract they can offer anything.' Next time when Bill saw Gilzean, he apologised and Gilzean said: 'I knew I was right.' Bill soon upped his bonuses for that season and in the next season he introduced bonuses for points on a sliding scale. The more games won in succession, the higher the rewards. Even so, his players weren't as well paid as those at Manchester United, Arsenal, Leeds and Everton.

Gilly proved a popular player in his nine years at White Hart Lane. He resembled Dimitar Berbatov, the Bulgarian striker who succeeded him 30-odd years later, both in appearance and as a player. Bill had high praise for him: 'He was easy to talk to, never moaned and got on with the job in an uncomplicated way. He was an unorthodox player, different in many ways from Bobby Smith. He was a more of a footballing centre forward and started his career as an inside left. He didn't head the ball full-on like Smithy, he preferred to glance it as he turned his head. It was not a style you could coach in anyone because the margin of error was so small, but it suited him and I never tried to change him. I never had any problems with him.

'Before every match he used to soak his boots in hot water to soften them up. I think that was a legacy from the old days when the toe-capped leather boots would be so stiff that they were painful to the feet unless softened in some way. Some players still did it out of habit.'

Jimmy Greaves loved playing with him. 'I don't think I was ever happier than when playing with him,' he said. 'He was a tremendously talented player and an unselfish one.'

Gilly would join the other players for drinks, but none of them knew much about what he did after he went home. He was looked on as a bit of a loner: he liked a drink but it never went too far, unlike his striking partner. These days, he is the only well-known former Tottenham player who doesn't attend the celebratory dinners. Phil Beal and Pat Jennings are employed by the club to meet supporters and Phil admitted: 'I don't know where Gilly is. No one knows.'

Gilly was sent off three times in Scottish football and was sent off soon after he arrived at White Hart Lane, but Bill came to his rescue. In the match against West Ham Gilly lost his temper and abused a linesman. Harry New, the referee from Portsmouth, showed him the red card. Gilly claimed that Bobby Moore handled the ball, not him, which led to the explosion of temper. Normally Bill never went to the referees' room to discuss these matters, but realising Gilly was the innocent party, he asked New for his reason.

'Gilly was reported to the FA and also me,' revealed Bill. 'But I heard no more of the matter. I never appeared at a disciplinary hearing in my life except one occasion when Bobby Robson, then manager of Ipswich, asked me to speak for George Burley in an appeal. I had seen Clive Thomas caution Burley and it was a ridiculous decision. It was a time when players could appeal against bookings and Burley's appeal was upheld.

'I met John Cobbold at the hearing and he mentioned that another player was appealing as well. His offence was kicking the ball away, ungentlemanly conduct. "Can you speak for him too?" asked John. "I can't do that," I answered, "I saw him kick the ball away. He was guilty." "Ah," said Cobbold, "but he didn't kick it very far, did he?"' Bill always had a laugh when he met this remarkable chairman.

Six months after the arrival of Gilzean, Bill paid Chelsea £80,000 for Terry Venables. He already had Alan Mullery on his staff but neither of them turned out to be another Blanchflower or a White and a proportion of the Tottenham crowd never accepted them. A combination of the two might have been the answer. Venables was the cheeky chappie at Stamford Bridge under the wise-cracking Tommy Docherty and he found himself in a new, tougher environment. He was soon put in his place by skipper Mackay.

'He was not backwards in coming forward,' said Mackay, 'and his forthright views had led to some differences with my old landlord, Tommy Docherty. They were two men from a similar mould and with hindsight, it was odds-on they would rub each other up the wrong way. There were no such problems between Terry and Bill, but we had a small run-in soon after Terry arrived. We were in the gym and I was adopting my favourite tactic of boxing a player in a corner and not allowing him to release the ball. Terry thought I was over-the-top and caught me with a cuff over my eye. He may have wore a signet ring and it cut me a little. I returned a couple of blows to areas of the body that did not bruise so easily and we soon became the best of friends.'

Both Blanchflower (19 in 219 appearances), and White (47 in 219) had reasonable goalscoring records for Tottenham as midfield players but Venables managed only 9 in his 141 appearances, while Mullery scored 30 in 373 appearances.

Bill's rebuilding of a side capable of winning more trophies took time and he was often frustrated. His team finished 8th in the 1965/6 season but they had played their best football for some time and he told a few of his players: 'Next season we'll win something, or else!'

But on 17 November 1965, his most reliable centre back – Maurice Norman – fell on his own and couldn't get up. He'd broken a leg. 'We were playing a friendly against a Hungarian Select, which we won 4-0, and one of their players was coming towards me, but he didn't touch me,' Norman recalled. 'I don't know how it happened, but it was a terrible injury. I had a plaster all down my leg for nine months and it was three years before I started getting about and I had a limp for some time. It ended my career at the age of 31.

'I was included in the World Cup side in 1958 and the 1962 one, and was looking forward to making it a hat trick. Luckily I was recommended to see a consultant named Newman, who performed surgery on Winston Churchill's hip, and he gave me hope. No one else at the time used his techniques and they worked for me. Now I get around well. I do a lot in the garden and play golf. No, I'm fine and I live in a 300-year-old house and it's wonderful.'

Phil Beal came on as a substitute for Maurice and said: 'His leg just buckled under him. It was very sad because we realised it was a serious injury.'

Dave Mackay was one of the first players to advise Maurice. 'Like me, Maurice fought to get fit again and though he resumed training after a long while, he never played competitive football again,' he said. 'He was a big, lovable man, who was an integral part of the Double winning side, and I shall always remember his long, loping runs up field to alarm all and sundry as he went forward for corners.'

At the time, Tottenham's players were not insured for injury though Bill was pressing the directors to introduce it. Eventually it happened, but it too late for Maurice Norman and many of his teammates. 'I was paid £8,000 compensation by the Professional

Footballers' Association and that helped Jackie and me to start a shop in Frinton,' he said.

Two other injured players – Micky Dulin, who had a bad knee, and Mel Hopkins, who had a broken nose, which never returned to its normal state – joined Maurice to organise a benefit match against an England XI at Enfield. 'A crowd of 7,000 turned up, a full house,' said Maurice, 'and the team was led by Billy Wright. I think it raised £1,000 and we shared the proceeds. When you were no longer on the staff, the club stopped our Christmas turkey and you didn't get invitations to matches. These days, the Tottenham Hotspur Trust pays for an annual John Lewis hamper, which is nice.'

Like most of Tottenham's players of that era, Maurice isn't envious of the ridiculously high salaries now paid to current players. Morris Keston, the club's number one supporter who organised most of the players' testimonials, said: 'Their attitude is that they say good luck to them.'

Bill always wanted a tall, strong centre-half to deal with high balls in his teams and subsequently signed Welsh international Mike England as Norman's replacement for a fee of £95,000. 'It was money well spent,' he said. 'Mike liked heading the ball, not everyone did, and that was one of the reasons I went for him.'

In the close season Tottenham must have been short of cash because they played 11 matches in Bermuda, Canada and the USA, the last one against Bayern Munich on 19 June, two weeks before the start of the next season. Bill missed the tour to stay behind to complete the signing of England. 'The reason why we used to go on these tours was because the club were short of money,' said Phil Beal. 'He would alternate, one year with the money going to the club and the other would be arranged so that the games were pretty easy and it was holiday for the players.'

Norman lasted 10 years and played 320 matches, scoring 16 goals while England survived for nine years, appearing in 369 matches and scoring 17 goals – almost identical records. Phil Beal, who partnered both, was signed by Bill at 15, having been spotted by Harry Evans while playing for Surrey Under-15s. 'The first thing I noticed about Bill was that he would always turn up to watch the juniors play on Saturday mornings or sometimes in the Southern Floodlit League. He never missed. No manager has ever done that. He came over as being stern, but I can't say anything bad about him. He was so helpful and he would come up to me after a game and say quietly, "Well done." It wasn't loud enough for the others to hear.

'Over the years the senior players used to call me his favourite because I came up through the ranks, but he didn't have favourites – he treated everyone the same. He ensured that everything was done right and if we didn't, he would keep us out on the training pitch until it was.

'The only time I fell out with him was when I had just married and wanted to move to a bigger house. I asked him if the club could give me a loan for a deposit and he said no. I said: "I joined as an apprentice from school and the expensive players who cost transfers were given houses, so why should I be denied for a loan?" He said the club had used all their money for that year. But I wasn't happy and I said to him: "If the club can't help me, I won't turn up for the game tomorrow at Leicester and I'll tell the story to the press." He seemed a bit surprised, but I wouldn't back down so he said he would ask the directors to treat me as an exception.

'A few days later he called me in and said the directors were agreeable to a loan. By that time I had the money available so the loan never transpired. I spent 11 years at Tottenham and I made a bad mistake joining Brighton. From going there, where Bill insisted on high standards and worked himself for anything up to 12 hours a day, to the Goldstone Ground was a big shock. On my first day I asked where Peter Taylor, the manager, was and someone said: "He'll be here later," and when he did come, I learned that he had spent the rest of the day looking at race cards and putting bets on.'

Though encouraged by his new buys, Bill wasn't overall happy about the way the game was going. He said: 'Inflation was worsening, forcing up costs and making it harder for clubs to exist; clubs were copying Alf Ramsey's 4-3-3 system, which he used to win the World Cup, and the game was more functional, less entertaining to watch. Teams were concentrating on stopping opponents and were happy with a draw. Goals were fewer and unless a team is winning, attendances were declining. The "professional" foul had started and I was one of many who were becoming disenchanted with the game around that time.'

CHAPTER THIRTEEN:
TOMMY DOCHERTY SLIPS UP

When it comes to great footballing battles, body language often reveals which team will win. On 20 May 1967, the FA Cup Final was billed by some newspapers as 'The Final of all Finals' and was the first all-London final of the century, the first to allow substitutes and the last to be televised in black and white. As the teams walked behind Dickie Bird – not the cricket umpire, but the shy, respectful FA official of the same name who always led the players out of the tunnel to their positions in front of the Royal Box – one team looked like winners: Tottenham Hotspur.

There is a picture of Bill, in his dark suit and club tie, gazing jauntily at a photographer with a wide-open smile and no sign of his normal, furrowed brow. Forty-eight, he hardly had a grey hair in his usual short back and sides. Chelsea's controversial 39-year-old manager Tommy Docherty, dressed similarly, had a solemn, pallbearer's look about him. Captain Ron Harris was behind him in his blue tracksuit and looking anxiously to the left, as though one of his guests had failed to arrive at the Chelsea End. Peter

Bonetti, third in line, appeared to be reliving a bad dream. Nicholson's cocky players were stripped for action: they had left their tracksuits behind and they meant business. Leading the line of his team in an all-white strip – the Real Madrid strip, which at that time dominated world club football – was a confident Dave Mackay, holding his hand downwards with the ball in his right hand. It was seen as a sign of strength.

The formbook showed that Tottenham had won all of their four FA Cup Finals and were bidding for a third in seven years. They were unbeaten for four months and finished level on points, with runners-up Nottingham Forest four points behind champions Manchester United. With their new and expensive players settled in, they were playing classical football, almost as refined as Danny Blanchflower's Double winners. Chelsea, who finished 9th, were wracked with arguments about Cup Final tickets and their bonuses. In his book *Chelsea: The Real Story* Brian Mears, later chairman, says: 'Before Tom spoke to the Board he told the players they would each receive a big bonus for winning the cup. The Board wouldn't bow to his demands. Bill Pratt, the chairman who soon departed, was furious, especially when Tom said "OK, well how much will you pay them for losing?" Bill said "Losing? We don't pay for losing. Only success." And that was the end of a very bitter boardroom row. The players remained up in arms and their dissatisfaction showed throughout the weeks leading up to the game, which I thought was appalling.'

Chelsea lost their charismatic centre forward Peter Osgood, who broke a leg a few weeks early, and the normally chirpy Docherty wasn't his usual self. He paid £100,000 for Tony Hateley to take Osgood's place and referring to Hateley's aerial ability, joked: 'If he turned him upside down, he would have been a star.' He could come up with caustic comments which upset some players but he was a highly qualified coach and did many good things. His weakness was to make sudden, dramatic changes for no apparent reason.

Later Bill said: 'He made a tactical mistake before the match and made our task easier. Docherty was then in his heyday, cracking jokes and constantly appearing in the newspapers, as he guided his young side towards Wembley. In previous matches he used Marvin Hinton as a sweeper and Chelsea took three out of four points off us in League matches [there were two points for a win then]. Our 0-3 defeat at Stamford Bridge was our heaviest of the season. Alan Gilzean didn't like playing against a sweeper and it showed in those matches. But just before the final, Docherty abandoned the idea and played an orthodox defensive system. When I heard that, I told my players: "He's done us a favour." Success in football comes from developing a system and sticking to it so the players know what is expected of them. Docherty had many fluctuations in his seven seasons at Chelsea and soon after the Final he left to join Second Division Rotherham.' Moving downwards proved a disastrous move for the Doc, almost in the same class as Bobby Smith dropping down to Brighton. In his long career he had 17 jobs and would say: 'I had more than Jack Nicklaus's golf clubs.'

In the lead up to the final, Bill's players were happier than they had been since 1960/1, if not more so. Jimmy Greaves recalled: 'We were playing pranks all the time. One was about getting an apprentice to deliver a message to Eddie Baily, who was Bill's assistant, saying, "Mr Baily, your brother Bill has telephoned to say he won't be coming home." The more we did it, the more irritated Eddie became. Another prank was to squeeze shampoo on someone's head as he was in the process of rinsing his hair of the shampoo he had already applied. We were in fits watching Frank Saul or Cyril Knowles frantically rinsing their hair and wondering why there was still so much shampoo. They would start singing with the rest of us and took turns to make up silly lyrics.'

You can't imagine the present Tottenham squad doing that today. The Chelsea players were also enjoying themselves. Ron Harris said: 'Tom decided to let us train in Brighton that week and he gave us £50 to go out for a night out on Thursday night with a midnight curfew. We stayed at the Dudley, just off the beach, and there was a room named after Compton, where we put a few bets and played cards.'

Bill considered it an ordinary final, notable for Mackay's third winner's medal. Jimmy Robertson, signed three years earlier, played 40 out of the 42 League matches that season, restricting Cliff Jones to only 20 appearances. Cliff was on the bench at Wembley and became the first substitute to qualify for a medal. Robertson scored the first goal in the 40th minute from a rebound off Allan Harris, brother of Ron. Bill said: 'Jimmy was 19 and had a reputation of being a quick, straightforward winger, who could score goals. He was at his best when he did things quickly. He could put over a great cross when under pressure, but give him time – he could be inaccurate.'

Frank Saul, who came up from the juniors and never really cemented a regular place in his six seasons, hooked in the second (67 minutes) from one of Dave Mackay's long throws. 'I was proud of my throws,' said Dave. 'I always thought most teams wasted theirs, and I practised and practised until I was able to reach almost the halfway line into goal.'

Five minutes from the end, Pat Jennings missed a cross from John Boyle and Bobby Tambling headed in a consolation goal. The 2-1 score didn't reflect the action, which was dominated by Mackay's men. Bobby Smith said: 'I wasn't really fit, but I had six injections before the game. I had two in the morning, two more just before the start and two more at half time. Five minutes from the end, the painkillers wore off and I could hardly walk.'

The after-match banquet was the best of the three, with Bill receiving a longstanding ovation after his brief speech. On the table where he was sitting was the FA Cup, and he got up and said: 'You eat a meal you don't want, so you can get up and tell a load of stories you can't remember to people who have already heard them. My father gave me the best advice on after-dinner speaking. Be sincere. Be brief. Be seated. That in mind, ladies and gentlemen, I give you the FA Cup!'

The directors was disappointed to learn that Morris Keston was having his own party for the players and some of them preferred his. It led to a breakdown between Keston and the directors that lasted for some years before normal relations were restored.

Tottenham's toughest opponents in the Cup run were Millwall, who had just come from the Fourth to the Second Division after being unbeaten for 59 home games, a League record. Bill warned that they were facing some highly determined and strong opponents such as goalkeeper Lawrie Leslie, Harry Cripps, Brian Snowdon and John Gilchrist; also 40,000 of the roughest, nosiest and hardest-swearing supporters in Britain. 'Their fans will try to intimidate us,' he predicted, and so it proved.

Benny Fenton, their manager, was well respected as a motivator by Bill and I knew him well. Earlier in the week, I called in at the Den to request an interview (in the days before organised press conferences you could do this) and the secretary told me that he was in the bath. 'Sit in his office, he won't be long,' she suggested, as she departed. Benny shouted, 'Come in, lad!' and as I entered the bathroom I saw that a tanned figure was just rising out of the bath, flexing his biceps. 'What do you think of that?' he asked. 'Reminds me of those statues at the Acropolis,' I said. Fortunately, he made no overtures to me and the interview was conducted while he dried himself and dressed. He was very pedantic about his appearance.

One of the features of the third round FA Cup tie, which finished goalless, was a fight in one part of the ground between the two sets of supporters. On a number of occasions the old Den was closed following fighting and it was like a smaller version of Boca Juniors, the often-closed stadium in the poor part of Buenos Aires. The replay at White Hart Lane, watched by 58,189, followed the same bear-baiting pattern of the first, with fans from both sides exchanging unpleasantries. Alan Gilzean scored the only goal and Bill was relieved. Bad teams can beat good ones by trying to scare them, but with Dave Mackay in charge out in the middle there was little chance of an upset.

One other story about the late Benny Fenton came from a rival manager, who revealed: 'He was the man who blocked Blackwall Tunnel once when he hit his wife while having an argument. The car stopped and the row continued, and it took some time to sort it out while horns were being hooted.'

Between 1982 and 1986, George Graham was manager of Millwall and he recalled: 'Bill was often at our games at the Den and I wondered why he turned up at a lower division club. It was an amazing number. I can't imagine that any First Division manager would watch so many matches outside of the top division, but Bill wanted to see players himself in every division. I got to know him pretty well and he was always helpful and friendly, a real gent. Frank McLintock and I used to park behind his house to go and see games at White Hart Lane when he played for Arsenal and we got on very well with his wife, Darkie.'

Portsmouth were disposed of 3-1 in the fourth round and the next opponents were Second Division Bristol City. This was the game where Mackay should have been sent off, for the only time in his career. The referee blew for a Tottenham foul when John Quigley, a Scot inside forward, suddenly threw the ball into Mackay's face. Mackay retaliated with a punch to Quigley's stomach, whereupon he collapsed. The referee came running towards the Tottenham skipper. As Quigley got up, he started to run away but Mackay grabbed him and told him: 'Now, tell the ref what you did.' Looking shaken, Quigley owned up and the referee warned both players. Neither was booked or sent off.

Mackay had a let-off from a similar incident in the opening League match of the season when Leeds were beaten 2-1 at White Hart Lane. Mackay thought Don Revie's side played classy football, '...but they spoilt themselves by playing very dirty football.' Most people outside of Elland Road would agree with that.

Billy Bremner was captain that day and within three minutes of the start, he floored Mackay. 'Billy was my pal in the Scots team but when he pulled his Leeds shirt on, he seemed to be a different man and for some reason he kicked me on my newly healed bad leg,' said Mackay. 'He could easily have broken my leg for a third time. I was enraged and I lost my rag for a few seconds and grabbed him by the front of his shirt and lifted him from the ground.'

It made for one of the finest sporting pictures of all time and a copy of Monte Fresco's photograph was framed and hung in the Tottenham boardroom for many years. The referee involved was Norman Burtenshaw, renowned for being closest to the action when he was in charge: 'I came up to them and said, "The game has just started and if you start doing that, we've got no chance. Cut it out and get on with the game – without the nastiness." I didn't even take their names. I couldn't really understand what they were saying – they had broad Scots accents, but they got the message. It turned out to be a wonderful game.'

Bill's luck held in the FA Cup draw: Birmingham City, another Second Division club, were his opponents in the quarter-final and they were walloped 6-0 in the replay on a rain-soaked pitch after a goalless draw at St Andrew's. The semi-final at Hillsborough against Nottingham Forest, one of the top four sides of that time, produced Bill's most satisfying FA Cup semi-final yet, a stirring game crowned with a great goal from Greaves – a rare, 25-yard grounder inside a post.

Jimmy's total of goals against Forest was 29, including four on three occasions, better than against any other club and Johnny Carey's side must have been intimidated by the sight of him. Carey was one of football's calmest characters, always smoking a pipe, but that goal must have jolted him. Again, the result – 2-1 – didn't tell the whole story. Before the match Forest's talkative coach Tommy Cavanagh insisted: 'We'll crush Spurs like grapes.' 'Some grapes!' said Mackay afterwards.

That season just under four million watched the FA Cup matches. Forty years later, the total had fallen to two million, yet sudden-death football is often more entertaining than League games. Fear is the reason why managers field weaker sides: they are desperate to avoid relegation and reluctant to go for the second prize, the FA Cup. Greaves once said: 'Now it seems that many people in the game are intent on killing it.' Bill Nicholson would second that.

One of the highest skills of management in football is to decide when to let valued players go and buy improving ones. Bill was top-class at picking the right time to jettison players and sometimes he could be ruthless, but he wasn't so good at clinching deals with players who wanted more money than he was prepared to offer them. In the 1967/8 season he saw signs of decline in Greaves and Mackay, and was lining up replacements.

Greaves admitted that he had lost his spark and a bout of hepatitis left him slower. For a time he was thinking of retirement at the age of 28. Years later, George Best felt the same way. Men of genius find that they can't do what they did before and their frustration leads to despair, often to the bottle. Winning a second European Cup Winners' Cup might have changed the thinking, but they went out limply in the second round against moderate French opposition in Olympique Lyonnais of Lyon.

Their first opponents were Hajduk Split, so-called after the romanticised bandits who were the Robin Hoods of Croatia olden times. Bill rated them as very strong opposition. Tottenham won 2-0 away and this led to some complacency despite exhortations to his players not to take them lightly. Play was continually held up by firecrackers being thrown onto the pitch and before the end some local fans set fire to the trainers' benches (the Tottenham contingent had left their seats by then).

In the second leg Hajduk conceded an early goal, but in the second half they were just 4-3 down, only for Tottenham to make the aggregate 6-3. Bill thought his players were slack and there was evidence of the wrong approach mentally in the first game in Lyon. The ground in the Gerland Stadium was less than a quarter full, yet the boisterous crowd started to behave appallingly and resorted to violence. There were several pitch invasions and Czech referee Dr Joseh Krnavek had difficulty in maintaining control.

Alan Mullery clashed with Andre Guy, the French international centre forward, and both men were sent off. Mullery claimed he was kicked in the face and therefore forced to retaliate. 'Unsavoury,' was how Bill described the game, which Lyon won 1-0. As the players went down the tunnel after the final whistle, Guy got into a skirmish with Alan Gilzean. In the return, a lethargic Tottenham side won 4-3, but went out on the away-goals' rule. 'I have no complaint about that,' stated Bill. 'It's a fair way of settling it.'

A 4-0 thumping at Highbury a few weeks earlier might have contributed to his team's state of mind and a bad run-up to Christmas virtually ended their title challenge. The eventual winners were Malcolm Allison's inspired Manchester City, who pipped Manchester United by two points.

Mullery had similar fiery qualities to Mackay. If someone whacked him, he would whack back. In June 1968, he was the first Englishman to be sent off in a full international. He has been happily married to his wife June for many years, but she is a forthright lady when she needs to be and when she heard the news, she rang and told him: 'You're a disgrace to the family.'

Two years later, he was involved in a much more potentially damaging incident. Not being the most popular player among the Tottenham fans, he occasionally found himself abused from the fans and on this occasion, he retaliated. A youth came up to him in the car park and shouted: 'Mullery, you're f****** useless!' Mullery was so incensed that he took off his coat, went up to the youth and laid him out. He then got back into his car and drove June to their home in Cheam. At midnight, two reporters from a Sunday newspaper knocked at the door to ask him for comments about the incident in the car park. Mullery told them if anything was written up, then he would take legal action.

Next day he bought all the papers and there was no mention of the fight but the youth who started the affair complained to the club and wanted to take it further. On the Monday morning, Bill called Mullery into his office and the youth was present. Bill told his player that he should apologise in return for the youth withdrawing any charges. Mullery did apologise with some grace then the two shook hands. That was Bill at his best.

Tottenham's hopes were raised with a third-round FA replay win over Manchester United, but were ended in the fifth round when they lost to a replay to Liverpool at Anfield. Seventh in the League wasn't good enough and Mackay admitted: 'If I had been manager in place of Bill, I would have dropped me and put me out to grass.'

After the last game of the season, a 2-1 defeat at Wolves, Mackay told a shocked Bill that he intended to retire. 'He thought I had another two seasons in me,' said Dave. Not long after, Bill rang him to say that Hearts wanted him as a player-manager. He was still mulling over the offer when the phone rang in his office at Dave Mackay Ties. I bought several dozen times around that time when I formed 'The Insignificant Seven' taken from the film, *The Magnificent Seven*. The seven members of our journalistic group were all number-two football writers for their newspapers and we had an annual dinner to present a cup to the 'Insignificant Manager of the Year' and also to the 'Insignificant Player'. Basil Hayward of Gillingham was the first recipient, but the player refused to join the festivities. When I met Dave some 20 years later to speak at a dinner at the Café Royal in honour of his career, I told him: 'We still haven't paid for them yet.' 'Forget it,' he told me – he is a very generous man.

The voice on the end of the line was Brian Clough and he said: 'Dave, I'm building a team at Derby County that will be in the First Division within two years and champions within five, and I want you to lead it. Interested?'

Dave said: 'Yes, I'm interested to hear more. Have you spoken to Bill?'

'No,' was his reply. 'I wanted to be sure you are interested and if so, I will call him and we can meet.'

At the time, Derby were 18th in the Second Division. Bill only wanted a token £5,000 for Mackay to make sure his captain had a good deal and it went through very quickly. Clough moved him to sweeper alongside Roy McFarland and at the end of the following season the Football Writers' Association made him Footballer of the Year with Tony Book of Manchester City, who tied with him. Derby went up in his first season and in four seasons, not five, they were League champions.

'Dave was my best signing,' said Bill. Clough's too, it transpired: 'Not only did he have everything as a player, he was the ideal skipper: a supreme example to everyone at the club. He brought a swagger to the team.'

Bill saw Graeme Souness as a possible successor to Mackay, whom he signed as a 16-year-old apprentice in 1970, but the wilful Scotsman didn't stay the course. In the FA Youth Cup against Coventry, he regarded Souness as outstanding and lavished praise on him. He scored goals from midfield and Bill commented: 'There was no mistaking his ability. He was a strong lad, but the problem was that he could be spiteful in the tackle. He didn't get on with Eddie Baily, who would throw his coat across the dressing room and curse. I said to him: "Souness will become a great player one day and it's worth being patient with him." He could have been Dave's successor, but he wanted to progress more quickly than I had planned for him.'

Twice Souness ran off to the family home in Edinburgh and Bill persuaded his father to send him back, but it never really worked out. Souness played in one Cup game, never appeared in a League game and was eventually sold to Middlesbrough where he became a huge success. He starred with Liverpool, Sampdoria and Glasgow Rangers, earned 54 Scottish caps and had variable acclaim as a manager of eight clubs between 1986 and 2006. Had he stayed on at White Hart Lane, perhaps he would have the same impact as Mackay and Bill's 16 years as manager might have lasted longer.

When he retired, Souness told one of his former Tottenham

colleagues: 'There are times when I think I should have stuck it out at White Hart Lane. If I had done that, I could have shown Bill and the fans that I turned out to be a pretty useful player.'

CHAPTER FOURTEEN:
MARTIN CHIVERS PLAYS UP

Martin Chivers gave Bill Nicholson more sleeping problems than any of the 79 players he used in his first team. He was 'Mr Awkward' for some time and Eddie Baily loathed him. Eddie would say to Bill: 'I don't know how you put up with it.'

Martin Harcourt Chivers was born in Southampton on 27 April 1945 and he was a self-starter in football. While attending Taunton's Grammar School in Southampton, he wrote to Southampton FC and asked for a trial. Ted Bates, the long-serving manager and a personal friend of Bill, liked the look of him. He was tall, well over 6ft, broad in shoulder and he struck the ball as hard as Bobby Charlton at his peak. At 17, he was a first team regular, scoring an enviable tally of goals in the Saints all-attacking side. Then, at 22, he wanted to go and with Mick Channon emerging, Bates was willing to release him but only for a record sum. In January 1968, Bill duly offered a British transfer record of £125,000 and the deal included Frank Saul as part-exchange.

Bill thought it was good business: he wanted a big, tough centre forward to take the strain off the rapidly-fading Jimmy Greaves and Alan Gilzean, who was never a target man of the Bobby Smith ilk. Chivers scored on his debut against Sheffield Wednesday in 1968. When he came into the away dressing room Cec Poynton, the kit and general factotum, threw him a bundle of clothes. Chivers was taken aback – he was used to having a neat pile of shirt, shorts and socks laid out for him. Bill Nicholson looked at him and said: 'Son, when you have proved to me that you are a good player, you can have a decent shirt'. Chivers followed up with two goals against Manchester United in his next game, but then his form slumped and Bill dropped him.

On 21 September 1968, Chivers fell and twisted his knee against Nottingham Forest. He was taken to hospital, where the doctor in charge discovered that his lower patella ligament had been severed. It kept him out of the side for a year and his mood became blacker and blacker. When he resumed training, Bill and his staff kept assuring him that he was a good player and they tried to toughen him up. 'He had an impressive physique, but seemed reluctant to use it to his advantage,' recalled Bill. 'We asked Mike England and Peter Collins, the centre halves in the first team squad, to play hard against him to goad him into a more physical approach. On one occasion, Chivers was so angry when England tackled him that it led to a scrap – they had to be pulled apart.'

Throughout his career Bill was always frank, and in his chapter about Chivers he became scathing. 'He was different from most players,' he continued. 'He had had a reasonably good education and could speak German because of his mother; he also had this stubborn streak, which made it difficult for us to advise him. Chivers was probably the only player I found it almost impossible to get along with because of his moods. He was the sort of player whose behaviour drains the enthusiasm of the manager – he would explode one minute and spend the rest of the day sulking. He was the opposite in temperament to the man he replaced as Tottenham's leading scorer, Jimmy Greaves. You could row with Jim and the next morning he would greet you with his customary smile; that wasn't the case with Chivers.'

Chivers was still out of the side on 4 December when Arsenal went to White Hart Lane to play the second leg of a League Cup semi-final, having scored the only goal at Highbury, and for Bill, it was embarrassing. A generation later Bob Wilson, Arsenal's much-battered goalkeeper, said in his autobiography, *Behind the Network*:

It was like sitting on the edge of a volcano. For those playing, it was unabashed hatred. Never before or since have I experienced the elbowing, disgraceful tackling and foul language that erupted out of the longstanding rivalry that was a north London derby. The stakes were too great – a Wembley place, local prestige and a passport to Europe. Twenty-two skilful players kicked lumps out of each other. In the modern game, only the keepers would have managed to avoid red cards. Experienced players lost their senses in the heat of the battle, Frank McLintock, Mike England, John Radford, Cyril Knowles and Terry Venables included. Only the two managers, Bertie Mee and the great Bill Nicholson, maintained any dignity with open condemnation of what had occurred. Bill is one of nature's gentlest creatures and he tried to defuse reaction to a style of play that was totally foreign to his and Spurs' philosophy. "Our injured are only in the heart," he said. "The game was too tense, too physical. It was like a series of explosions."

Near the end, after Arsenal went through 2-1 on aggregate, Bob Wilson thought he had broken a leg following a wild tackle from Gilzean. He was carried into the Tottenham medical room and Bill took an active part in organising his treatment. An X-ray showed no break and he was able to play the following Saturday. When he later became chairman of the London Football Coaches

Association, held at Highbury, Wilson always invited Bill as chief guest. He looked on him as a footballing idol, a symbol of fair play and decency.

In his first two seasons at White Hart Lane Chivers achieved little, but with Bill often challenging him to play for his personal pride, his form slowly returned. It took a lot of time and effort, and many managers would have cut their losses and sold him. In 1969/70, Tottenham were virtually mastless and drifting towards the rocks. A 1-0 defeat by a colourless Crystal Palace side in the replay of a fourth round FA Cup tie at Selhurst Park launched a torrent of criticism from the media and Bill dropped Greaves, among others. Jimmy was never picked again and instead, spent the rest of the season scoring plenty of goals in the reserve side, which topped the Football Combination.

He had played his first game for the club against Plymouth in 1961 and his last opponent was the same club, in a rearranged reserve game in 1970. Bill's obstinacy in leaving him out when the Press kept asking for his recall was explained by several factors, including Jimmy's expanding business interests, his decision to take part in the London to Mexico Rally and his drinking. Greaves wanted to see Bill in his office and when they met, they decided to keep every option open. There were three: sell him to another club, stay for the remaining 18 months of his contract or retire. A third party made an approach and said that Brian Clough wanted to sign him, but Jimmy hastily rejected the overture. 'I think I got that wrong,' he admitted later. 'Cloughie would have been just the man to get hold of me and motivate me.'

Invariably the decision was taken by Bill, who rang him on 16 March 1970, the transfer deadline day, to tell him that he had Martin Peters with him and he had agreed to sign for Spurs for £200,000. As part of the deal, Bill was prepared to let Greaves go to West Ham and his value was put at £54,000. Jimmy was livid: it was the day he was moving house and he hadn't been consulted. He had never earned more than £100 a week; the other sums he received came from bonuses. But the new house was only 15 minutes from the West Ham training ground and after chatting to his wife Irene, he decided to go.

Bill's handling of the transfer showed his ruthlessness. Like all the great managers, he had to act swiftly to do what he did in the interests of his club. Jimmy was dismayed by the lax training at Upton Park compared to the strict regime at White Hart Lane; with his drink problem also gaining momentum, he ended a remarkable career less than two years later, at the age of 31. It was far too young to go.

Bill said of Peters: 'Martin did a good job for Tottenham. He was a quiet, honest and reliable person, and for some time our supporters failed to appreciate his worth as they had done with so many players in my time, including Terry Venables and Alan Mullery. These men had one thing in common: they were all midfield players. Some of our older supporters never let them forget they were playing in competition with the memories of Mackay and Blanchflower, and that was unfair.'

Peters was 27 and was happy to stay at West Ham, but with the team sinking towards the relegation zone, Ron Greenwood set up the record-breaking transfer deal. The two managers met outside the deserted Walthamstow Greyhound Stadium and sat together in Bill's car. No one recognised them. No agent or advisor was involved and it took 30 minutes to clinch it. An hour or so later, Greenwood told Peters the details and said he would make £10,000 himself as five per cent of the transfer. As he was only earning £147 a week, Peters took the offer. He was about to join the Football League side at Coventry that night and he rang Alf Ramsey, who was in charge, to ask if he could be late. Alf okayed it and told him: 'You'll be going to a great club, and a great manager. They've got a lot of outstanding players and you won't be an automatic first choice.'

A few days later, Peters called in at Bill's small office, next to the High Road, and Bill asked him: 'How much do you want?' He told him he was happy to take the same salary. Bill was delighted and said: 'What about the contract? Three and three?' That meant three years on contract with an option of a further three. 'That's fine. I'll leave it to you,' replied Peters. All of Bill's deals were conducted that way, without haggling.

Peters hadn't met him before and he said in his book, *A Man for All Seasons*: 'I was a bit in awe of him. He was one of the great managers of all time – a strait-laced Yorkshireman from the old school, firm, friendly and very correct. He seemed to share the same kind of values as Alf Ramsey. That was good enough for me. I thought that the Manchester United side that won the European Cup in 1968 was a great one but I think Bill's Double side was better. No one messed about in his presence. He was a manager of authority, who enjoyed the full respect of his players. I felt that the demands for success were greater at Spurs than at West Ham, but Bill didn't put any pressure on me.'

Peters went on to play for England in 67 internationals, 10 more than Greaves, but that was no criticism of Jimmy as Bill willingly admitted. The new signing formed a good relationship with Chivers and that helped the striker's confidence. Peters said: 'I like to think my arrival had something to do with him regaining his best form. For three or four years I considered him to be the best centre forward in Europe and I was surprised he didn't win more than 24 caps. The fans loved him and still do. They remember him for his goals, his surging runs and his super-long throws.'

As Cliff Jones was no longer with the club, Bill searched in vain for match-winning wingers. Jimmy Pearce and Jimmy Neighbour, both nice guys with low self-esteem, were introduced and Bill observed: 'They were useful players and good team men, but didn't quite measure up to it and I was forced to go out and sign Roger Morgan from QPR for £110,000. Roger turned out to be an unsatisfactory buy through no fault of his own – he had a lot of injuries and had to retire early because of knee trouble.'

One player told a good story about Roger: 'His identical twin

Above: Bill coaching in Bratislava (with a disinterested Brian Clough on the left).

Below: Bill at his uncluttered desk.

Above: The 1960/1 FA Cup winners. *Back row*: Bill Brown, Cliff Jones, Peter Baker, Danny Blanchflower (*with trophy*), Bobby Smith, John White, Dave Mackay, Maurice Norman. *Front row*: Ron Henry, Terry Dyson, Les Allen.

Below: After clinching the League championship by beating Sheffield Wednesday 2-1 on 17 April 1961.

Above: Cliff Jones gets a word in while Danny Blanchflower discourses on the way the game went.

Below left: Dave Mackay holds the Cup..

Below right: Bill in earnest conversation with Chelsea manager Tommy Docherty at the 1967 FA Cup final.

Above: Bill pictured at White Hart Lane.

Below: Bill in a happy mood. Ken Montgomery, the late secretary of the Football Writers' Association, is to his right, with Julie Welch (*above right*).

Above: Bill and Darkie with Spurs players and their wives.

Below: With fellow Double-winning manager Bertie Mee, who performed the feat with Arsenal in 1970/1.

Above: A handshake from Jimmy Greaves at Bill's first testimonial in 1983.

Below: Bill with Martin Chivers at his second testimonial, in 2001.

Above: Bill's father Joe on Scarborough sea front and, *Below*, Bill and Darkie returning to Bill's roots with a trip to Scarborough in 1998.

Above left: Bill with his grandchildren, Richard, Shaun and Colin.

Above right: Playing with son-in-law Steve (*right*) and grandson Colin on the family pool table.

Below: Bill and Darkie at home. Sadly Bill died on 23 October 2004, and Darkie passed away on 30 July 2007.

Ian once took his place because Roger couldn't get there, and no one noticed.'

In 2009, Jimmy Neighbour died at the age of 58. Ralph Coates was one of his best friends and he said: 'Jimmy went into hospital to have a hip operation and next day he died of a heart attack. It was shocking.'

Eleventh position in 1969/70 wasn't good enough for Bill. In most of his 11 seasons since he took over he ran a team challenging for the title, but in the next season a touch on the accelerator soon changed things around again. Chivers scored 21 goals in his 42 appearances and despite losing twice to their Double successors Arsenal, Tottenham finished third, 13 points behind Bertie Mee's side. They also won the League Cup. The emergence of Steve Perryman added the quality that some of the bigger names lacked: the determination to keep running throughout the 90 minutes of each game and keep harrying opponents.

Perryman was born in a council house in Northolt, the third son of a loader at Heathrow Airport, and fell in love with football at a very young age. He used to run the two miles to school and back every day and was reckoned to be an outstanding runner. After passing the 11-plus he was accepted by the Elliotts Green Grammar School to learn that the sports master, a basketball coach, only permitted competitive sport in basketball because it was a non-contact sport. Also, the playground was so small that playing with normal-size balls was prohibited. It meant using tennis balls, and later in life he attributed his skill on the ball to kicking tennis balls at every opportunity.

When the sports master left, competition in contact sports was reintroduced and Perryman's career soon advanced at a fast rate. He starred in a game for Ealing against Harrow and Charlie Faulkner, the Tottenham scout who was one of Bill's closest friends, was observing the action. This led to an invitation to attend training twice a week. Soon a host of clubs wanted him, including Arsenal, West Ham, QPR, Chelsea and the two Manchester clubs.

'Without exaggeration, more than 30 clubs wanted me,' he said. 'I could have had a lot of money, but I agreed to sign for Tottenham for nothing. I hadn't seen them play, but I joined them because of Bill. He was a very, very impressive man and he was so honest and I believe in honesty. There was no sweet talk, no flannel, no spin and he gave it to you straight, sometimes when you didn't like it. He told me I would be treated the same way as any other player on the staff and I was just 16.'

If there was any inducement, it came when Nicholson told him: 'If you don't sign now, I can't give you an FA Cup ticket' before the 1967 FA Cup Final. Tommy Docherty offered him and his family the chance to travel to the final on their team coach. 'Coming from Northolt to White Hart Lane meant a 12-hour day,' he continued. 'In pre-season, with morning and afternoon sessions, it meant leaving home at 6.45 and taking one bus, then an underground trip to Manor House and taking another bus, a journey of two hours. I wasn't back home until seven or more.

'In those days no one ever talked about football, to my knowledge anyway. I used to see card schools, hear chat about birds and money, cars and going out, and see a phenomenal amount of mickey-taking, but no football talk. But it was as if Bill said: "That's how we played" and there was nothing to discuss. Yet it was a very friendly club when you were on the inside. Bill and Eddie Baily changed with the players, something which is unusual in my experience. Training started at ten and Bill would be in there at 9.45, changing with us, and he would have a shower with us afterwards. He was there all the time.

'There was the dourness and discipline, the aggressive masculine values of the dressing rooms, where even in training Eddie would talk about getting the bayonets out and sticking your head or your body in front of shots before you went out. "Get hit, get hurt, that's what this game's about, but afterwards, you'll laugh about it. You need G and T – Guts and Tenacity."

'No one ever overstepped the mark with Bill. The basis of his teaching was that he would take a weakness from a game and that would be the basis of one or two days' coaching.'

The apprentices were given strict orders and trainer Johnny Wallis would call for volunteers, who often had to perform the worst tasks. It was almost like being in the Army, but it turned Perryman into a key player.

Bill was one of the pioneers who used mind games to bring players into line. When his first contract was nearing an end, Perryman went to see him about a rise. 'I'd played almost every game for three seasons and I roomed with Alan Gilzean. Gilly was on £95 and I was on £28, so I said: "Can I get £30?" He said: "What, you want to be paid £30 a week for Tottenham Football Club?" He insinuated that any player should be proud to play for the club, irrespective of his wage. "I'll put these two questions to you," he said. "First, how many people would want to pay money to see you and second, have you seen yourself playing recently?"'

Perryman was taken aback. 'I dunno,' he said. This was the days before videos so except for short clips on sports programmes, he had no opportunity to study himself on film. By this time Perryman was ready to take anything, but Bill said: 'Okay, you're on £30, but keep working hard to improve your game.'

John Pratt played in the same era as Perryman and although he didn't have the same gloss he worked just as harder, or even harder. 'Bill always stressed quality, not quantity,' he recalled. 'If he wanted to do some sprints, he wanted us to give it everything. Six quality ones was better than a dozen half-hearted ones. A lot of people today haven't got a clue about him and his achievements. He was an institution and I put him into the top four, along with Stein, Busby and Shankly. In those days it was all about the players and you rarely saw interviews with Bill in the papers and he was rarely heard on radio or seen on television. Today it's swung round: it's all about the managers today.

'Bill was so far ahead of his rivals with his methods, his work on the training pitch, and even diet. He was the first to introduce chicken and rice, and even Mars bars for energy. He was hot on getting a good education before you became a professional. I was an only child and my parents put me into a private school – Clark College in Enfield – and I didn't leave before I was 17. Terry Medwin coached there and that's why I joined Tottenham.'

When his first contract ended, Pratt went into see Bill and asked for a rise of £5. 'Why do you want money?' he asked. 'Well, to eat, live and stick some petrol in my car,' was his reply. Bill said: 'Pat Jennings has been in for a rise, so has Martin Chivers, Alan Gilzean and Mike England, and there is no money left from this year's budget.' After thinking it over, John agreed to sign for the same money. 'I realised that he had put it quite well,' he explained. 'The big names had made it and I hadn't – I had to try a bit harder next time.'

When he retired, John Pratt worked as a window cleaner for 20 years until a fall from a ladder curtailed this. Between 1984 and 1986 he was assistant coach under Peter Shreeves, the Neath-born coach whose career with Reading ended with a broken leg.

Tottenham had four comparatively easy home wins in the 1971 League Cup and overcoming Bristol City in the two-legged semi-final, they expected to take on Manchester United, but Third Division Aston Villa beat Wilf McGuinness's troubled side. The general opinion was that their 2-0 win over Villa, with two goals coming from Martin Chivers, was a bad game, maintaining Tottenham's poor run in Wembley finals. Two days later, the north London derby took place at White Hart Lane and Bill desperately wanted to beat Arsenal to prevent them from emulating his team's Double.

After matches his players always wanted to know the Arsenal result first and Bill put a prohibition on using red in any form: it was red phobia at its worst. Perryman said: 'Bill would always mention Arsenal. Whatever problems one had during a season, beating Arsenal made up for it.' The snag about denying Arsenal in that deciding match was that a scoring draw would let Leeds in to take the title and Bill didn't like Leeds and their dirty tricks. Ray Kennedy scored an early goal for Arsenal and Alan Gilzean missed a chance near the end, which would have given Leeds the trophy. Thousands were locked out and Arsenal's biff-bang 1-0 win, played out in a fraught, tense atmosphere, wasn't quite robbery, but maybe a lesser charge of larceny.

Bill missed the last game of the season, at Stoke, to meet the Burnley manager Jimmy Adamson to discuss the signing of Ralph Coates in the Post House Hotel, Staffordshire, just off the M6. After he parked his car, he went in and was immediately recognised by the hotel manager. 'Let's talk outside,' he told Adamson. So they trooped outside to his car and sorted out the deal in his usual style, just under half an hour.

In many ways, it was the one of the most overpaid transfers Bill ever conducted. The suspicion was that Bob Lord, the Burnley chairman, railroaded him into it. Lord, who wore a hearing aid, was a dodgy character who made a lot of money from the club to keep his butcher's business thriving and in Bill's book, he quoted Lord as saying: 'Look, Bill, we are making Coates available and the fee is £190,000. I am prepared to give you 48 hours to think about it. After that, I'll have to tell other interested clubs. No one knows at present.'

Tottenham had good relations with Burnley and Bill thought that Lord had been honest and fair with him. Arsenal were interested and Bill didn't want him to lose Coates to his bitter rival, so the deal was rushed through with some of the directors and players wondering why the club had paid a record fee for a player who never established himself as an international. Chairman Sidney Wale – he was always called Sidney – was a retired chartered accountant and he told Hunter Davies: 'You have to pay money to get the star player. You just can't replace a team of the quality of Spurs purely from homegrown players, so you have to buy. On balance, I think it is a good thing to buy. A bit of competition does no harm – it makes the existing players that bit keener to keep their place.'

Ralph knew Bill from a previous England Under-23 tour of the Far East. 'He was a brilliant manager and he had a deep love for the game and didn't want to harm it,' he recalled. 'I learned so much from him and I didn't hesitate to sign for him, but in my first season I found it difficult to settle for a variety of reasons. At Burnley I was playing in midfield and that suited me. I was always in the thick of it.'

For a while Coates wasn't sleeping too well and was forced to take sleeping tablets. He continued: 'I went to see him before the next season and he said he had plenty of midfield players and he was looking for wingers. Eventually he let me play in the middle and after that, it was fine. I really enjoyed my football playing under him and I think the fans helped to lift me. They were very knowledgeable and when they saw someone giving 100 per cent, they would forgive someone for making a few mistakes. I look at some of today's players and many of them are not giving everything, which is terrible because they earn so much money.'

Steve Perryman said of the club's most expensive player: 'The fans liked him because he was all-action, with his short legs going like pistons, and he used to sweat a lot but he didn't really produce the quality Tottenham expected as a return for the money.'

Coates was Bill's last big buy and the manager said later: 'When Ralph started pre-season training it was clear to me that some of the players didn't think he was worth the money. He was hard-working and earnest, but his skills were inferior to some of the more experienced players and his shooting wasn't up to the standard I had been led to expect after seeing him strike a fantastic goal in Turkey once. Some of them were inclined to poke fun at him and I said to them: "You are being unfair. Who used to give us the most problems when we played Burnley? It was Coatsey. Give him a chance."

'His total of 13 goals in 188 League matches may not have justified the outlay but I always said to the doubters that Stanley Matthews's scoring record was no better.'

Sorry, Bill: you were wrong on Coates about assists. Matthews had more assists than anyone in his time but Ralph couldn't match Stan's tally. Ralph could be loosely compared to Carlos Tevez – the Argentinian who when he first played in the Premier League ran and ran without scoring many goals – except Tevez has more skill than Coates at his best.

But Darkie liked Ralph Coates. She didn't see him in action much but she thought him a nice, young man and he tried hard on the field. Ralph said: 'I blame Darkie for that because she was quoted in an article saying that and when the other players read it, they called me the favourite of Bill and Darkie. Bill used to joke about it saying, "She's signed you, not me."

'I got to know her and she was wonderfully supportive of Bill. No manager could have a better wife. I went to her funeral, three years after Bill, and there was a very big turnout.'

Ralph always had an upbeat, enthusiastic approach to life and put a lot back into the game. He was coaching at schools in St Albans almost until he died and was a popular host at Tottenham's corporate lounges. Ten ex-Spurs players are employed by the club. In April 2009, Coates had a total replacement of his left knee and the consultant who performed it, Dr Fares Haddad, operated on my knee the previous November in the same Princess Grace Hospital off Euston Road. 'I blame Tommy Smith, Norman Hunter, Chopper Harris and his mates for my knee,' Coates joked. A few months later, he spent three weeks in the Watford General Hospital and had a heart pacer fitted. Finally he collapsed from a stroke and failed to beat the count. He was given a tremendous farewell at his funeral with the packed audience giving standing ovations to the six speakers.

At the time when Coates played, the directors were resolutely against any advertising around the ground and also shirt advertising. They had a budget for each season and Bill's job was to keep within it. None of them were paid and they met every fortnight. Bill always presented a report and almost without exception, they accepted it. Each season they tried to balance the books by earning money from pre-season, or post-season tours.

At the end of the 1970/1 season, the team spent two weeks in Japan: three matches were played against a rather feeble All Japan XI and they were won by 6-0, 7-2 and 3-0. There were few restrictions and most of the players enjoyed themselves. One had a geisha girl living in his room and the cleaning staff complained of not being allowed in the room.

CHAPTER FIFTEEN:

EXPOSED BY HUNTER DAVIES

There is hardly a single football club in the country that would open its doors and allow a professional journalist to sit in on almost all their activities for a whole season. Certainly not Tottenham Hotspur FC. Even today, the club is still circumspect about issuing news, but in Bill's time it was almost like the Kremlin. They had no press officer and it was difficult to drag out a comment about the most innocuous of stories.

In the weeks leading up to the 1971/2 season a Scots feature writer with an English accent named Hunter Davies, who worked for various newspapers including the *Sunday Times*, had the idea to be a footballing Boswell embedded into a major club. He was a Tottenham fan and wrote to the club, but not surprisingly, he had no response. Davies played a few matches for Brian Glanville's team Chelsea Casuals and Glanville said to him: 'You were stupid to approach Spurs – their board are the most unhelpful and old fashioned and Bill Nicholson is dour and unco-operative.'

Davies, one of the 'Titanium Men' after having a new knee in

2005, tried Arsenal and Chelsea without any result; he then persuaded the *Sunday Times* to take a trial piece about a Tottenham game, interviewing a number of staff. In his book *The Beatles, Football and Me*, he said: 'Nobody at the club objected when the article appeared, so at the beginning of the 1971/2 season, I turned up on the first day, 15 July 1971, for their four weeks of pre-season training at their training ground. I had no contract with the club, either with the chairman or with Bill Nick – I just gave the impression to each of them that the other had agreed to my project – but I had promised both of them that they could read the finished book before publication. I also told the nineteen players in the first team pool that they would share 50% of the book's proceeds, so there might be a few bob in it for them. There was a few hundred pounds each and in those days it was a reasonable sum. I was treated like a feature writer, not a football writer; otherwise I wouldn't have been let in.

'At first, I stood on the touchline, watching Bill talking to the players then doing a few exercises. I followed them afterwards into the changing room and no one stopped me. Next day, I went straight into the changing room. That day, they were going on a cross country and I went on it. Someone threw me a Spurs training kit. At 34, I didn't stand out and I played a lot of Sunday morning football and kept myself fit. Soon I got on well with the players and when the season started, I was able to infiltrate myself into the dressing room before and after most matches, walking in and out as if I were a part of the squad. I went to the home games and some of the away games when we travelled on trains in a reserved section and went on most of the European trips. In a game against Nantes, I am described in a photo as one of the players. That was a highlight. Over the season there were times when I thought my game might be up and I could be ejected, such as half time in one game where Bill Nick was furious with Martin Chivers.'

His book *The Glory Game* was, and still is, a classic of its kind and Mainstream updated it several times. Most of the tastiest bits were serialised in the *Sunday Times* and the *People* and some of the directors were furious. Eddie Baily was incensed after being quoted as an Alf Garnett type racist.

'I got a letter from Lord Goodman of Goodman & Derrick, the most feared firm of libel lawyers at the time,' recalled Davies. 'Fortunately, both Bill and Sidney Wale, the chairman, had read the manuscript and I could prove it. The chairman had even made pencil marks in the margin. I was able to prove that each player had read the bits about himself and had not objected. I never heard anything further. Today, such a book would be practically impossible. All Premiership clubs and players have hordes of lawyers, accountants, agents, plus endless corporate deals and sponsorship arrangements. They wouldn't, or couldn't say hello to you without charging a fortune. Probably they wouldn't be bothered anyway with a book like mine as they are all so rich.'

It was remarkable that one of the most secretive of all clubs should be exposed to such blinding revelations. Steve Perryman said: 'It was astonishing that he should be given such access. Tottenham was a club almost impossible for outsiders to penetrate. Soon he became like a part of the scenery and no one thought of him as a reporter.'

Several changes were made, but the book reflected Bill's honesty and though he had some reservations he was happy with the finished work, describing it as 'exceptionally good.' In his own book, he said: 'In my view the dressing room must always be a private place. Permission was not given by me but someone else at the club. In hindsight, I should have objected and overruled the decision. I know Davies's work was highly acclaimed but after one particular match I was forced to keep quiet when I wanted to say a lot of things straightaway. I remember feeling, "I am the manager, yet I am not doing my job tonight because he is there." Chivers later admitted to Davies that perhaps he needed geeing up, so I could have been right.'

There was only one book similar to *The Glory Game* and it was written by another Davies, no relation – *All Played Out, the Story of Italia 90* by Pete Davies. The other Davies spent nine months with the blessing of the FA, following Bobby Robson and his squad in the World Cup in 1990 and filling 437 pages, 100 more than Hunter's which had an index. Pete's didn't have one and that annoyed the players, who wanted to find out what had been said about them. The journalists were particularly critical: mainly through being jealous because the author beat them to it.

Inside journalism of this type is virtually extinct in modern football. The people who run it have so much to hide for obvious reasons and they employ press officers to control the news emanating from their club. Most of it is extremely mundane and leads to speculative journalism. If the writers aren't told the truth, they start embellishing it.

One of the most quoted parts of Hunter's work was his survey of the views of players. One question – 'would you become a manager?' – provoked some interesting replies. Of the 19 players in the squad, 11 said no, with one even declaring: 'Not bloody likely! I've seen Bill Nicholson after a game and I couldn't stand it – I'd end up in a loony bin.' Most were undecided and only one, Martin Peters, thought he might take up the reins. Peters was briefly player-manager of Sheffield United and later went into insurance; he is now a director at Tottenham, a much safer haven. Nine – Mullery, England, Steve Perryman, Martin Chivers, Joe Kinnear, Phil Holder, Graeme Souness, Glenn Hoddle and Cyril Knowles – became managers and only Perryman is still in charge of a club (Exeter, where he is director of football).

Cec Poynton was 70 when *The Glory Game* was written and no longer first team trainer, but he was in the background giving advice about injuries. An incident involving Roger Morgan brilliantly portrayed the way players were given medical treatment. Morgan's knee started to swell up and Poynton told him to sit down and bend it as far as it could go. Morgan screamed out in pain. 'It's nothing,' insisted Poynton. 'Cliff

Jones's was four times as big as that.' 'They should have taken out the cartilage,' continued Morgan. Poynton countered: 'If you believe you're going to limp, you will limp. Dave Mackay still limps from his two breaks in the same leg but it's never stopped him playing, has it?' Morgan responded: 'It's on fire! What shall I do?' Ever-practical Poynton replied: 'Go and cool it. Get yon hosepipe over there and turn it on.'

The water was cold and Morgan sprayed it on the injured joint. It made little difference, but it was probably just as effective as today's expensive equipment.

Eighteen of the players in the first team admitted to being highly superstitious – Pat Jennings was the exception, which was unusual because he is an Irishman – and Morgan's pre-match ritual was to take a piece of chewing gum from his mouth as he went on to the pitch. He would then toss it into the air and kick it. If it was a good kick, with the gum going some distance, he felt confident he would have a good game. In that season he obviously failed to kick the gum very far and an operation loomed.

Hunter Davies was lucky because Tottenham were having a good season when he chose to write about them. They won the UEFA Cup (the trophy that took over from the Inter-Cities Fairs Cup and which has recently been rebranded into the Europa League), finished sixth in the League and reached the semi-final of the League Cup and the quarter-finals of the FA Cup. Chivers was back to form, setting a club record of 44 goals in 64 appearances. But Bill wasn't happy about their League form: 'For such an experienced team, a lot the players weren't consistent,' he said. Wale and his directors enjoyed the six trips abroad, but he too was concerned about the League form, saying: 'It's our bread and butter.'

They even entered the superfluous Ango-Italian League Cup Winners Cup, a mini competition dreamed up by Gigi Peronace, the persuasive agent who won the confidence of the FA and most of England's managers. Torino were the Italian Cup winners and

Tottenham beat them 1-0 away and 2-0 at home; another award filled the already-bulging trophy case.

Davies started to label Chivers 'Mr Chivers' in his chapter about him, possibly because most of the players thought him arrogant. Chivers recalled: 'Despite all my success, I'd always been a timid player. At Southampton I'd had to fight because everything had come easy – it was the way I'd been brought up. I'd had a very easy-going childhood and schooldays: I did everything without really trying. People called me a "gentle giant", which was true. It's always the little fellers who do all the fighting, in football as in other things; they're trying to prove how good they are. Big players like me, and I suppose John Charles, don't continually have to prove anything.'

Icelandic amateur side Keflavik were Tottenham's first opponents in the UEFA Cup and they were like a Southern League conference side without the gale force winds and the ice. Some of the players visited the geysers, but declined the chance to dip into the outdoor hot springs. They were told to keep away from the drinking houses, which were filled with drunken young people of both sexes. On one trip to training, a woman in her thirties staggered on to the team coach and refused to get off. The players found it very amusing and it took some time to remove her.

Keflavik were outclassed 6-1 and Chivers scored a hat trick in Tottenham's 9-0 win in the second leg. Even Ralph Coates scored, his first since arriving two months previously. Ten journalists, including me, were permitted to travel with the team's aircraft to Nantes in the next round and only one, Hunter Davies, was allowed in the dressing room. Bill picked a modest, medium-sized hotel as if to remind his players that it wasn't to be a holiday but a serious job of work. In recent times, Nantes had twice been French champions and he expected a tough match.

Before the first night's dinner, Bill went through the menu with the players. It took almost an hour to complete the orders for the next three days. Hunter Davies, the club's Boswell, wrote: 'It was a job Johnny Wallis [the club's general factotum] could have done, or Alan Mullery, or the head waiter, or anyone.'

Bill barred alcohol until the match was over. When the players were served their steaks, they removed any trace of garlic and Phil Beal declared: 'I hate it.' Most of the time, they played cards while they waited for their food. Invited to tour around the town, one or two started out, but decided it was too boring and returned to the hotel to resume their card games. Even today, football teams go through this excruciatingly boring ritual on away trips, though games consoles have taken over from the full-time playing of cards.

On the second day, the players still moaned about the hotel, the food and the lack of booze while the directors and the journalists were treated to a slap-up reception at a smart restaurant 10km out of town. Some of the directors were tipsy by then, but there was more drinking to be done at the ground. Davies sat with the team for Bill's pep talk and it lasted 90 minutes. 'They were all fed up and bored rigid with it,' he said. Perhaps this was a sign that Bill might be losing his grip.

The dressing room, like the small stadium, was Spartan and on the benches there were wrapped bars of soap and a new blue towel for each player. Most of them pocketed the soap, with one saying: 'Another free present for the wife.' The home club had presents for each of the players and the gifts turned out to be a Waterman propelling pencil wrapped up in green paper and tied with a bow. Bill said: 'They asked me for a list of things you'd like, but I don't know which one they chose. If it had been me, I'd have given you a comb and a pair of scissors.' But the players ignored his joke – they'd heard it so many times.

There was no ventilation and when Bill went out, after telling Eddie Baily to lock the door, the atmosphere in the room became hot and fetid with embrocation. A few minutes later, Bill knocked three times to regain admission and started cursing. 'They've changed their bloody strip!' he said. 'They told me last week they'd play in yellow, which is why they're called the bloody canaries.'

The French TV wanted Nantes to play in yellow and fortunately Pat Jennings had a spare jersey because his green one would have clashed. His calmness contrasted to Bill's increasing frenzy. Bill launched into his final exhortation: 'You remember what happened when we last played in France,' he said. 'We lost to Lyons and we were knocked out. Keep your feet down. It you raise a boot, this referee will book you.'

After this, he went off to wash his hands – he always had a ritual of doing that before every match. He also patted each player on the back, wished them good luck and used their Christian names as they went out. It was a courtly way of conducting himself. The crowd kept up a barrage of noise as the all-French team piled on to the attack and Eddie Baily never stopped – cajoling, screaming and shouting. Once he even shouted: 'Bloody frogs!'

Meanwhile, Bill was shouting, mainly at Chivers, urging him to get moving. 'Bloody [a stronger word might well have been used] internationals!' yelled Eddie. 'Look at them. Play for England, but they won't play for us. Get moving: don't bloody stand there! Too much publicity, it's gone to their heads – they won't try any more.'

At half time, the verbal bombardment from manager and coach continued: the players were upset that they didn't have their usual tea, only Vichy water. The second half was a repeat of the first and Bill brought on the recently-fit Morgan for the final minutes. Morgan ran so hard that when it was all over, he sat on the bench: 'like a defeated racehorse, frothing and streaming from being pushed almost beyond endurance,' in the words of Davies-cum-Boswell. He goes right to the heart of football, a form of journalism we never read these days. It has been replaced by sanitised journalism and the intention of those running the sport is to avoid controversy.

Davies went on to describe the bitter exchanges between Chivers, the star player, and the fuming manager in the dressing room afterwards. The result was 0-0. Normally a draw away from home would be considered a decent result, but Bill was very unhappy about his players.

After a brief lull, Chivers said: 'A poor team.' Bill reacted aggressively: 'I never said they were a good team.' Chivers came back: 'They were a bad team.' 'You mean, we had some poor players?' Bill replied. Suddenly Chivers blew up like a screeching kettle. 'What do you know about it? You never praise us when we do well, you never do – you weren't out there! It is easy for you to say we didn't do well.' Bill insisted: 'I've bloody well been out there! I know what it is like: I've been through it. We had some poor players tonight – that's what I am saying. Some of our players weren't trying, that's what I'm saying.'

Eddie Baily tossed a towel across the room to one of the players and accidentally knocked a glass cup onto the floor, shattering it into pieces. He and Bill bent down to pick them up. A valuable player could have cut a foot and put him out of the next game. The other players filed out to the showers leaving the sullen Chivers sitting alone, staring at the floor. Mullery started singing: 'Oh What A Beautiful Morning!' Mike England, who was looked on as a musical upstart, whistled a piece from Tchaikovsky's 'The Nutcracker Suite'.

I was one of four journalists allowed in for some reason and we chatted to Mullery and Chivers, neither of whom disclosed any information about the bust-up. Sidney Wale and his directors were allowed in as well. None of us had ever known such an experience – inviting the press and the directors in at the same time.

As the players trooped on to the coach Bill announced the whole squad would attend a reception given by the Mayor of Nantes at the Château des Ducs, a castle in the middle of the city. It was the finest occasion of its type that I've experienced and the other writers felt the same way. The buffet was sumptuous, served by powdered flunkeys.

Sidney Wale praised the Mayor and his staff, saying: 'Our club has visited dozens of football clubs all over the world and your hospitality tonight is the best we've ever known.' Half an hour on, the players decided they wanted to go back to the hotel, forsaking the chance to experience some history. These days, clubs never entertain opposing sides after matches, chiefly because of cost and also, they want to fly their players back home as quickly as possible.

Back at the hotel, the players bought themselves pints of lager and went to bed without any more inquests. On the mid-morning flight they were served champagne for some reason, but most declined. By then, Chivers had calmed down: he admitted nothing went right for him. Davies asked Bill if he thought that shouting at his players was counterproductive.

Scenes like that are commonplace at most matches today, probably more so than in Bill's time because more than half the Premiership players are mercenaries, with most of them showing little or no loyalty to their club. Apoplectic managers can't shout for more skill, but only call for greater effort. If one player makes a mistake through lack of concentration or effort, the team can lose the match so the managers and coaches will keep up the pressure on their players at the expense of their health. Jock Stein died while at a game and it's amazing more managers don't die from sudden heart attacks.

Bill's explanation was very rational: 'Players can easily become too confident and arrogant,' he told Hunter. 'I don't mind confidence but it leads to lack of self-criticism. That was wrong with some of them last night. Good players like that shouldn't make mistakes, ever – that should be the aim. But if they do make one mistake, that should be it. They should be so furious with themselves that they vow never to do it again but they won't make mistakes, so they don't try harder and do better. Everyone can do better.'

Tottenham's form up to Christmas was satisfactory, with seven wins out of ten, but a pattern seemed to be forming: a bad run would appear in the New Year, particularly in the Championship. Wale agreed with Bill that the team was too inconsistent. Some players raised their game in Cup games whereas they treated League games as a chore.

On 8 December the team beat Rapid Bucharest 3-0 in the next round of the UEFA Cup in an uneventful tie, but the return game a week later was termed 'The Battle of Bucharest'. Bill did some detailed research on the Rapid players and learned that most of them had poor disciplinary records. He told his own team just before the kick-off: 'I want no retaliation – you've got to keep your tempers. It will be hard, but you'll be penalised if you step out of line. So no retaliation.'

Bill Stevens, the club's assistant secretary, was sent round the butchers' shops in the Tottenham area to buy up a supply of chicken, steak and lamb. This was to be stowed away in a deep-freeze container to send out in the BEA aircraft. 'We've heard the food out there is a bit dodgy,' he explained.

The players were each given £10 in local currency but when they arrived, they were told it was useless. Not that there was anything to buy – the shops were virtually empty. Unlike Nantes, Rapid didn't lay on a reception or even a tour. On most of these trips, particularly behind the Iron Curtain, the British Ambassador would invite the club to a drinks party at the Embassy and Bill and his directors came along. Davies recalled: 'Bill was the centre of attention. It was strange to watch him, with his broad Yorkshire accent and no-nonsense manner, surrounded by a gaggle of Oxbridge faces, yet perfectly at ease and in command. They were hanging on to his words, especially some of the women.'

The away dressing room looked more like a country-house parlour than a football dressing room, with wall-to-wall green carpeting and pot plants on a large antique table in the centre. There were no baths or showers. A home official brought in dressing gowns and explained that the two showers were at the end of a corridor. Naturally, the players didn't think much of that. The August 23 Stadium, named after the start of the Republic of Romania in 1947, had a capacity of 80,000 yet no more than 10,000 turned up. But they made enough noise for 80,000, with a continuous, almost hysterical hubbub of hostility aimed at Tottenham's players.

Right from the start, the players were kicked and punched off the ball and the Italian referee failed to send anyone off until late on, when he sent off a Rapid defender and Jimmy Pearce, who scored the first goal, for trying to punch each other. Perryman had his testicles squeezed, Gilzean was punched in the kidneys and Chivers kicked in the leg, not just once, but several times. Perryman went off after dislocating a shoulder, but gallantly returned to the action, and the number of Tottenham players injured reached seven. Chivers scored a second goal – a brilliant solo effort from a narrow angle to make it 2-0 – and Tottenham went through an aggregate of 5-0.

Eddie Baily, who had been shouting abuse for most of the game, yelled: 'You're great, brilliant!' Chivers ignored him. Davies called it 'a sordid game' and described the scene in the away dressing room as being 'like a hospital casualty ward.' Meanwhile, Bill congratulated his players. 'I'm proud of you,' he told them. 'You showed them how to do it – you didn't retaliate, we've had the last laugh. Well done!' His players sat there, stunned. He warned them to be careful in making comments to the press, but he surprised them again, saying: 'It was the dirtiest team I've seen in 30 years. Diabolical! I've never seen such dirty fouls.' Bernard Joy, the former Arsenal centre half who was chief football writer on the *Evening Standard*, asked if that was on the record, to which he replied: 'Yes, quote me.'

The match was televised live in Romania, but TV companies in the UK were denied the opportunity to show it at home. Phil Beal recalled: 'That was without doubt the toughest side we ever played against. Bill said he'd never seen a game, or a place, like it in his life, with those huge perimeter fences to keep away the crowd.'

For unexplained reasons some clubs and countries keep drawing against the same opponents in international competitions and tournaments. Frequently, England face countries such as Poland, Norway and the former countries of the USSR. Tottenham were always sent to the furthest outposts, like Rumania, Poland and

Georgia, and after surviving the visit to Bucharest, UEFA officials gave them another Romanian club, UT Arad, an industrial town near the Hungarian border. Told the news, the players shouted their disbelief.

I went on that trip, too, and Arad was more dreary and depressing than Bucharest, except the people were far friendlier. Thousands turned up to welcome our party. Arad had no foulers in their ranks and Tottenham won 2-0 through goals from Cyril Knowles and Martin Chivers, who were both booked. The ground was jam-packed and the British press had to sit on trestle tables along the side of the pitch. My ordered telephone failed to turn up and with little time to write a report after the final whistle – the Tottenham party departed half an hour later – I borrowed one from John Oakley of the *Evening News*. Without his kindness, and his speed at which he ad-libbed his final piece, I could have been left behind. A number of residents in the many houses surrounding the stadium removed slates on their roofs to get a grandstand view. The return match was a placid affair, ending 1-1.

Alan Mullery missed four months of that season due to a pelvic strain. When he recovered, Bill left him in the reserves. Mullery had been on the staff for eight years and was still an England regular and he felt he should be brought back. He came to see Bill and asked if he could come on as a substitute. 'I don't do that, Alan,' he was told. 'I'm not sentimental. There is no room for sentiment in professional football.' The miffed Mullery asked if he could go on loan to his old club Fulham. Bill was more understanding about that and with hardly a 'good luck' or even a 'keep in touch', Mullery was back at Craven Cottage for a month's loan.

AC Milan were Tottenham's UEFA Cup semi-final opponents and with John Pratt breaking his nose and the team facing four games in six days over Easter with the final one at home against AC Milan, Bill appealed to UEFA to ask for a delay but he was turned down. He rang Mullery and told him that he wanted him back. Next day he called him over and said: 'You're in the team and you're the captain.' The tie was eventually won 2-1 through two extraordinary long-range goals from Perryman, who said of Mullery's performance: 'He had something to prove and he roared around the pitch like a raging bull.'

The 42,000-capacity crowd greeted him with chants of 'Ra-ra-ra-Mullery' and that helped to spur him on. Bill had told him: 'I want 90 minutes from you, and don't get booked.' Mullery satisfied him on both counts and at the end of a pulsating, niggly game, he declared: 'We'll see who the big men are out there' meaning the second leg in the San Siro. Though Mullery didn't have the same skill as Mackay, he had the same passion for winning and he was an inspirational leader.

One of Bill's greatest strengths was his pre-match preparation. He acted like a General Montgomery, covering every eventuality, and before the second leg he heard that Inter Milan might be willing to loan him their opulent training camp at Lake Como. The feeling between the two Milan clubs was, and still is, far worse than the relationship between Arsenal and Tottenham – they hate each other. Bill contacted their general secretary and was delighted when he was told that their training camp, which included a cinema and a games room, would be open house to Tottenham. On visiting the camp, however, he found that half the rooms were below ground level. He felt it was too depressing, so Inter offered accommodation at a nearby golf club for only 20 people, which proved another masterstroke. 'We had the privacy we needed,' he said.

Each day, I went to the training pitch and Eddie Baily organised daily skill tests. One was to chip the ball at a range of 30 yards to make sure it bounces back off the crossbar. All the members of the squad took part and the one with the most hits was 48-year-old Eddie. Many were irked by his continual criticism but they respected him as a football man of high quality.

The team coach left early for the match, but the traffic was so heavy that they reached the stadium just 40 minutes before kick-off, risking in a fine from UEFA. Roads in the vicinity were blocked and the police escort unable to stop dozens of crazed AC supporters, who banged at the windows of the coach, shouting abuse. The players took cover, with Gilzean observing wryly: 'On the way back it will be bricks.' Fortunately it never happened. At this stage, Gilzean wasn't fit: he was there for the ride. In the dressing room, he told his fellow players: 'Come on, lads, I need the bonus – I've got a wife, two kids and a budgie to keep!' Someone else shouted: 'and a pub!'

The players seemed more relaxed than normal, as was Bill. 'I want you back 10 yards at every free kick,' he told his men. 'Don't give the referee a chance to take your name – I want no dissent of any sort.'

One wonders how many of today's managers would say the same to their players. Most of them moan about referees in front of their team instead of supporting the officials. I have covered two major matches at the San Siro, which was built in a similar style to the Coliseum, and in the words of Peter Ball, Steve Perryman's ghost: 'It seems to go straight up and you wonder if you're in danger from the hundreds of fireworks and firecrackers going off.'

The incessant chants of 'Mee-lan, Mee-lan' were almost terrifying and it was impossible to have a conversation. In the Tottenham game I spent the whole 90 minutes on the phone trying to dictate copy to the *Daily Mail*, but the poor copytaker could hardly get a single word. It was the same at the semi-final of the World Cup in 1990 when the great Luciano Pavarotti sang 'Nessun Dorma' and the 83,000 crowd started their own unchecked mass choir which never stopped.

Bill picked out the hardy Romeo Benetti – who scored in the first game – as the main threat and asked Pratt and Perryman to mark him and Gianni Rivera. Eddie Baily urged Bill to switch to short corners, to upset their man-to-man marking system, and this turned out to be a successful ploy. After a jittery start, Perryman laid a perfect sideways pass into the path of Mullery in the seventh minute and the ball rocketed into the net.

'I've belted a few balls in my time, but I've never connected with the power I produced that night,' enthused Mullery. 'It was perfect. I had never hit a ball better, or with more intent.'

Rivera equalised from a penalty, but Tottenham's more determined players held on. In the dressing room the directors, accompanied by other members of staff, entered the vast dressing room to offer their congratulations. Cyril Broderick from Thomas Cook, who arranged all Tottenham's tours, was splashed with water by the players and responded by stripping off and jumping into the bath with them. Seeing his skinny build, John Pratt observed: 'I thought Belsen had closed.'

Wolves won through to the final by beating the Hungarian side Ferencvaros in the other semi-final: it was the first time that two English clubs were in a European Final. Their manager Bill McGarry had many similarities with Bill Nicholson. Both were hard-tackling wing halves, who believed in strict discipline but whereas Bill could often control his temper, the red-haired McGarry lost his on too many occasions. His players joked that he only became bald because he tore out his hair in rage.

That season Bill Nicholson's players had flown 10,238 miles in Europe, had sleepless nights in uncomfortable beds and were bored rigid, as one admitted, with all the hanging around. Taking a two-hour train ride up to Wolverhampton suited them better and they knew the ground at Molineux and were familiar with the likes of Derek Dougan and Dave Wagstaff, the tricky winger who always gave Joe Kinnear and John Richards, among others, a hard time.

Bill thought too much of the pre-match publicity was placed on the two centre forwards: showman Irishman Dougan, who was the chairman of the Professional Footballers Association, and Martin Chivers. 'If Dougan had concentrated on using his ability to the best advantage, he could have been an even better player,' he commented. 'Chivers scored both goals in our 2-1 win and both were beauties. But there's no justice in football. If I was Bill McGarry, I'd be in tears. Never mind the result, our performance was awful.'

Chivers hadn't done a lot, except score the goals, but Eddie Baily volunteered to lie down in the dressing room afterwards and let him walk all over him. 'You've knocked me out, Martin,' he told his teammate. 'I'm out for the count. Martin, what can I say?' Chivers smiled and said: 'Thanks, Ed', but declined the offer.

The return match was another middling affair with most of the experts saying that Wolves were the better side. Mullery knocked himself heading his side's only goal and Bill congratulated Pat Jennings on a marvellous save to stop a shot from Wagstaffe, who scored the earlier Wolves' goal. The crowd of 54,303 was the biggest of the season and they weren't bothered about the quality, only the win. Bill pronounced: 'Once again, our performance hadn't quite matched the occasion.'

In the dressing room, the champagne was open and the players pushed Mullery out onto the pitch to parade the heavyweight UEFA Cup on his own. Mullery said: 'It was unbelievable madness, but I loved every minute of it and I never once let go of the Cup, even though it weighed a ton!'

By then, Mullery was 30 and he desperately needed a rest: he wrote to Alf Ramsey, saying that he had played his last game for England – his 35th. He then went to see Bill and told him he was quitting the club – 'and leaving behind glorious, happy memories.' Bill made no effort to keep his captain. As Perryman said, years later: 'That was Bill, and Tottenham were never good at goodbyes.' Mullery went on to sign for Fulham, his first club, and played a further 164 matches, many of them successful.

In his autobiography, Bill recalled: 'Attendances were falling at White Hart Lane and despite our successes in Cup competitions, we had less money to spend on players. I found it almost impossible to buy the ones I wanted. It was around this time that football plummeted to a level never before experienced in this country. There was a meanness about the way the game was played. I had to admit I didn't enjoy watching it. There were fewer goals and more arguments, more dissension, more professional fouls.'

Tottenham staged 70 matches that season and none of the players were ever present in the League side. Bill had won seven major trophies in 12 seasons and only one, winning the ECWC in 1963, brought him contentment. The budget was overspent again and the directors voted for advertising around the ground and opened a club shop selling, among other things, underpants for men and knickers for women: in white with the Spurs cockerel on the front. It was no longer a football club but a business, the pressure on the manager growing all the time.

Hunter Davies once said of managers: 'They have complete power over their charges (not today, though!) but when it really matters, they are helpless. Most players do forget once they get out there playing, but a manager has few releases, few safety valves. Their agony is constant.'

Speaking at the Ladies Night of the Football Writers' Association dinner at the Savoy on 15 January 2005, Arsène Wenger described his efforts to achieve perfection on the field: 'You always want to improve players and you want your team to be the best it can be, but that maybe only happens once or twice a season and I apologise if I get frustrated when it doesn't happen. There is another question: who motivates the motivator? It is our job to work with the players and raise confidence, and when the work is done, you are left on your own – it can be a lonely life.

'I look at the body language of the men in charge and when they lose, some of them show their feelings and are down, and that transmits to their players. But if you can present yourself for interviews in the same way, whether the match is won or lost, it can reassure players and you can maintain strength.'

For much of his long coaching career, Bill Nicholson stayed strong but his strength was slowly ebbing away in the early seventies.

One of the saner voices in the game – Dr Neil Phillips, honorary medical officer to the FA – told Brian James of the *Daily Mail* in 1972: 'We just don't know about the strains and stresses put on our elite of players, the stars who are important to the top ten sides in the country and the same people on whom the burdens fall in international football. Playing Saturday, Wednesday, Saturday... week in and week out, year after year, in a highly competitive atmosphere at a high level of physical commitment can impose appalling strains. Players don't have time to recover from minor injuries and chronic conditions develop from small ones. We have seen evidence of the pelvic disorders suffered by men like Alan Ball, Alan Mullery and Bob McNab.

'I have noticed the change in top players, a sort of disenchantment with the game. A lack of sparkle. One finds oneself looking around a dressing room like an officer looking at his men in the trenches in the First World War: which ones will crack when the shelling starts, and which will still have the nerve to go over the top?'

Some of these problems have been solved by the injection of huge amounts of cash from television, enabling a handful of clubs to field two sides to suit themselves and defy the FA, which has a rule insisting each club must put out its strongest side. The remaining clubs with limited resources are cheated of the chance of winning a trophy; the supporters also denied. The 'meanness of the game', as Bill Nicholson once described it, has deepened. It is now a philosophy of 'every man for himself' and that is not fair, not right.

CHAPTER SIXTEEN:
DISILLUSIONMENT SETS IN

In 1973, the pressure on Bill Nicholson was mounting, and a lot of it was self-inflicted. For the second season in a row, he was unable to sign a new player. Instead, he found himself in a dilemma – the acute shortage of talented players was forcing transfer fees up to record heights. On three occasions, he set records himself, buying Jimmy Greaves, Martin Peters and Ralph Coates, and as Phil Soar said: 'Armed with more than a quarter of a million pounds as the rich pickings of Spurs' crusades in Europe, he had more than enough to do it again. On this occasion, however, he became the victim of his own big spending.'

The fans were eager for new names and he could have calmed things down, had he bought one or two players no better than the ones he already had, but he considered that bad business – the directors wouldn't be happy when they realised he was wasting the club's resources – so he held firm and suffered in silence. Today's talkative manager would have mounted a clever PR campaign to defend his position and win the critics over, but Bill was never like that. Sidney Wale tried to fill in the PR gaps and said: 'I wish the crowd would see what we are trying to do and stop living in the past. It is far more satisfying to produce your own players than go out and pay out £1m for one. The fans are still judging us by the Double team and we cannot possibly match that.'

If Bill took the same approach to the media as Bobby Robson then his managerial career might have lasted a few more years. Bobby loved football, but he also loved football people, including many journalists and commentators. This helped him to keep his job as England manager for eight years when he was under prolonged attack from the competing redtop newspapers, the *Daily Mirror* and the *Sun*, in the eighties. Nigel Clarke of the *Mirror* once said: 'My job is to fry Bobby Robson,' but he never managed it, mainly because Sir Bobby courted the other, more responsible, newspapers.

When he played for Fulham, he fell in love with Tottenham's style of football and over the years built up a wholesome relationship with Bill, who was one of his idols. In his first of several autobiographies, entitled *Time on the Grass* and published in 1982, he wrote:

I spent a lot of time in my formative years on the terraces at White Hart Lane watching that great Spurs side of Danny Blanchflower, Dave Mackay, Jimmy Greaves and Bobby Smith. The players worked together so well. Smith was the ideal foil for Greaves. Blanchflower complemented Mackay. The blend was sensational and in my view is one of the basic ingredients of the truly great side: blend. You can have good players but they won't necessarily make a good side unless they fit each other like pieces of a jigsaw.

I used to get off the bus at Seven Sisters and practically run to White Hart Lane. The atmosphere at the ground almost dragged you there. It was like a powerful stimulant. To me, there was no thrill in football to match it. I was there the night they outclassed Gornik 8-1 in the European Cup after losing in Poland. What a night that was! Would Spurs side have been as successful in today's conditions? I think so. Of course the game is more compacted now. There is less space because the play is pressed into a narrow strip in the centre of the pitch, but I am sure those fine players would have adapted. They were so good at using the width of the pitch, so economical in their passes. Arsenal's Double winning side in 1971 cannot be discounted but they lacked the artistry of Bill Nicholson's team and they failed to stay at the top very long.

The man who took the decision to sack Robson when he was manager of Fulham in 1968 was Sir Eric Miller, chairman of Peachey Property, and the following year he committed suicide. In 2009, it was revealed that MI6 had investigated insider dealings with shares owned by former Prime Minister Harold Wilson, who had earlier knighted Miller in controversial circumstances. Some of Wilson's private papers were stolen and just after his 60th anniversary, he surprised the nation by suddenly resigning.

In 1972 Bill had problems when nine players whose contracts were coming to an end rejected his offers. Most of them were internationals and when they went on such duties, they had plenty of time to discuss comparative wages with the other players in the squad. One complained: 'We've discovered that Tottenham aren't in the top ten in wages in the First Division. And as for Arsenal, some of their players earn twice as much as ours.'

Somebody leaked the details to a newspaper and Sidney Wale and his directors were angry, accusing those responsible of being disloyal. The basic wages of the players were among the lowest, but Bill had drawn up a payments scale related to success. The more points they won, the higher sum they received at the end of the season. He said: 'Often the wages reputed to be paid to players were grossly over-estimated, yet stories at international gatherings of footballers were all too often given credence. Some of the

211

newspapers built it up as a pay revolt, but it was never that. We had some sensible people on the staff then, and the matter was resolved with both sides making concessions.

'No doubt the players concerned would say I should have given them more money and that the club was stingy, but I have never heard one say he was better off elsewhere, or that Tottenham was not a good club. Many I met in subsequent years told me that their best days were spent at White Hart Lane so we cannot have been too far behind the best paying clubs.'

Mike England represented the players in the negotiations and did a good job. He was one of the sensible ones.

Tottenham played a taxing 23 cup ties in the 1972/3 season, taking their total games for the season to 69. Unlike today when the current top clubs often use 30 players or more in a season they had just 20. Tottenham's first two opponents in the UEFA Cup were of indifferent quality. Lyn of Oslo went out on an aggregate score of 13-2, while Olympiakos of Piraeus were summarily dismissed by a 4-1 aggregate. The first leg was routine, with Tottenham winning 4-0 at home.

Arriving in Athens at their individual bungalows in a beautiful setting, the Tottenham party were delighted – but the mood changed when they got to the ground. Steve Perryman said: 'The game was ugly and the hostility of the crowd was frightening. It was an afternoon kick-off and very hot. We went out on to the pitch beforehand and were greeted with a hissing, spitting noise from the fans, who jabbed their fingers at us in an extraordinary gesture, which together with the noise I assumed to have something to do with the devil. On the way back to the dressing room, Joe Kinnear made the gesture back to them and they went even more berserk than they had been before.'

The clubs in Greece and Turkey still have passionate, intimidating supporters, but once the visiting sides gain control they revert to almost silence, which happened on this occasion. Olympiakos managed just one goal and the game ended without incident.

Red Star of Belgrade were next in line and in the following weeks, Bill was happier than he had been for some time. He had made a friend: Miljan Miljanic, Red Star's manager who later coached the Yugoslav squad. Miljanic was extremely helpful and although their language difficulties caused problems, they developed a good relationship. David Miller helped Miljanic to arrange interviews with Chelsea and Arsenal, and Miljanic was keen to become the first overseas manager of a First Division club. In the end, he backed off, though. Bill commented: 'He was a very good coach, who had been successful at all levels, but he might have found working in England too different from what he had been used to, and that was probably why he didn't go.'

Before the home game against Red Star at White Hart Lane, Bill flew to Belgrade to see Yugoslavia v Greece with the intention of watching the four Red Star players in the national side. Though his English was indifferent, Miljanic invited him to his home for a meal and they spent a few pleasurable hours at his flat in the old part of the city. Two days later, the club invited Bill to a pre-match lunch and together, they walked to the stadium.

'Mixing with such friendly people, and talking about and watching football made it one of the most enjoyable days of my managerial career,' Bill recalled. 'I struck up a firm friendship with Miljanic and when he came to England, which was fairly often, he would visit us at Cheshunt and watch us training. Miljanic was one of the most honest men I knew, which was another reason why I admired him. On my trip to Belgrade, I asked him if he could give me the pen pictures of his first team squad for the Tottenham programme. He duly supplied me with photographs and details of all 16 players and he picked out the 11, set them out on a table and said: 'This will be my team.' I was astounded.

'At first I thought he might have been trying to kid me but when he arrived, two weeks later, for the match and handed his team sheet to the referee, he had kept to the 11 he had nominated, and also the substitutes.'

No manager would do that today. With the aid of Miljanic, Tottenham duly won the first match 2-0, but lost the return 1-0.

Tottenham were still dropping points in the League yet they were able to raise their game in European matches. In the fourth round their opponents were Vitoria Setubal, a small club in a fishing town in Portugal, which is pronounced 'Stewball'. They had neat, skilful players who kept possession of the ball and they restricted Tottenham to a 1-0 lead after the first game. Morale was low because four days earlier Tottenham's players were castigated for their performances in one of the worst Cup Finals ever played at Wembley: the League Cup Final that resulted in a 1-0 success over an unenterprising Norwich side.

The players needed a fillip and in the return at Setubal, two weeks later, the trip turned out to be one of the most relaxed and funniest they went on during that era. Phil Beal recalled: 'A few of us went out for a meal and just as my fish arrived, a call came through and I had to go to the phone. When I returned, one of the players said, "The waiters have kept your fish hot for you, mate." When I lifted the lid, I saw a fish head, a tail and a long bone connecting the two. Everyone started to laugh and soon the whole group were in fits of laughter.

'Next day I was walking around the harbour when I spotted a local man selling fish heads. I asked him to put four into a plastic bag for me and took them back to the hotel. When I got back, I asked for the key to the room shared by Cyril Knowles and Pat Jennings, and placed the heads under their pillows. They slept in that room all right, in between searching high and low for the revolting smell that filled the room. The next morning it absolutely reeked and they had to leave the room smelling like Billingsgate Market, with the heads still there. All the lads couldn't believe how bad the smell was and it didn't take them long to guess who had got his own back. That might be where the phrase "done like a kipper" came from.'

Phil Beal was the club's chief prankster. He would ring up new players and pose as a journalist, asking them personal questions. One player who fell for it was Martin Peters: 'You had to be careful when Phil was about because he had a reputation as the dressing-room joker,' he said.

Perryman said: 'The Setubal game stands out because they had a midfield player who was really putting himself about, whether as a result of something in the first leg, I can't remember, and even Bill got upset about it, which was very unlike him. He said to us at half time: "If one of you don't sort out that big so-and-so, I'm going to get up off the bench and do it myself," which was very strong for him because he usually appreciated good players on the other side and he must have realised the lad was doing a good job for his team.'

Chivers scored 34 goals in the previous season and his relationship with Bill had improved, although there were still times when rows broke out. He scored from a 35-yard free kick late in the tie after the Portuguese side scored twice and Tottenham squeezed through on an aggregate of 2-2 by the away goals rule. Bill and Eddie Bailey made a point of going up to congratulate him. Another of Bill's strengths was to study the laws and regulations. Many players didn't have that knowledge and when the game ended, he told them that Tottenham were through to the next round. That was before penalty shoot-outs.

Two 1-1 draws in the League with Manchester United and Liverpool, plus a 1-0 victory over Chelsea revived spirits before the UEFA semi-final against Liverpool. Bill never admitted it in public, but their chances of winning a second trophy were evaporating because his side had to play 11 matches in the last 33 days of a crowded season. His squad simply wasn't strong enough. Liverpool had greater resources and they won the League title, 15 points ahead of Tottenham: it was the start of the Scouse domination in English football.

A 1-0 defeat at Anfield in the first leg should have given Tottenham the advantage, especially as the rejuvenated Chivers scored both goals in the return match. Ray Clemence reckoned it was one of his greatest games. Then Steve Heighway, the Irish winger, broke away to score and the result of 2-1 ended the run by the same away-goals rule. Bill Shankly's side went on to win the Cup, beating Borussia Mönchengladbach 3-2 on aggregate, and Bill Nicholson was one of the first to congratulate him.

Earlier, Tottenham marched towards Wembley in the League Cup with victories over Huddersfield, Middlesbrough in a replay, Millwall, Liverpool in a replay and Wolves in the two-leg semi-final. Beating Liverpool in the quarter-final replay was one of the side's finest performances of the campaign. They swept to a 3-0 lead after only 20 minutes and it showed there was little between the two clubs. Semi-finalists Wolves were tricky, testing opponents. A spectacular goal from John Pratt helped Tottenham to win 2-1 at Molineux. In the return, an own goal from Terry Naylor left the aggregate 2-2 at normal time. Chivers, inevitably, scored the winner in extra time.

He signed for Tottenham in 1968 – the same week Arsenal signed Bobby Gould, who later managed Bristol Rovers, Coventry, Wimbledon, WBA and Wales. Gould said: 'We stopped in the same hotel, the Alexandra National Hotel in north London, and I didn't warm to him. He could be moody, but in 2009 I played cricket with him for Bob Wilson and he was a different man, a lovely guy. I said to him: "You move quicker now than you did 40 years ago!"'

When a big club meets a tiny one fighting relegation often the players tend to lose their edge and that happened in the final on 3 March. Norwich, a folksy club founded in 1905, had never reached a final before. The closest was when Ron Ashman led them to the semi-final of the 1959 FA Cup. Ron Saunders was in charge and within the game he was rated one of the outstanding managers of his time.

Born in Birkenhead, he was a Bobby Smith-style centre forward and as a manager, an unyielding, blunt and strict disciplinarian of the Stan Cullis mould. In *Football Managers*, written by Dennis Turner and Alex White, his style was described as 'dull and unimaginative and his dour image did not endear him to the public, but he knew his job inside out and was greatly respected by the players in his charge.' Bill warned his players that Norwich would provide stiff opposition but subconsciously, they ignored the advice. It turned out to be a non-game, as he freely admitted.

Saunders took Norwich into the First Division in the previous season and if three up and three down had been brought in – it was introduced the next season – they would have gone straight down. Doug Livermore played in their final line-up and admitted: 'I agree it wasn't a good game for the fans, but Ron organised the side very well. He didn't go out to defend and with Tottenham not playing are their best, it turned out to be an ordinary match. We had great respect for Ron – he'd done a good job to get us where we did, without money to buy better players.'

John Pratt, Tottenham's most big-hearted player, was appearing in his first final and was injured early on. Ralph Coates came on in his place and scored the goal, mopping up most of the headlines afterwards. Some players emerge as folk heroes and one of them is Coates. 'That goal changed my life and I never looked back,' he revealed. 'It was like removing a ton weight on my shoulders. Even now people come up to me in supermarkets and shake my hand and congratulate me for the goal. And it's still being shown at White Hart Lane in the build before games. I had tremendous fan mail after that. Before then some folk hadn't accepted me.'

Perryman described the game as '…a dreadful let-down. We were all relieved that Ralph managed to score. Only masochists would have wanted to sit through the game any longer than they had to. Ron Saunders had really just set out to stop us playing, but again we didn't play well, and I was surprised by how some of the big names failed to cope with the occasion.'

Still, three Cups in three seasons wasn't too bad. Perryman was 21, sometimes he was appointed captain, and in that month he married his childhood sweetheart Cherrill. He said: 'Bill always encouraged us to get married, but he wasn't very pleased about the date – he just couldn't believe that I was getting married in the season. And I didn't help matters by saying: "Well, I don't want to mess the summer up, Bill." He went berserk and I didn't ask him or Eddie to the wedding, although I can't remember why not. We should have invited them.'

Bill was becoming disillusioned about many things, including 'bungs', cheating by players and the rapid fall in attendances, particularly at White Hart Lane. In two seasons the average home gate dropped from 38,000 in the 1971/2 UEFA Cup winning season to 26,000 in 1973/4 and a profit of £300,000 fell to £35,000.

Perryman felt he was being turned into a harrier and tackler, not the all-round midfield player he thought he should be: 'I thought he should be helping me, and I was feeling oppressed by him. Players always say the manager is always picking on them, but at that stage I felt his critical eyes were on me the whole time. And I thought that people like Chivers, who were causing a lot of ructions at the time, should have been the target rather than me. But I suppose because of what I gave to the team I was never dropped.'

One day Bill called him into his office to tell him that he was thinking of leaving him out. Perryman replied: 'Suit yourself' and left. He went home and put his feet up, thinking he had been dropped. Graeme Souness was lined up, but to his surprise, Bill stuck with Perryman. But it was a gee-up for him and he was relieved that his record was left intact.

Bill was becoming desperate to sign another Greaves or Smith and realising no one of that class was available, he started looking at the likes of Duncan McKenzie, who specialised in trying to upset Brian Clough with his antics at Nottingham Forest. He was once photographed jumping over a Mini, and also apparently threw a golf ball from one end of a football pitch to the other. He had immense talent but rarely seemed to use it on the football field, which explains why Clough eventually sold him. As well as McKenzie, Bill also considered Chelsea's Bill Garner. McKenzie preferred to join Leeds. Garner was similar in style to Tony Hateley – he was good in the air, but his skills on the ground were minimal.

When Bill met him, Garner asked for a tax-free payment. Sidney Wale was furious and wanted to leak the story to the press, but Bill told him that it was legal to pay these so-called 'underhand' payments so long as they were detailed in the player's contract and spread out over the period of the contract. In reality, what it meant was that the club was signing two men: the player and the taxman, who made nearly as much out of the deal as the player.

In Alan Gilzean's last four seasons, his goal tally was 9, 11, 5 and 3, so no longer could he be termed a regular scorer. And that was Bill's biggest worry: finding another Gilly, or similar.

CHAPTER SEVENTEEN:
'GET YOUR HAIR CUT!'

During the Nicholson reign, many of Tottenham's players had long hair and the taciturn Pat Jennings still has that style in his sixties. But to Bill Nicholson, long hair was an anathema. 'It sickened me,' he said. 'Besides the risk of having their hair fall across their eyes, I always maintained that it gave the wrong image. Long hair is fine in the pop world but not in football. Players began bringing hair-driers to matches and I didn't approve of that, either. It was a source of mickey-taking. But now it is accepted and clubs provide the necessary electric points, up-to-the-mark hair-driers and mirrors.'

Bill himself usually had his hair cut just around the corner from the ground and he never varied the style. It was short back and sides, exactly the same cut as he was given in the Army.

In 1974, his difficulties in signing new players took a new, worrying turn when he finally relented and signed Alfie Conn from Glasgow Rangers for £150,000. It was Bill's last big transfer before he resigned. The move was doomed for failure, but not because of

Alfie's extraordinarily long hair and sideburns. Alfie's father had the same name and was one of the most popular Scots players north of the border, scoring nearly a goal a game for Hearts. Alfie Senior was bald, but Junior, with his exotic hairstyle, wasn't in the same class as a goalscorer. He was more of a dribbler and a teaser, although he did have a powerful shot.

With brutal candour, Bill admitted that he had made a mistake in signing him: 'With good footballers unavailable, I had to aim lower down the scale and that explained why I bought Conn, who was also not really my type of player. He did not come up to my expectations, though he was popular with our crowd. I find that most crowds, including ours, understand the game and applaud the right things, but there are a certain number of players who sometimes may not deserve such treatment. I felt Conn came into that category. Our crowd had a similar rapport with Steve Archibald: they invented the refrain: "We'll take good care of you, Archibald."'

Archibald was a far better player than Conn Junior and Bill had a grudging admiration for him. In his second season, Conn flashed across the night sky like a meteor, scoring a number of match-winning games and enabling Tottenham to stay up, but injury sapped his speed and after scoring six goals in 38 matches, he was sold.

Around this time Bill was quoted as saying that large payments were being paid to certain players in transfers and he felt it was bad for the game. Conn was on £15 a week at Glasgow Rangers and when he joined Tottenham, he was paid £7,000 as a signing-on fee and his weekly wage was £180. It was against Bill's instincts to pay such a large sum, especially as a further £4–5,000 went to the taxman, and it showed just how desperate he was to sign a charismatic and talented player to bring back the dwindling crowd. Conn had a certain appeal but his talent didn't extend to finding space, using the ball accurately and blending into the team – he was too much of an individualist.

The 1973/4 season, Bill's last full season, started with a

disastrous 4-1 defeat at Ajax in a friendly and his team went out in the League Cup and the FA Cup at the first attempt, finishing 11th in the League. Now the club which scored a record 111 goals in a League season was down to 45 goals, equalling the figure in 1912/13, which was the worst in its history. The match at Amsterdam was staged for a benefit with the proceeds going to a retiring player, Jackie Swart. Bill said: 'It's a bit early to meet this kind of opposition and our opponents reckon we will be beaten easily.'

Indeed, Ajax swept to a 4-0 lead inside 10 minutes and Johan Cruyff, then at the top of his game, strutted around the pitch like a peacock. Ajax were renowned for their receptions after ceremonial matches, but they forgot to lay on a table for the Tottenham party and the players were very upset when they had to stand.

Two home defeats against Leeds and Burnley added to the gloom but there was some relief in the UEFA Cup. Swiss side Grasshoppers were knocked out on an aggregate of 9-2 in the first round and Pat Jennings had an outstanding game in the second leg. Then Aberdeen lost 5-2 on the two legs in the second round.

On 28 November, the party was transported to Tbilisi in Georgia, south of the then USSR, in a creaky, uncomfortable Aeroflot aircraft that caused considerable concern to everyone, including the press. It thudded onto the uneven tarmac and by the time the players left the airport, it was nearing midnight. On arrival at the hotel, everyone sat down for dinner at 1.30am, but all the players wanted to do was go to bed.

The next day, they were asked to attend a display of Cossack dancing while the directors were treated to a four-hour banquet. Every few minutes, someone or other would get up to propose a toast and by the end, most of the directors were somewhat inebriated. Eddie Baily had been on a spying mission and reported back that the Tbilisi players – particularly Kipriani, their midfield general – were world-class.

The ground was packed with excited supporters, almost half of them soldiers, and at one corner a gallows was set up, on which a cockerel was strung. They had done their research. It was an intimidating place with the temperature just over the freezing mark. As often happened on Tottenham excursions abroad, they scored an early goal and the better team, Tbilisi, had to be satisfied with a 1-1 draw.

Kipriani looked like Gilzean in appearance and they struck up a good relationship at the reception held at a restaurant on a mountaintop. Though somewhat sceptical about going up and down the funicular railway, after a few glasses of Georgian champagne and caviar, the players began to enjoy themselves. The Georgians were well beaten in the return – 5-1 – with most of the goals coming from set pieces, well prepared as usual, by Bill Nicholson. Afterwards, Gilzean and some of his colleagues took the Georgians out in London. These days it would never happen: players are whisked away to the airport and taken home during the night to avoid drinking after matches.

As the year ended, Bill's qualms deepened when a crowd of 14,034 saw his team beat Stoke 2-1, the lowest attendance in 20 years. Alarm bells rang loudly and the directors showed signs of panic.

When the winter break ended in Europe, the next UEFA opponents were FC Cologne, where the home side hadn't lost for many years in a Euro tie. Cologne had players of the class of Schumacher, Cullmann, Flohe, Dieter Muller and Overath, but they were soundly beaten 2-1, and then in the second leg, by 3-0. Bill thought their next opponents – the skilful Lokomotif of Leipzig, East Germany – superior to Cologne, but they were beaten 2-1 and 2-0.

In the League, three of the last four games were won. Had they had been lost, the team could have finished 20th. Two matches remained against their good friends Feyenoord in the final in May. Another Cup success to add to Bill's unbeaten record would save face for the ailing club, but he knew that Feyenoord had just won the Dutch championship and they were formidable and skilled opponents. One fear for both camps was that a number of hooligan groups were promising 'action' off the field and for several months, British and Dutch police had been working on methods to deal with the trouble, if it came.

The first leg, played in heavy rain, saw a number of skirmishes outside White Hart Lane and several coaches taking Feyenoord supporters were stoned. By hooligan standards of that time, it wasn't severe. Several hundred police officers were on duty and the visiting fans limited to a small area. Traditionally, European clubs do not take vast numbers of travelling fans, unlike English clubs.

Bill considered his team more handicapped than the Dutch by the conditions and he was impressed with the physical strength and resilience of his opponents. Feyenoord used the offside trap frequently and he conceded: 'We needed one of our better performances, but it wasn't forthcoming. We need to sort our tactics against their offsides. We were caught far too often.' It was disturbing that the match hadn't been a sellout for Tottenham – the crowd of 46,281 was around 8,000 short of the capacity.

The team took a long time to open up and it was late in the first half when Mike England ran round the back of the home defenders to head in the first goal. Stocky Wim Van Hanegem equalised from a classical 25-yard free kick off the woodwork and Bill described it as 'a left-foot curler, reminiscent of Glenn Hoddle's for England in Budapest in 1983.' Earlier, Van Hanegem was cautioned for dissent and banned from the second match. An own goal from Van Daele made it 2-1, but four minutes from normal time, Theo de Jong brushed past Steve Perryman to beat Pat Jennings. Perryman blamed himself. He was one of that rare breed – always one of the first to hold up a hand when he made a mistake. A 2-2 result had given the advantage to the Dutch side.

After twisting an ankle Phil Beal went off, saying: 'A lot of teams have come here and jacked it in when we go ahead but they took everything we gave them and gave us a bit more back. One of them even hit me in the neck. I thought they were brilliant – easily the best side in the competition.'

The same day Ronald Crowther, the Northern football writer on the *Daily Mail*, reported that Stan Bowles was ready to join Tottenham in exchange for Martin Chivers. Ron was usually right and on this occasion, he was spot-on. The deal was underway until the unscrupulous Jim Gregory, chairman of QPR, vetoed it. A car dealer and varied businessman, Gregory had a habit of ringing up his enemies and threatening them by saying: 'I'm sending someone round to kneecap you.'

Bill also wanted Gerry Francis and Don Givens, but admitted: 'Stan Bowles was the one I liked most. I considered him to be one of the most skilful players in the country.' Later manager of Tottenham (between 1994 and 1997), Francis said: 'Gregory didn't want to lose his best players and I once signed a contract with Dave Sexton, when Dave was manager of Manchester United, and when I showed the form to Gregory, he tore it up and threw it into the bin.'

Bowles would have been a better buy than Conn, but Bowles stayed on at QPR for a further five years. When Francis succeeded Ossie Ardiles at White Hart Lane he had numerous conversations with Bill, who by then was a consultant at the club. 'It was always a pleasure to sit down and chat with him,' he said. 'He had so much wisdom and he was always helpful.'

On a number of occasions Bill tried to sell Chivers, but he never succeeded. In 1975, Terry Neill sold him to the Swiss side Servette for £80,000 when he took over. Bill later recalled: 'An amazing change occurred in him after that. No doubt it was inspired by the realisation that Tottenham had been good to him and he had spent his best years with them. He became no longer moody and sulky – he became a very likeable and personable man. He would ring me for advice, or to socialise.'

Bill's eldest daughter Linda was working for Procter and Gamble in Geneva at the time and knowing that her parents were going to spend a few days there, she rang Chivers and asked if he could let her have four tickets for one of Servette's matches. Chivers duly obliged and a few days later he invited Linda and her parents to join him for dinner. Bill said: 'Darkie couldn't believe the change in him. She said to me: "He's the bloke who has given you more aggro than any other player yet he was so pleasant and we all had such a marvellous evening." I am sure she thought I had been making it up when I spoke to her about my problems in the past. I tried to handle Chivers as a special case and that was contrary to my principles of management – I believe they all should be treated equally and I got that wrong with Chivers.'

Chivers went on to join Norwich in 1978 and then Dorchester in 1980, before taking a hotel in Brookman's Park in 1982. He asked Bill to open it and he duly obliged – it was a good night.

The return leg in Feyenoord incited some of the worst hooliganism for years. The shock of seeing his own supporters create such havoc had a profound effect on Bill and was one of several reasons why he resigned. In the days before the match there were incidents on ferries, with hundreds of drunken yobs causing damage. Similar scenes happened through the day and night in Rotterdam, with marauding gangs of Dutch hooligans joining in the battle. Shops were looted and the town centre, rebuilt after German bombers destroyed much of it in 1940, looked like a war zone.

Feyenoord always insisted they never had any problems up until then, but they had a number of hooligan groups who were bent on trouble. And although Tottenham hadn't been involved in a serious hooligan outbreak, they too had their gangs of hoodlums. How it started, no one knew: Tottenham travelled all over Europe and the USSR in three successive seasons and there wasn't a single arrest until then.

Tottenham took an army of 5,000 supporters, including four planeloads. Many of them appeared to be intoxicated. I walked the last mile and a half to the stadium and it was obvious that the local police were having difficulty in restoring and keeping order – they only had 20 dogs with them and there should have been more. Sports writers rarely make the front page, but the next day I had the whole of the front page of the *Daily Mail* under the headline 'RIOTING FANS SHAME BRITAIN'. The word 'hooligan' came from an unruly family from the Elephant and Castle in the 1880s – someone should have thought up a better name for their descendants.

The three-tiered stadium was filled to capacity with 62,988 supporters and when the match started some of Tottenham's players glanced anxiously at the club's end, where the fans were sitting in the middle tier. They expected trouble and it happened when Wim Rijsbergen scored the first goal in Feyenoord's 2-0 win to give an aggregate of 4-2. Suddenly scores of Englishmen turned on the Dutch ranks alongside and below, hurling bottles, tearing out seats and throwing them in their direction. A thin line of police proved powerless and after a few futile attempts at baton charging, they withdrew. Shocked home officials asked Sidney Wale to speak to the supporters and he did so. 'You are disgracing the British people, yourselves and your club,' he told them. In response, they screamed 'F*** off! You ****!'

More bottles and seats cascaded on the Dutchmen. For the first time in his managerial career, Bill was unable to give a half-time talk. Eddie Baily did it instead. He told the Feyenoord officials: 'I'll go out there to the middle and ask them to behave themselves.' He was handed a mike and shaking with anger, he shouted: 'Will you listen? This is the manager of Tottenham Hotspur speaking. You hooligans are a disgrace to Tottenham Hotspur and England. It is a game of football, not a war.'

Martin Peters, the captain, tried to wave a placatory arm from the pitch but he was shouted down. By this time many of the troublemakers filed out of the three exits on that side of the ground and police moved in. Outside the stadium, scores of fights broke out between the respective groups. On the field, Italian referee Concetto Lo Bello booked Ray Evans and Perryman for dissent and when Peters was hacked down, there were fears that the English louts would smash down the two-metre high fence. Luckily, it didn't happen. Seven minutes from the end, Peter Ressel scored the second goal.

Bill's proud record of never losing a Cup Final was gone. More than 200 people were injured, 70 or more arrested. Jan Van Nass, the President of Feyenoord, issued a statement: 'We are very sorry for Tottenham. In all their years in Europe they have never been in any kind of trouble. It is not the fault of their players or officials but they have been let down by several hundred of their mad supporters. This kind of thing is unknown in our country. We have one of the most security-conscious stadiums in Europe but despite all precautions, we were powerless to stop it.'

Bill's daughter Jean, accompanied by husband Steve, went on the trip. 'It was absolutely awful,' she recalled. 'We travelled in a train from King's Cross and people with six-packs were getting drunk and smashing up the carriage. Then we went on an overnight ferry and they continued behaving appallingly, like throwing fire extinguishers into the sea; it was terrifying. I was 25 and I never encountered such mayhem.

'At the ground we were seats in a lower terrace and the Spurs fans were above, and when the first goal went in, they hurled cans, bottles and coins down on those below. They started breaking up the seats and throwing them, with the police not being able to stop it. I listened to my dad's words on the tannoy and I could see later that he was totally devastated by what had happened. After the game, we returned to the coach and when it drove off, someone threw a brick and broke a window. Fortunately no one was hurt.'

Bill said: 'Having to speak to the crowd meant I had no chance to speak to the players at half-time, but I don't think that contributed to our first defeat in a major Cup for 73 years. We were beaten by a better side. I was so angry that English fans had tried to smash up part of our opponents' very fine stadium. The local people tried to say it wasn't our fault and that we shouldn't worry, but I saw it as a national disgrace, as indeed it is every time hooliganism is repeated by English "supporters" abroad.

Looking back in his 1984 autobiography, he said: 'Since 1974 the authorities have done their best to ensure that fans travel in approved groups and don't arrive too early in the town. Sports ministers of the European countries have worked out guidelines for their police forces. Everything was done in advance, but vandalism continues. The perpetrators are not lovers of football – they see the game as an excuse for them to provoke trouble and start fights. Having away legs relayed back on close-circuit TV, as we did in 1983 from Feyenoord and Munich, could take us part of the way to a solution, but even that wouldn't stop people travelling. Only withdrawing their passports, or turning them back at the ports and air terminals, would do so, but the EC rules prevent that being used as a deterrent.

'These people have no discipline in their lives and they carry on pillaging and looting and causing mayhem because they know they are reasonably certain to get away with it. If the same severity was applied against soccer offenders as it is against those who break the motoring laws, I feel sure the incidence of offences would drop.'

Steve Perryman said of the Feyenood riot:: 'Before the kick-off, I looked out of the dressing-room window and saw people throwing beer over passers by. By half time, it had developed into a serious riot. Bill came in at half time, but went quickly out again to try and calm things down. People said it was the final straw for him and when he came back, there were tears in his eyes and I remember thinking, "That's probably the end for him."

'My father was in the stand where the rioters were ripping out seats and using them as missiles and he said it was terrible. The club had flown the wives out and we met them at a hotel afterwards and we were very depressed. Next day we went on a trip to Delph to see the pottery and had lunch. What would have been a lovely day was completely tarnished. One felt ashamed to be English, ashamed of being connected with football. Feyenoord didn't think much of us either because when we exchanged shirts at the end of the match, the ones they gave us were old and full of holes. They had obviously changed at half time.'

UEFA, the ruling body of European Football, ordered Tottenham to play their next two European home ties at least 250km from White Hart Lane and they were fined a moderate sum. Both penalties were on the light side. In 1980, when Tottenham were still out of European competitions, UEFA granted an amnesty to all clubs who were convicted after breaking the rules, but Tottenham were left out. Geoff Richardson, son of the former chairman Arthur, appealed and eventually the club was included. 'I think they just forgot about us,' he said.

By 2016 Feyenoord hope to have finished a new 80,000-capacity ground from a design that will, they think, eliminate the kind of riot that besmirched their name back in 1974. Tottenham, meanwhile, aim to build their new 54,000-capacity ground in 2011.

CHAPTER EIGHTEEN:
ON HIS BIKE

When Bill Nicholson started work as manager of Tottenham in October 1958, Danny Blanchflower asked: 'How long do you think you will be the manager at White Hart Lane?' 'Five years at the most, the way I am going,' was his reply. As always, he underestimated himself – he was virtually in charge of the first team from 1956, so in effect, he was the boss for 18 years. He was a worrier and did most of the jobs which are now shared by a host of others at the club.

Though Tottenham are now a medium-sized business, they are dealing with a smaller attendance, down 20 per cent from the sixties figure, and fewer professional players. You need to be a Charles Atlas to take up that weight of work. Bill had just two members of staff on the secretarial side: a secretary and Mrs Barbara Wallace, his personal assistant. He dictated nearly all the letters himself and often answered the phone. There was a club secretary and an assistant, the rest of the staff part-time.

Bill would arrive at work around 8am and except for a short

break when he sometimes walked home for lunch, he was back at the ground until late in the evening. On Sundays he was there as well. He usually had a two-week holiday, but was never away for other breaks. Eddie Baily was his first team coach and number two, Cec Poynton, was the trainer and physio. Johnny Wallis was the baggage man and general factotum. There was no goalkeeping coach, no condition trainer, no sports psychologist, no nutritionist, no commercial manager and no press officers.

Ken Friar, OBE, currently a director of Arsenal, but known throughout the game as 'Mr Arsenal', said: 'The only person I have known that has been so dedicated as Bill is Arsène Wenger. Bill was a good friend, and he was a superb guy and the like of which it would be almost impossible to find today. He was so honest and full of integrity that he would find it difficult fitting in.'

In 1946, Ken started work part-time at the age of 12 and his record of longevity with one club is unlikely to be beaten. He succeeded Bob Wall as Arsenal's secretary in 1973, later becoming managing director and overseeing the move to the Emirates Stadium.

With so many problems weighing on his mind, Bill thought of resigning after the UEFA Cup Final, thinking that if Tottenham won it, he would be given the chance to go out as a winner, thus preserving his remarkable Cup record. But the defeat in Rotterdam left him in turmoil. Most days Sidney Wale popped in to see him and they talked about moving him up to general manager and bringing in a younger manager with experience. Wale said: 'There will have to be changes one day: it is a question of time and timing.'

Eddie Baily was 49, six years younger than Bill, and they were similar personalities – total perfectionists. There was an acute need for a younger man to join the coaching staff with a view to assuming control later.

Asked by a Sunday newspaper correspondent who was on his 'Okay List', Bill said: 'It is more difficult to get loyalty, respect and honesty from players.' He was becoming more and more disenchanted, and with the extra burden of having to drive long distances to look at players, he was also feeling the strain. Chivers was after a new contract and when he wasn't offered the sum he wanted, he gave an interview saying it was rubbish and asked for a transfer. Four possible transfer deals collapsed and the 1974/5 season started with four successive defeats, the worst start to a season for 62 years. One defeat was at the hands of newly promoted Carlisle, who beat Bill's fast falling side 1-0.

When questioned about what he intended to do, Bill insisted: 'Work harder. Being in such a state was entirely my own fault. No one asked me to work all day and every day, but I ran the club and wouldn't trust the smallest job to anyone else. I wouldn't delegate, which perhaps was wrong, but it was my way of working and it had been successful. I had felt it was essential to have organisation and method, but now that wasn't enough. New thoughts and ideas were needed. I believed a new manager would provide them and also the motivation which I felt was no longer coming from me.

'It was said that one of the chief reasons I resigned was that I lost touch with the players. That was not the case. My relations with them were not much different from what they had been when I first took over. I had no favourites – if there are slack attitudes in a club, the team becomes slack and inefficient. We had a book of rules, which I insisted had to be observed, but just as I never put a soldier on a charge when I was in the Army, so I cannot remember having taken serious disciplinary action against any player. In the Army, the rule was five minutes before time and I insisted on that.

'There were silly little things in the rulebook, like telling players not to drop towels on the dressing-room floor and stand on the duckboards when drying themselves because it was unhygienic. The boards were there to cut down the amount of washing we did. I put myself in the players' position and looked at every problem from their viewpoint. I discouraged selfishness and thoughtlessness, reminding them of their responsibilities to each other.'

The rebellious Chivers was recalled for the home game against

Manchester City and the ever-loyal John Pratt dropped and replaced by Chris McGrath, who turned out to be a bit-part player. Pratt summed up the feelings of the younger players, saying: 'I hated to say it, but I thought Bill was becoming too negative. His team talks were getting longer and longer.'

City won 2-1, and according to Phil Soar's history of the club, he went to see Wale that evening to announce his resignation. 'The pressures had been building up for several months,' recalled Wale. 'Few people knew it at the time, but Bill was under a lot of strain. He'd had a bad time over contracts and some players really got him down. The opening results of the season finished him – he felt he just couldn't take it any more.'

Three days later he confirmed that he was leaving his post, but stayed on until 13 September. A 4-0 home defeat in the League Cup by Middlesbrough was a sickener for him. 'Even Darkie didn't know about my resignation,' he admitted. 'She heard about it on the radio next morning. Mr Wale didn't want me to leave – he asked me to stay and so did his charming wife Cynthia, when I attended a private cocktail party at his house in Hadley Wood the following Sunday, but my mind was made up. He asked me to stay on for two weeks until a successor could be found and I agreed.

'One of the most touching moments was when the players asked me to reconsider. A delegation led by Martin Peters and Phil Beal tried to change my mind. I was surprised and heartened about how the attitude of the players towards me had altered. I suppose it is true that people are vastly different when they are relaxed from when they are working under stress.'

Martin Peters organised a petition and only one player refused to sign it because he believed Bill had been trying to sell him. Peters said: 'I went on TV and told Jimmy Hill that the Spurs players wanted Bill to stay. But he didn't, and after what he'd achieved in the game, you had to respect his decision.

'I had the greatest respect for him: he'd taken a big gamble when he broke the transfer record to sign me. Under his leadership, I'd enjoyed a lot of success with him and he made me captain. In many ways he was similar to Alf Ramsey. He cherished such old fashioned values as loyalty and humility, qualities that were vanishing from the professional game. Even so, he was always protective towards his players. He treated us all equally with firmness and understanding, but I know that months of protracted contract talks with some key players had frustrated him. We had a few jokers and he didn't always appreciate their humour, and he didn't like swearing and asked the players to watch their language if children turned up at the training ground. And he was sickened by the increase in hooliganism and felt players were becoming more mercenary.'

Linda expressed her feelings after her father's resignation, saying: 'I was a bit shocked, as everyone else – he had done so much for the club. It was strange afterwards to see him putting his name to sports columns and analysing matches instead of still being manager of Tottenham.'

One myth about Bill was that he never enjoyed a laugh when he was working. Eddie Baily recalled an incident when the team were on their way to a match in Germany: 'We were in a coach, going pretty fast on an autobahn, when suddenly a wheel flew off and was spinning along the road on its own. Bill looked up and said, "Well, there goes our meals on wheels."' Everyone roared with laughter.

A few days before Bill resigned, Ron Greenwood, one of his best friends with similar beliefs, resigned as manager and moved up to general manager at West Ham, leaving John Lyall in charge of the team. In his book, *Yours Sincerely*, Greenwood observed: 'A manager can stay in a job too long and I was becoming increasingly angry at the way the game was developing. John was a strong character with a Scottish background and he cared passionately about the club and the game, and he was the perfect man to take over.'

Lyall, who became a wages clerk at Upton Park when his career ended at 23 through injury, was a scrupulously honest man, like Greenwood and Nicholson. Not many of them were left. On 12 July of that year Bill Shankly, another OBE and a worrier like Bill Nicholson, suddenly announced that he was resigning as manager of Liverpool at the age of 60 after 15 years. As he departed, Shankly said similar things to Greenwood and Nicholson, decrying modern players and saying: 'When I hear of the money that is bandied around, it makes my blood boil. There are men with tennis courts and swimming pools, who haven't even got a championship medal!'

Nicholson enjoyed a fine relationship with the Liverpool manager: 'He was the best motivator in the game. He had a fervour about him, like a bottle of pop, full of effervescence. He never said, "I don't know" – he always did know. He couldn't stand slackers or what he called "flash Harrys." He spoke in a harsh Scots brogue and gave the appearance of being a severe man, but underneath that exterior he was warm and humorous. He built up his players when they were in the team but when they weren't, he had less time for them and that made them all the more determined to get back in.'

Like Bill Nicholson, Shankly was addicted to football and when he resigned, he thought he would still have a role to play at Anfield. After turning up at the training ground at Bellefield, near his semi-detached house, and at Anfield on many occasions, upsetting the new manager Bob Paisley, the directors instructed him not to go to the ground any more. He was mortified and became a bitter man. In 1981, at the early age of 67, this unique and much-loved character died of a massive heart attack.

Realising they had treated him badly, the directors paid for the 15-foot-high Shankly Gates to be built, inscribed 'You'll never Walk Alone', but when a seven-foot statue of him was unveiled in 1997, it was paid for by Carlsberg, the sponsor, not the club. Bill Nicholson might have met the same fate but for the intervention of Keith Burkinshaw, who invited him back to White Hart Lane in 1976.

The fourth member of the quartet who quit around the same time was Joe Mercer, who resigned at Coventry. He too was a straight and upright man, who was much loved and he had more to give, but for his illness at the end. They were all OBEs, highly respected, great managers. Joe acted as caretaker of the England team for a short spell when Revie resigned and brought a smile to English football. Bill Nicholson had always been a great supporter of Greenwood and he felt that he would be the best man to take over. The FA got that right when they appointed him in 1977.

If there was ever a date when English football turned into the wrong road then it was 4 July 1974, the day when another OBE, Don Revie, was appointed manager of England in succession to Alf Ramsey, one of the straightest men in the game. FA secretary Ted Croker admitted that he didn't know Revie too well, but he should have been suspicious when Revie rang and told him that he wanted to be the England manager but didn't want to apply for it. No one else was interviewed and the FA blundered into swift action without much thought.

In his book, *The First Voice You Will Hear Is...*, Croker said: 'Revie's record bore comparison with any manager in the game and was in the class of Bill Nicholson and Bill Shankly, both of whom were about to announce their retirement.'

Alan Hardaker, the hard-nosed secretary of the Football League and a former Naval Commander, warned Croker that his candidate ought not to be considered because of his bungs and other excesses. The FA ignored that advice and after the appointment was confirmed, Hardaker told Croker: 'You must be off your heads.' Six months later, Croker admitted: 'I realised Hardaker was right. Also, I thought it was a mistake that Revie didn't have a FA Full Badge. Revie only had our preliminary certificate and that made a mockery of our coaching system.'

Three years later Revie walked out of his job to coach in Dubai and the FA subsequently banned him for 10 years for acting in breach of his contract. In late 1979, Revie's appeal was heard in the

High Court and the ban was lifted because Sir Harold Thompson, the FA chairman, insisted on acting as prosecutor in the FA hearing and acting as a judge to decide that Revie was guilty. Croker warned that he couldn't do it, but the headstrong Thompson ploughed on and despite Mr Justice Cantley calling Revie a liar, the former Leeds manager was allowed back into English football. It was like flashing a green light to all the others who were dabbling with bungs and 30 years later, the authorities have yet to clean up the game as Nicholson, Shankly, Greenwood and Mercer wanted. It is doubtful whether Bill Nicholson would have been interested in the England post, especially after his earlier experience with England in the previous World Cup.

Bill's resignation led to a rift with his loyal assistant Eddie Baily, who worked with him for 12 years. When I saw Eddie at his home he said he was advised not to have more operations after surgery on his hip and back, because he had a heart condition. 'I can't jump up to the high balls', he said. Not long after he died at the age of 85 on October 13, 2010. I attended his funeral and one of his daughters said 'He was a bit of a bugger but we all loved him!' I spent two hours with him on our final meeting and his mind was needle sharp. 'Bill was a bit of a cloak-and-dagger man, he would keep a lot of things to himself,' he said. 'That 4-0 defeat at Middlesbrough really affected him and he told me he wasn't going to stay on. He'd had enough. I asked him, "What about me? I've been doing most of the coaching for many years, what about recommending me for the job?" He didn't tell me at the time that he was interviewing Danny Blanchflower for it, but Danny didn't get on with the chairman. He interviewed Johnny Giles of Leeds as well, and also Gordon Jago at QPR.

'I told him I ought to be manager, not any of them, and he said: 'You've had too many ups and downs with the directors and they wouldn't give it to you.' Bill obviously thought he was going to have a part in the appointment, but the chairman made it clear the directors would find a new manager – and they did.'

Blanchflower was 47 and had been out of the game for 10 years – the board wasn't going to appoint someone who spent much of his time criticising both Tottenham and the game itself. Wale said: 'He didn't apply for the job, which is why we didn't consider him.'

Bill had been planning to do a deal with Jago, letting him have Martin Chivers in exchange with Gerry Francis and Don Givens, but this failed to materialise. Baily said: 'A few days later I saw a headline in the *Evening News*, which said: 'Terry Neill may be the next Spurs manager'. I saw Bill and he said, "I think that's right. They want Neill, with Wilf Dixon as his assistant. And Neill is an Arsenal man – that won't go down well with our fans."'

On Friday, 14 September, the bespectacled Wale called a press conference at White Hart Lane to announce the shattering news.

John Barnwell, a teammate of Neill's at Highbury, revealed: 'I threw my arms up in horror when I heard the news. Terry talked a good game, but I don't think he was right for the job.'

I was at the ground covering the day's events with the *Daily Mail* and the next day's edition carried two photographs, which brilliantly told the story. On the left was a picture of Bill in his tweed jacket, flannels and tie, leaning ill at ease against the brick wall in the indoor gym, and in front of him, facing the other way, an unsmiling Martin Chivers. Big Chiv was the man who caused most of the trouble in Bill's reign, but that wasn't the whole reason why he quit. The other picture showed a slimline Terry Neill, shirtsleeves rolled down, talking to Wale, who had his hands in his trouser pockets.

Bill was just approaching on the right and about to pass without being invited to join in the discussions. From being the big chief he was now downgraded to someone they didn't want around any more. The headline was: 'LONELINESS OF A MAN WHO IS NO LONGER WANTED'.

Wale told the press conference: 'I've had some sleepless nights over this. It's been a traumatic three weeks and you don't take a decision like this lightly. Bill came to us first and hinted he might want to go. We tried to talk him out of it. The first time he made it definite was on Bank Holiday and having decided to accept his resignation, we had to look for a new man and let him run things. It wouldn't work to have Bill and Eddie still there.'

Bill believed that one of the senior directors had raised the Sir Matt Busby scenario: when Busby relinquished the manager's job at Old Trafford, he stayed on and was branded, very unfairly, as someone who interfered too much. Bill said: 'I would never have done that, and that showed when I came back working with Keith Burkinshaw.'

He pleaded with Wale to retain Baily as the coach, stating: 'He's a bloody good coach. He may be a bit funny at times, but he could still do this club a service. I felt very concerned that they were letting Eddie go like this. We've been through a lot of campaigns together and we've had a fair bit of success. I knew I was a Mr Nobody here from the moment the directors started sifting through the applications for my job. I thought they would ask me for some advice, but they didn't.'

Instead Wale wanted a clean break, leaving the Nicholson-Baily duo out of the way. Neither man was offered a golden handshake. Baily was legally entitled to redundancy, but with Nicholson resigning, he wasn't entitled to any. Wale said: 'We will not be arranging a testimonial for them – we already have three players due for ones,' adding, 'We have said we intend to make Bill a suitable payment. I cannot reveal any figures.'

In 2009, Eddie revealed the exact figure: 'It was £10,000 for his 16 years, when we produced one of the finest attacking football teams of all time. I got £4,000 from my redundancy and that worked out to £333 a year. On the Monday I went round to the Labour Exchange to sign on. Bill signed on at his Labour Exchange as well and someone took a picture of him turning up and put it in a newspaper. What a comedown!

'Today, managers walk out with millions. Bill was too honest, too mean. I'd go to his office and claim 18/6d for my fare to a game and he would open a drawer with cash and dole out the

18/6d. I'd say, "Give me a pound, they won't mind", but he always insisted on the exact amounts. I felt very let down by him and for some time afterwards we didn't speak. Ron Suart, the former Blackpool manager who was working at Chelsea, got me to do some scouting and I took a job as the PE master at a school in Enfield; that just about kept Elsie and me going. We've been married 62 years [the Nicholsons' marriage lasted the same length of time] and Elsie knows her football. She always teased Bill when he used to get too regimental.'

It was typical Bill when Terry Neill, then manager of Hull City, rang and asked whether he had any chance of taking the job. Bill told him to write in and Neill said: 'I don't have time.' He was ringing from a Heathrow hotel and Bill told him: 'Get some writing paper and an envelope in your room and write the letter as soon as possible, stick a first-class stamp on it and go down and post it.'

Neill did just that and several days later, he was asked to attend an interview at Wale's home. They wanted a young man – at 32, Neill was the youngest to be appointed to a First Division club – who had a more upbeat approach: '...lifting them up, not smacking them down,' as he put it. Two days later, after the 4-0 defeat by Middlesbrough, the directors signed him up. If Neill hadn't followed Bill's advice, he might not have been appointed. The directors didn't even want Bill as a guest at matches and for two years, he didn't go to White Hart Lane. One former player and scout said at the time: 'He was like a fish out of water. He always looked after his garden, but you can't spend all day, every day on it. He starting taking Darkie out more and even took her to matches.'

Eddie didn't return to White Hart Lane until 1983, when he played in a veterans' match before Bill's first testimonial. 'Some time before I was scouting and the game was at Luton, and whoever was giving out the tickets, they put me next to Bill and Darkie, thinking that we were good mates still,' he said. 'When I sat down, Bill said: "How are you?" and I said: "Well, I'm not too happy about things, but I get a living." We started chatting and still I had the hump about him, but eventually the hump worked through the system. Bill used to come along with me to matches after that, before Keith Burkinshaw took him back as a consultant. I went to his funeral and I went to Darkie's as well. I did have a benefit, but not at White Hart Lane: Enfield played a Spurs XI and I was very grateful for it.'

Bill wrote in his autobiography: 'Eventually we resumed our relationship again, which pleased me. Eddie is a typical East Ender, amusing, sometimes barbed in his comments, but a loyal friend. He was the man who geed up the players before matches, employing a variety of similes, most of which were related to his time in the War.'

For some years, Baily refused to speak to Neill but on a spying trip to Copenhagen, he found himself in a hotel room next to Neill and his assistant Don Howe, when they were in charge at Highbury. They started talking, but it was a strained atmosphere. Right up until his death, Baily was still upset about what happened when he was fired. Neill said in his book, *Revelations of a Football Manager*: 'Despite his sometimes brutal forthrightness, which has upset players, Eddie has made an outstanding contribution to the British game.'

Ultimately, Neill lasted just two years at White Hart Lane, keeping them up with Tottenham, finishing 19th in his first season and lifting them to 9th in the second. He surprised football again when he succeeded Bertie Mee as Arsenal manager with more success than he had at Nicholson's club. For seven years (1976–83), he remained at Highbury and was the tenth longest-serving Arsenal manager out of 19.

In 1985, there was an interesting sequel when Sidgwick and Jackson published his book. Harry Harris and I wrote it, and it was a well-received publication with plenty of stories about backhanders, fisticuffs in the dressing rooms, gambling, drinking and sex in the home dressing room of a leading club. The *News of the World* offered £50,000 for the serialisation rights and it was all going ahead until Terry sold subsidiary rights to a sex magazine for a much lower figure. The 'Screws' – Britain's biggest-selling newspaper – promptly withdrew their offer and the book subsequently failed to make the bestseller list.

Bill had the urge to get back into the game and started visiting the training grounds of the London clubs. Most coaches went to Cheshunt to see his methods when he was in charge, so he felt it was only fair that he should look at the ideas of the other clubs' coaches. One day he was at Chadwell Heath, West Ham's training ground, when Ron Greenwood asked him what was he doing. 'Not a lot,' he admitted. Ron offered him a job as consultant and Bill was delighted to accept: 'They'd won the FA Cup and was in Europe and it was a good time to be there.'

Wally St Pier, West Ham's chief scout, soon left and Greenwood asked him to take over. After serious thought, he felt it was too much for him but suggested Eddie Baily for the post and Baily jumped at it. 'We were lucky to have someone of his quality,' said Greenwood. Bill spent a happy year with West Ham until the call came from Burkinshaw to take up a similar consultancy at White Hart Lane.

Eddie left West Ham after 14 years as the chief scout and since then his relations with Martin Chivers changed abruptly. Chivers lived 250 yards from him in Brookman's Park and just before he died, Eddie said: 'He can't do enough for me now. One of my grandsons is a very good golfer with a handicap of 5 and Martin takes me to his golf club occasionally and we get on well. I told him, "You were lazy, arrogant and a big I am" and he agreed, but he's a changed man now. He was a very good player when he was in the mood and he had a short backlift, which a big advantage – Charlie George was the same.' Eddie also lived near to Steve and Jean Bell – it is extraordinary that three protagonists in the Bill Nicholson story should have ended up so close to each other.

CHAPTER NINETEEN:
BACK ON HOME SOIL AGAIN

Bill Nicholson's love affair with Tottenham Hotspur, rudely interrupted when he was heartlessly eased out of White Hart Lane in September 1974, resumed in July 1976 when Keith Burkinshaw succeeded Terry Neill as manager. 'I think we needed his experience and wisdom,' said Keith. 'So I rang him up and he invited me round to his house. We got on very well and he was only too pleased to come back to the club as a consultant.'

The two men were astonishingly similar in almost every respect. Sixteen years younger than Bill, Burkinshaw was born in Higham, south Yorkshire. Like Bill, he also believed in playing attacking football and didn't like cheats. He was totally honest and never minced his words: he gave it to them straight. Happily married to Joyce, he did his work conscientiously and without advertising himself. Burkinshaw started out by transporting tubs of coal from the pit face in a local coal mine and this experience helped him to learn the right values in life. He was never going to be a top-class player: he was a hardworking wing half whose greatest asset was his determination.

After playing for the juniors at Wolves, he joined Liverpool and played only one game in the first team in 1955 before being shunted down the League to Workington, where he played under Joe Harvey, who later became manager of Newcastle. He had three years playing at another footballing outpost, Scunthorpe, and it was then that he went into coaching, gaining the FA Full Badge. Following this, he went off to coach in Zambia. Harvey needed a coach at St James's Park and signed him as the reserve team coach. Soon he was promoted to the first team and his expertise helped Newcastle to reach the FA Cup Final in 1974. Not long after, the popular and inventive coach was sacked.

Wilf Dixon, Terry Neill's assistant manager, lacked top-class coaching knowledge and with Tottenham foundering, Neill needed another coach at White Hart Lane. He said: 'I'd been on a coaching course with Keith and although we were not close, I had a good impression of him. I was spurred on by the news that he had been sacked after Newcastle got to Wembley. Even to this day I didn't know the inside story of why they got rid of this very capable man. I invited him to lunch and over five hours, we established a good understanding and he accepted my offer. We both enjoyed a glass or two of wine and had the first of many good times.'

Burkinshaw soon realised that Tottenham's reputation for meanness was a deserved one and when the club went on a nine-match tour to Canada, Fiji, New Zealand and Australia at the end of the 1975/6 season, he found that his bonus for taking part in a successful season came to just £300. The British Government had imposed a pay restraint and the directors used that as an excuse. Neill was incensed and this, together with several other instances of mean-mindedness, meant that he clashed continually with the management. Meanwhile, Geoff Jones, the club's diligent secretary, was on the same salary as a reserve player and his office car was a banger.

Finally, Neill resigned after learning that Bertie Mee was leaving Highbury. Dennis Hill-Wood, the Old Etonian chairman of

Arsenal, was the complete opposite to the Tottenham directors – he was one of the most generous of men and like his son Peter, who is still on the board, a staunch Corinthian – and he soon appointed Neill as Mee's successor. Burkinshaw had never managed a top club, but Wale wanted him as the next Tottenham manager: 'On the tour I got the chance to get to know him and I found him hardworking, honest and I knew he was well liked by the players,' he said. 'He did the work while Terry appeared on TV.'

There was a feeling of guilt throughout the club, basically because Bill Nicholson was never given his due reward after 38 years on the books; he wasn't even offered a testimonial. Burkinshaw soon brought up the subject with Wale and at the next directors' meeting, it was agreed to bring Bill back as a consultant on a modest salary. 'I realised there might have been a worry that I would interfere, but that never materialised,' said Bill. 'Keith wanted to use my experience and when he sought advice, I gave it – I didn't volunteer it. Football is a matter of judgment about players. You can be sure in your own mind about a player, but it is valuable to have the backing of an older, more experienced person. I did a lot of scouting, looking at players of all types to see if they could suit Tottenham. I enjoyed my time and whatever was achieved it was down to Keith, not me.'

In that 1976/7 season Tottenham were relegated for the first time since 1934/5, but Burkinshaw was retained. 'I didn't expect to be sacked,' he admitted. 'I knew we were going the right way.' Wale said: 'Keith showed many of the qualities of Bill Nicholson. Like him, he was never a publicity seeker. He was hardworking and more the sort of manager we'd been used to, and we liked.'

Tottenham clawed their way back to the First Division in their first season, chiefly by playing adventurous football that brought 83 goals, the highest total since 1965.

Bill's main job was to help with the scouting system. He had scores of contacts throughout the British Isles and he watched four of five matches a week. 'I probably covered more miles than when

I was manager,' he admitted. One of his finest discoveries was Tony Galvin, whom Tottenham signed for £30,000 in 1978. He recalled: 'Tony was recommended to me by Doug Tingle, our scout in Scunthorpe when Keith was there. Doug said Tony was playing for Goole Town and was worth looking at. The next match he was due to play was at Buxton in the Peak District and I decided to drive there. Darkie came along to accompany me and it was raining when I set off, then it turned into sleet and snow. Road signs warned of floods in the Derbyshire hills and with the sleet and snow turning to slush, the roads were very hazardous. It crossed my mind that perhaps we would be better advised to turn back, but we stuck it out hoping the match would still be on.

'By the time we arrived at the ground, the pitch was covered in an inch of snow. A handful of spectators huddled at the back of the grandstand, away from the driving sleet. To my surprise the game went ahead and Tony played well enough to suggest he had potential for us to work on if we signed him. He had good pace for a big, strong lad and a powerful shot in both feet. I told Keith that we should get him and he agreed. It turned out to be a wise investment.'

Galvin was 22 when he joined and was a popular, one-club man, playing in 201 first team games between 1978 and 1987. As for Bill, not many managers would take his wife on a 340-mile round trip in such appalling weather conditions. The Nicholsons' only sustenance was their homemade sandwiches, which they ate sitting in the car and drinking tea from a flask. It must have been true love!

An even more remarkable signing was the way Bill plucked Graham Roberts out of the arms of Ron Atkinson, the then West Bromwich Albion manager, in 1980. Peter Shreeves, who worked under Burkinshaw, revealed: 'Graham had been playing in non-League in Dorset and Bill had a tip to go and see him and liked the look of him. Later on, Graham was up before an FA Disciplinary Committee at Lancaster Gate and Bill heard about it, and turned up there and persuaded him to sign for us. Ron Atkinson had him lined up to sign, but Spurs beat him to it and Ron was very upset.'

Spurs paid only £20,000 to Weymouth and Roberts went on to make 209 appearances for Tottenham and played six times for England. Bill recalled how he first heard of the combative and strong-tackling Roberts: 'I was going to see a player at Swindon, but hadn't been well and Darkie told me to stay at home. She said it was unwise to think of driving, so I went by train instead. The match was uninteresting and the player I was watching hadn't impressed. I left just before the end to catch my train and there were a few people standing on the platform.

'A man was standing with a transistor listening to the football results and I asked him: "Do you mind if I listen?" He said he didn't mind – he hadn't recognised me. We started talking after the results ended and he asked me whether I had seen the game. I said yes and I asked him who he supported. "I pick a game which appeals to me and go and see it," he said. "I go to a ground I haven't been to, or watch a certain player who appeals to me."

'I asked if he watched non-League football. "Quite a lot," he said. I asked him which was the best non-League side of the day. "Weymouth," he said. "Why Weymouth?" "Because they are a strong team with a few outstanding young players." "How young?" "In their early twenties." "Anyone really good?" "Yes, one chap called Graham Roberts and there's another one, but I can't remember his name."

'When I arrived at my office on Monday I made some enquiries and discovered Weymouth were at home on the following Saturday. It was an arduous journey across the New Forest and I arrived ten minutes before the kick-off. I paid to go in and sneaked into the ground, hoping no one would recognise me. Just as the man on the platform said, Graham Roberts looked a fine player. He scored two goals, one a header which reminded me of Cliff Jones in his prime. He played in midfield, controlling the game and knocking it about with great assurance.

'I made one or two more enquiries and later told Keith that it would be a good idea to make an offer for him. Stuart Morgan [now a coach at Tottenham] was the manager of Weymouth and proved an easy person to do business with. Graham made such speedy progress that he soon established himself in the side, playing in a number of positions. In a short space of time he played for England. Weymouth presented me with a lobster when I was invited me back to open a new club room and Darkie was delighted – she loved lobsters.'

Roberts was born in Southampton and his hometown club signed him as a schoolboy, but let him go. Bournemouth, managed by Harry Redknapp, then signed him as an apprentice before releasing him. Then Portsmouth took him on and when Ian St John was sacked as their manager, Roberts found himself being shown the door by the new man in charge: Jimmy Dickinson, one of football's gentlemen. Three knockbacks would be enough to daunt anyone but the steely Roberts kept going, playing a season with Dorchester before Weymouth paid £6,000 for him.

Roberts revealed: 'Bill contacted me and I was shocked – one of the game's legends, the best manager Tottenham ever had, coming on to me. I called him "Mr Nicholson". He was a lovely, approachable man. That season I'd run up around 15 bookings and I had to appear at the FA to explain myself. They gave me a ticking-off, which pleased me. I didn't want to start at my new club being suspended. When I was introduced to Keith Burkinshaw, he said to me: "What position do you play?" He didn't know. He signed without knowing that, relying on Bill's word. That showed how he trusted Bill and how he respected him. Over the next few years I would meet him and he always had time to speak and pass on any advice. I will never forget him.'

Roberts was still playing as a professional with Slough Town when he was 40 and is now looking to manage a club after being in charge at Yeovil and Clyde. He also played for Glasgow Rangers and Chelsea, and his League career ended at WBA, the club he missed out on at the beginning. In 2006, he led Clyde to success, beating Celtic in the Scottish Cup Final. Shortly afterwards he was sacked as manager over allegations of him making racist remarks, which proved to be unfounded. He was tried by the Scottish FA disciplinary committee, but received no punishment.

By amazing coincidence, Ron Atkinson's career had been ruined two years earlier after he was overheard making a reference to Marcel Desailly using the term 'f****** lazy thick n*****' when he thought a microphone had been switched off. Atkinson had to resign from his job as an analyst on ITV and the *Guardian* cancelled his weekly column. Roberts said: 'I'm still determined to get a manager's job. It's more about who you know than what you know.'

Another coup for Bill as a finder of talent was the arrival of Gary Mabbutt at Tottenham in 1982. One day Peter Anderson, the articulate manager of Millwall, rang and asked his opinion of a certain player. Bill said: 'I told him what I thought about the player and he asked about Gary Mabbutt. I said he was a fine player, but Millwall couldn't afford him. I was surprised when he said it would be around £100–120,000, not the £300,000 I thought. I contacted Bobby Gould, who was the manager of Gary's club Bristol Rovers, and the figure Peter quoted was right. Naturally, I didn't express any surprise to Bobby. I always found Bobby to be a very genuine person.

'Keith was watching the World Cup in Spain and I telephoned him and urged him to act. He asked me what I thought was Mabbutt's position. "I don't know," I said. "He is so versatile he can play in a number of positions." I said he would be invaluable at White Hart Lane, especially as we had so many injuries. As all-rounder, he would be very desirable. Keith said Mabbutt was going off on holiday and he was so keen to join us that he came back early from his holiday. The deal cost £120,000 and was completed very quickly. He proved to be a great acquisition and he was soon in the England side.'

Gary comes from a footballing family in Bristol – his father Ray played for Bristol Rovers and Newport, while his brother Kevin played for Bristol City and Crystal Palace. He played 482 matches for the club in 16 years and was capped 16 times by England. By looking after himself, following a strict diet and injecting himself with insulin on time (he is a diabetic) and not drinking, he was one of the fittest and most admired footballers in the country. Gary's feelings about Bill were expressed at his second testimonial when he said: 'He had the same incredible aura as Bill Shankly and Matt Busby. He was respected throughout the whole country, not just for what he achieved, but for the way he did it. When I won a lifetime achievement award at a PFA dinner once, it was Bill who presented it to me and when I was the subject of a *This Is Your Life* programme, Bill was the star, not me. I was proud to know him.'

Not all Bill's recommendations were successful, however. In 1977 he was asked to watch Alan Hansen, a tall, rangy defender who played for Partick Thistle. Keith Burkinshaw said: 'Bill didn't fancy him – he said he was neither one or the other, meaning a defender or a midfielder. Liverpool were watching Alan as well and they signed him soon after. We could have done with a Hansen!'

In the height of the summer of 1978, Bill played the key part in one of the most sensational, and successful, transfer coups in the history of English football. He had friends dotted all around Britain and one of them, Harry Haslam – the Manchester-born full back who managed Luton and Sheffield United – rang him on 29 June to say that two of the Argentinians who helped their country win the World Cup in Buenos Aires four days previously, Osvaldo Ardiles and the bearded Ricardo Villa, wanted to play for a club in England. Harry said: 'Oscar Arce, who is on my staff at Bramall Lane, told me about them and I don't think we could afford the money. They wanted £400,000 and it's got to be a big club like yours, or Arsenal.' He warned that it might be difficult to conclude a deal because the Professional Footballers Association was against admitting foreign players that would deny opportunities to their members.

Today, of course, the PFA have taken a different stance. They agreed to accept a limit – overseas players have to play 75 per cent of international matches to qualify – but over the years the barrier has failed to hold back the stampede. Earlier, the Department of Employment lifted the ban on foreign players and Southampton's Lawrie McMenemy signed Ivan Golac, a full back, from Partizan Belgrade.

Bill watched all Argentina's World Cup matches on TV at his home and was highly impressed by Ardiles. 'He was obviously a player who would improve our side,' he said. 'Any inspiring midfield player would have learned a lot from playing with, or against him, or even watching him. Though a small man, he was quick and brave and his passing, particularly when under pressure, was an object lesson. His balance was such that he could ride most tackles and still find a way through the tightest of defences. He was an artist and there haven't been too many of those playing in England in recent years.

'I hadn't seen much of Villa, who came on as a substitute in two matches, but Antonio Rattin, captain of the Argentine side that lost to England in the World Cup in 1966 when it took eight minutes to get him off the pitch when he was shown a red card for violent conduct – Harry said that he had given him a strong personal recommendation on his behalf. Harry said he'd rung Terry Neill at Arsenal and they were thinking about making a bid. He also said Manchester City had been alerted as well, but dropped out: they didn't have the cash.'

When Bill's conversation with Harry ended, he called Keith to tell him the news. 'He was just as excited as I was,' he said. The directors were meeting that day and Keith knocked at the boardroom door and told the dramatic story to a startled Wale. Within minutes, the directors sanctioned Keith and Harry Haslam's trip to Buenos Aires. Keith said: 'The following Friday we caught the night flight and we were on our way. Harry brought along Tony Pritchett, a football reporter on the *Sheffield Star*, which was a bit unusual but he was a cheery lad who had a good sense of humour. Rattin was at the airport to meet us and I was surprised to discover that he was a very nice, humble man – much different to the way he was portrayed in England so many years ago.

'Arsenal had dropped out. Their board didn't want foreign players, a bit different to today's attitude when they sometimes put out a side without an Englishman! A meeting was arranged with Ossie, who spoke little English, and there was no agent involved. It took just 20 minutes. Rattin wanted $640,000 deposited in a bank out there and for some reason, we paid the cash in Canadian dollars, which saved the club a few thousand dollars because of the different exchange rates. It was one of those occasions when immediately you know something is right. There was an instant rapport between us. It was the best thing I ever did.'

Burkinshaw didn't realise that he had to buy Villa as well. But the £350,000 for Ardiles, compared to the £950,000 Manchester United paid Leeds for Gordon McQueen earlier in the summer when Burkinshaw failed to sign him, was really a bargain and so he readily agreed to take Ardiles' friend as the makeweight in the deal. The money for Villa was the same, but he wasn't too concerned. One great world-class player plus a reasonable, skilful player who wouldn't make a regular place in Tottenham's side made wonderful business sense.

On Sunday afternoon, Buenos Aires time, Burkinshaw called Wale to ask permission to go ahead. 'We need a decision right away,' he told him. Before he died in 2001, Wale told Phil Soar: 'I worked out how much the bank would allow us on overdraft, how much extra we could expect to raise from season ticket sales with all the interest that was bound to be aroused, so I gave Keith the go ahead. We were both putting our heads on the chopping block. It was a big gamble to take, but looking back on it now, it was the best decision I ever made.'

Villa agreed terms even quicker than Ardiles. Soar said: 'Not only were Spurs able to pay cash on the nail, but in the best traditions of Nicholson's cloak-and-dagger transfers, not a word came out about the true nature of the historic deal until Burkinshaw was ready to announce it.'

The speed with which the deal was concluded was explained by the wretched state of the economy in Argentina at that time – most of the football clubs were broke and today they are in exactly the same position. In the autumn of 2009 the clubs were bailed out by the Government or professional football might well have collapsed: no wonder Ossie and Ricky couldn't leave fast enough!

The story broke on 7 July, eight days later after Haslam's telephone call, when Jeff Powell described it as the most sensational deal in British soccer history in the *Daily Mail* and David Lacey said in the *Guardian*: 'When Keith Burkinshaw went out shopping and brought Ardiles back, it was as if the janitor had gone to buy a tin of paint and had returned with a Velázquez. Astonishment that the Argentinians were coming at all is equalled by the incredulity that they were going to play for Spurs, who seemed to have lost faith in major transfers following the muted success of such purchases as Coates, Conn and Peter Taylor.'

Keith said: 'When they finally got to London, we fixed them up in big houses and had English tutors to help them. Ossie is a very intelligent man and soon picked it up, but Ricky wasn't so good, but he could get by.'

In arranging the deal, Haslam made a considerable amount for himself and he impressed Keith with his sense of fun. He was a natural comic, raconteur and a larger-than-life character. When Bobby Robson was manager of Fulham in 1968, he appointed Harry, then manager of Tonbridge, as chief scout and when Robson was sacked in 1969 in a ruthless way – he was driving home when he saw an evening newspaper placard saying 'Fulham manager sacked' – he went as well. If you look through all the job details of managers and coaches, most of them have been appointed through recommendations from friends and teammates. That camaraderie in the game, helping each other, is now being stifled because the managers from abroad don't have those contacts. They are mercenaries, trying to make money as quickly as they can before moving on to another highly paid job in Spain or Italy, or wherever.

Bill's time working with Burkinshaw between 1976 and 1984 was one of the happiest of his life. He spent more time with Darkie, who often went on his scouting missions, and he loved being with his grandchildren. 'His eyes lit up when he saw them,' said his daughters. Everyone spoke highly of him. The players called him 'the Legend' and many of them called in at his office to talk about football. One who liked to pop in for a chat was Gary Stevens, who had seven years with the club before a crude tackle from Vinnie Jones virtually finished his career in 1990.

Gary was 21 when he was one of Brighton's heroes in the 1983 FA Cup Final and Bill recommended that the club should buy him. 'Keith was away when I went to White Hart Lane to sign and Peter Shreeves did the talking,' he recalled. 'He called in Bill and I was thrilled to be in the company of such a great manager. Bill suggested that I should be taken to Cheshunt, the training ground, and off we went. He talked about the current players – Ossie, Ray Clemence, Glenn Hoddle and others – and even introduced me to the groundsman. He was such a humble, very approachable gentleman and I was immensely proud to be with him. On the way back, he said: "I'll show up the back doubles to avoid the traffic hold-up" – and he did.

'I remember one conversation I had with Keith and he said to me: "Who's the next person behind the most important man in a football club?" I said: "The chairman?" "No," he said. "The captain?" "No." "The chief scout," he said. "He's the man who brings in the players and that's Bill."

'Bill was sceptical about all the stretching and warming up before matches. "They get more strains than we did," he said. He believed in building up stomach muscles and he would often tell us: "Don't forget your stomachs!" He was also critical about the increasing number of staff in the dressing room – coaches, fitness trainers, goalkeeper's coach, and so on. "There's no room to move," he would say.'

Under Burkinshaw, Tottenham never really mounted a realistic challenge for the title, but his success in knockout football earned him a deserved reputation as the second most successful manager of the club. Bill was at Wembley in 1981 when Ricky Villa scored that memorable goal in the FA Cup replay against Manchester City. 'I doubt whether there was a more stirring goal in an FA Cup Final than that,' he said. 'He had a little luck as he rounded Tommy Caton, Ray Ranson and Nicky Reid before shooting past Joe Corrigan, but the goal typified what he could do when he had the confidence to do it.' Two FA Cup wins in succession – 1981 and 1982 – and winning the UEFA Cup in 1984 wasn't enough to extend Burkinshaw's reign, though. The victorious penalty shoot-out in the second leg against Anderlecht was his last game in charge and as he left, to sign a two-year contract to coach the Bahrain national squad, he came up with that immortal phrase: 'There used to be a football club there.' He resigned, much to the chagrin of Bill, because of a principle. 'Irving Scholar wanted to buy the players and handle the financial side and I told him he was doing my job,' he explained.

Two property developers, Scholar and his friend Paul Bobroff, took over the club from the Wale family in 1982 and floated the company on the Stock Exchange: a public limited company was now running the football club which diversified into leisurewear, computers, tickets and other matters, many of which lost money. No longer was it the football club that Bill and his fellow professionals knew. Enthusiastic amateurs who made money from their businesses, they thought they knew better.

Ten years later – mainly exciting years, one has to admit – they were proved wrong. Scholar, a tax exile, was a lifelong fan of Spurs and had an encyclopaedic memory about the club. Years later, after

Scholar did the decent thing in agreeing to let Burkinshaw have a benefit match – an England XI played Spurs and he made £30,000 from it – Burkinshaw told an extraordinary story about the way Sidney Wale relinquished his control over the club, purely out of pique. 'It was an honest club, not a political club,' he said. 'After the end of the 1982/3 we went on a tour to Japan, Hong Kong and Bahrain, and I said to Sidney Wale: "We're going to make a lot of money from that, why don't we take the wives and children to Bermuda, to show our appreciation?" He agreed rather reluctantly, but said he didn't want the other directors to go – only his wife and him. It went off swimmingly well. The directors were up in arms when they heard and they started to oust him. Sid was livid and he had the majority of the shares and proceeded to sell them to Scholar for £270,000, a ridiculous sum.

'The club went haywire. Scholar wanted me to stay and he invited me and Joyce to see him in Monte Carlo, where he still lives, and booked us into the most expensive hotel to impress us. He told us what he intended and then asked my views. "I am the manager of a club that makes profits and you should let me do my job and you ought to sit in the background," I said. He didn't agree. He wanted to buy the players and arrange their contracts. I wouldn't budge and he made it clear that he wouldn't budge either so that was the end of our relationship.'

Scholar had a high regard for Bill and he sanctioned the staging of his first testimonial match when a Tottenham team drew 1-1 with his old club West Ham on Sunday, 21 August 1983. The warm-up game was between two teams of ex-Spurs players. It lasted 20 minutes each way and there were many laughs and funny moments. Scholar said of Bill: 'Every time this ground is open, someone, somewhere, thinks about you.' The profits from Bill's testimonial, sadly, were only £25,000.

Shreeves, a devotee of Bill's, managed the side from 1984–86 and David Pleat took over in that high-scoring time of 1986/7. Pleat said: 'Bill was scouring the country for recruits and being 100 per cent involved with everything that took place at the club, from the chairman to the youngest apprentice. One day I spent an enlightened afternoon with him in his back garden, reminiscing. In the days of his management, players were scouted thoroughly; there were no videos then. The manager had to vet the player himself and find out all the little points, such as his diet, whether he was of good character, on and off the field, and so on. Once I sent him to see a player and he came back and was most scathing. "Whoever recommended that player...!" he shouted. Calmly, I told him we had had a couple of good reports on him. Bill replied: "Well, you should check your scouts because the player doesn't even prepare himself correctly to play the ball." It was a small point, succinctly made.

'On another occasion, at a managers' dinner, Bill was in the audience and he was the main attraction, winning thunderous applause when introduced. Every year he was the main guest at the London Coaches Association dinner. Again, the audience, many of them young coaches who did not have the opportunity to see his teams, revered his presence. He was a man without airs and graces and set standards in the days when football was untouched by overexposure on TV, avaricious agents, a frenzy of foreign players, a hyperactive press and excessive player salaries.'

In Bill's reign as manager, there was stability and loyalty, 16 years of joy with few crises. When Burkinshaw quit, eight managers were hired in the same period, with one crisis after another, finally ending up in the High Court. Alan Sugar found it very disquieting and the club only reached a state of normality when Daniel Levy and his colleagues took over.

It is always true that a good man is only truly appreciated when he has left his post and the same applied to Bill. Scholar and Bobroff were eager to make amends in their 10 years at the helm and appointed Bill as club president in 1991. When Terry Venables took over as manager (1987–91), Ted Buxton was appointed scout and Ted often drove him to matches. His mind was undimmed, but his body slowly wearing out. He retired as a scout in 1997, at the age of 78. In December 1998, he received the Freedom of the Borough from Haringey Council and the road outside White Hart Lane, measuring just 46 yards, was renamed Bill Nicholson Way.

In later years he was shaky on his feet and one supporter told a wonderful story about him. Sean Humphrey said: 'I was standing near the entrance of a school, just wide enough for one or two to pass. I stopped to let this old man pass and he suddenly toppled over and fell. I bent down to help him up and he said he was okay. He was wearing a long, navy Spurs coat and as he got up, his accent seemed out of place. It was then that I realised it was "Sir" Bill I was helping up and all I could blurt out was "F*** me, Billy Nic!" He smiled and laughed, and said: "All right son, thanks very much."

'I told him it was my pleasure and kissed his hand a number of times to thank him for everything, the club I love. He was so humble and said that was his pleasure, as he also loved them. I'll never forget how warm it made me feel. My friends and I still talk about that evening and how lucky I was in assisting him up.'

Under the more caring leadership of Daniel Levy, Bill was granted a second testimonial in 2001 and it was a tremendous success, making up the shortfall of his first testimonial of 18 years earlier. A crowd of 35,877 turned up to watch Tottenham take on Fiorentina, managed by Roberto Mancini and the proceeds were considerable, almost as much as the weekly salary of one of today's Tottenham stars. It was more like a pop concert than a football match with the idolising worshippers cheering and clapping the star.

As he was presented to the two teams, the man holding his arm to keep him upright was Martin Chivers. The two of them waved to all parts of Bill's former kingdom and the noise continued unabated for a long time. It was as though they were reaching out to him to say: 'Thanks for everything, we love you!' One fan wrote: 'I took my seat in the Park Lane upper, feeling a humbleness that rarely experienced in my life. As a small lad, Bill's teams enchanted and mesmerised, enticing us like a moth to a very bright lamp. After experiencing such a great era in my chosen football team's history, then living through the sheer torture of the last dozen or so years, my eyes started to fill up.

'The famous old words "Mine eyes have seen the glory of White Hart Lane" – well, for a few moments I couldn't really see anything. I tried to hold back the tears as I sprang to my feet as the great man took to the pitch. This man had affected my childhood, even more than my own father. In many ways, it was an important pivotal point in the future of our great club. With Bill there, loved by all, with new owners, I genuinely feel we are on the way back to their rightful places at the head of British football.'

A year later, Bill and Darkie moved out of Creighton Road into a warden-controlled flat at Potters Bar. The building was opened by the Beverley Sisters and Joy, wife of Billy Wright – the man who restricted Bill to just one international cap by his consistency – went up to Bill and hugged him.

His last appearance was at the inaugural dinner for the Hall of Fame at the club in March 2004. Six months later he died and as Steve Bell said in his appreciation at the packed funeral: 'He passed away peacefully at 5am on Saturday, 23 October 2004 – no fuss, no bother – a match day, inevitably. The family knew his time was close, although we were a little surprised that he didn't keep going until he could check all the football results. He was a strong believer in teamwork and to the end, he expressed his gratitude, along with his family, to the doctors and nurses who cared for him, especially at the Potters Bar Community Hospital. The family feel that we all owe something to the memory of this great man. If we are to correctly celebrate the life of William Edward Nicholson, he would want us to do it properly, so please do, but most of all, do it his way: with some style!'

CHAPTER TWENTY:

THE FINAL FAREWELL

Brian Clough's memorial service took place on 21 October – Trafalgar Day – in 2004, 48 hours before Bill Nicholson passed away at the age of 85. Clough had died of cancer at the age of 69 on 20 September and his service, attended by around 10,000 at the Nottingham Forest ground, was a sombre affair whereas Bill's, on Sunday, 7 November, was a joyous celebration of a great life, untainted by corruption and deceit.

Bill was as honest as an archbishop, but Clough was always taking cuts from transfers and his clubs' close season tours. The two great managers had similar props to their hectic life – their families. Once, Clough was about to set off for the Baseball Ground to attend Derby's sixth round FA Cup tie against Leeds when he was told that his mother was ill. He missed the match and went to see his mother instead, saying: 'She means more to me than any Cup tie.'

Brian Moore, one of his best friends, once told me: 'During those rampaging days at Derby, the unreal ones at Brighton, and the short-lived ones at Leeds, he struck me as someone who revelled in the strident headline – which more than often he helped to create – but who wanted the private home life as well.'

Clough, who loved driving a top-of-the-range Mercedes, was generally late for appointments. Bill Nicholson was the opposite: he was never late and he drove a Rover, the symbol of stability or, latterly, a Vauxhall Cavalier. Nicholson looked on Clough as 'a bit of a loner.' He said: 'I didn't have much to do with him. Most managers like socialising after a match and I always invited the opposing manager to the Blue Room at White Hart Lane for a drink – I used to like circulating. I couldn't remember Clough taking up my invitation. From what I was told, his players didn't see him much either, but that didn't affect his ability as a manager. There is no one way to be a winner as a manager.'

Many of Bill's potential buys failed to sign for Tottenham because he refused to pay under-the-counter bungs. Clough had no scruples about taking money, or indeed paying it out, and David Pleat recalled: 'Brian used to talk about his top drawer. He'd say to the players: "You ought to put something away in your top drawer. You should speak to your chairman."'

Clough's standoffishness with Nicholson may well stemmed from an incident in Bucharest in 1958, when Bill was in charge of the England Under-23 side which toured Bulgaria, Rumania and Czechoslovakia. England lost 2-1 and Nicholson was unhappy with Clough's work rate. 'Clough is an intelligent positional player, but I felt he didn't put enough into his game,' he explained. 'He didn't look keen so I left him out against the Romanians. I realised that he was the only orthodox centre forward in the party and I told Walter Winterbottom, the senior manager, "You watch him in training and you'll see what I mean." Winterbottom watched the training later and said, "You're right." I like players who are thoroughly committed and I had the impression that Clough was inclined to be lazy. I didn't dispute that he was a good player with a good scoring record.'

Later on the tour, Bill told his errant centre forward not to speak to foreigners. 'You never know what might happen,' he said. A few hours later Clough was seen in conversation with several men, not players. 'Come on, Brian,' said Nicholson. 'You know what I told you!' Clough wasn't the usual footballer: he wanted to find out about people of all types and life generally. As managers, Nicholson and Clough always insisted on playing quality football, with effort, not the way Charles Hughes, the FA guru, advocated the use of the long-ball style. 'If God put grass high above the clouds we'd kick it high and long, but he didn't,' Clough would say.

Like Bill, Clough gained his FA Full Badge at a young age but his son Nigel, now manager of Derby County, is one of the very few coaches in the Football League who haven't any coaching qualifications.

After I completed the bulk of the writing of Bill's autobiography in 1984, I sent a copy to Clough senior as a goodwill gesture. He sent me an odd letter by return. 'Dear Mr Scovell,' it read, 'Thank you very much for sending me the copy of Bill Nicholson's book which I look forward to reading. Yours sincerely, B. Clough.'

Over the years he had always called me 'young man'. On the Nottingham Forest FC notepaper the manager's name was down as 'Brian H. Clough'. I never heard back from him. He might have been upset to read of Bill's criticism of his work rate in Bucharest and failed to mention his omission from the next game in Romania in his autobiography *Clough*, published in 1994. Jimmy Armfield was the captain of the U23 squad and he said: 'I have great memories of that trip. Conditions were terrible and Bill made light of everything. The hotel in Sofia was unbelievable and Bill arranged the room arrangements by the alphabet. I was in the first room with Alan Acourt, the next one with Brian Clough and Bryan Douglas, and so on. Bill came round to see us and each room had two iron camp beds, a rug on the bare floorboards and a bare bulb in the ceiling, and that's about all, but in between our beds a big black beetle was on the floor and Bill laughed and said: "Someone has beaten us to it – it's like being back in the Army!" We'd all done National Service so you knew what to expect.

'The food was awful and someone suggested that Jimmy Bloomfield, a lovely man who had trained in the Catering Service, ought to be recruited to help out. So Bill went to the manager and persuaded him to let Jimmy cook the breakfast and the manager agreed. It could be a trip of moans and groans, but Bill wouldn't let that happen. He joked his way through the tour. He was a terrific bloke, dead honest and a supreme realist.

'There was a lot of anti-Western feeling in those countries at the time and I remember one of the interpreters trying to lecture on the virtues of Communism. In Bucharest, a Polish women's gymnastic team were staying on the same floor of our hotel preparing for the European Championship and we watched them train. Bill said: "I hope your lot are going to be as frisky as these girls!" Coming from Blackpool and him from Scarborough we were always pulling each other's legs about how cold their hometown was, and Bill always reckoned there was a stronger wind on the West side. He was a lovely man. I met him on coaching trips at Lilleshall and I admired the way he worked with young players. I am pretty certain he could have gone on to manage England, but he wouldn't have liked all the fuss. He didn't like publicity. He liked to be in the background. He built a terrific team in the early sixties and he got just the right blend.'

The sun shone brightly on Bill's memorial service and 8,000 turned up and sat in the Paxton Road Stand with Bill's ex-players and working colleagues, numbering 289, sitting in the front rows of the lower East Stand. Darkie sat proudly in the first row of the podium and she said: 'I wore black at the funeral, but I decided to wear my Tottenham blue-and-white blouse today. Bill would have approved. It was a good life. I'm not sad, why should I be?'

Cheekily, someone asked her if she had biked there – she travelled by bike for most of her married life. 'Oh no,' she replied with a chuckle, 'Several of my bikes were pinched over the years, especially at supermarkets. But when we moved out at Creighton Road to go to live in Potters Bar I gave my last one to a neighbour. Next time I saw him, he told me he'd sold it! What a cheek! Once another bike was damaged and I couldn't ride it home, and I told Bill about it and asked him if he could do anything about it. He said: "I'm busy."'

She said her father Alf was one of a minority of English soldiers to survive the Battle of the Somme and he had a specially converted bike to accommodate his stiff right leg. Behind her, some yards away, Terry Neill sat self-consciously – many Spurs fans hated him for taking over from Bill as manager and for being an Arsenal player – with his wife Sandra, who looked stunning.

Darkie and his daughters Jean and Linda chose a typically smiling picture of Bill for the front page of the simple, four-page service card. He was wearing his Tottenham tie and a light green suit and there was a box saying: 'The Nicholson family and the Club would like to thank you all for attending this celebration of the life of Bill Nicholson'. The hymns – Bill's favourites – were 'Abide With Me' and 'Jerusalem'. Linda said: 'He loved singing at home and he knew the words of many ditties. And he often sang hymns.' Nearly all his players stood and sang with gusto.

The day before the Frenchman Jacques Santini had resigned as manager after only 13 games in charge, the shortest term of office of any of the Tottenham managers. Steve Perryman had a theory about it. 'I think it might have been a set-up,' he said. 'They'd been saying they were going to appoint a big name and if they gave it to Martin Jol from the start, they wouldn't have called him a big name. So Santini filled in for a while. I don't know. The directors appointed four foreigners to run the first team and two have left, but Bill did the lot himself.'

Later, speaking at the annual meeting of the club, Jol spoke about 'the way Jim [sic] Nicholson played the game and I wanted to follow that.' It must have been a slip of the tongue!

The service was brilliantly organised, with chairman Daniel

Levy's wife Tracey taking a leading part. Six speakers, all Tottenham players, addressed the audience and the big screen showed some of the finest moments of Bill's career. They were loudly applauded, and with great reverence. Glenn Hoddle's goal when he dribbled from the halfway line, gliding past two defenders and dummying the goalkeeper, like Pelé, before rolling the ball over the line, was the highlight. Arjen Robben, the former Chelsea winger, had scored a similar goal against Everton the day before and he was the kind of player Bill might well have tried to buy in a different era. The fans accorded the loudest cheers to Hoddle, the player most of them believed to be the man who typified Nicholson's appreciation of the highest form of footballing art – except his work rate.

'I never played under Bill and I very much regretted that,' said Hoddle. 'But I had four years training under him and we had the total respect of every player, without exception. I soon learned a lesson from him. I was playing in a Youth tie once and I had scored a hat trick and on the following morning he said: "Young Hoddle, your third goal – you took a risk with that. You should have passed the ball. It's a team game, you know." I never forgot that. He was a humble and honest man, a true football legend. His new life lives on in spirit, still influencing us.'

Perryman spoke of Bill's footballing beliefs, his insistence on playing simple football. 'The first thing he taught me was to play quick, easy and accurate. He'd say things like "Play the way you are facing," and "When the ball dies, you come alive."' He described his military-style discipline and style of dress. 'I never saw a hair out of place,' he said. 'He used the same hairstyle when he first played. He had the shiniest shoes, creases in his trousers you could cut with and a hatred of anything red.'

David Dein and Ken Friar, sitting nearby, smiled wryly: Arsenal were playing at White Hart Lane that following Saturday.

Cliff Jones and Jimmy Greaves stepped onto the blue carpet and walked out to the podium. Greaves, a much bulkier figure than in the sixties, spoke with feeling. 'From the day he took the helm at White Hart Lane he was the great man of the club,' he said. 'He gave a generation of fans something they will never, never forget. He arrived at my flat in Milan wearing a Trilby, tweed coat and thick gloves, and from the day he signed me from AC Milan I had nothing but the deepest respect for him and I can safely say that is a fact for all my teammates, too. He was a dour Yorkshireman – on the outside. But he was a great man with many values who did have a humorous side.

'Like all great managers, he was one of the lads when he wanted to be and the boss when he needed to be. His final words to the players in the dressing room as they waited to go out onto the pitch were often something along these lines: "Remember, you are going to run out in front of the people who pay your wages. Their expectancy of you is high and their opinion of you is high, so do not let them down. Entertain them and you can only do that by being honest with yourself, respecting your teammates and your opponents and by, as a team, playing as one." He gave me something which I carry every day, a sense of respect for a fellow man.'

Jones, as slim as in his Double days, took up the mike and said: 'I remember feeling really pleased with myself after playing what I thought was a good game until Bill said: "Remember son, a pat on the back is only two feet away from a kick up the backside!" He didn't waste words, but he paid strict attention to detail. He managed the club from the bootroom to the boardroom. He insisted that the most important people at the club were not the directors, management or players but the supporters. When I first played for him, he looked at my studs and said: "They'll let you down." And he was right. I was in a good position, slipped and missed scoring. In the dressing room afterwards, he said: "That was a good lesson – wear proper studs."'

Martin Chivers probably had more rows with his old manager than any of the players, but he was the man who supported him as he hobbled out of the tunnel for his second testimonial at White

Hart Lane in 2002. 'He was walking on his stick and I said to him: "You don't want to be seen with a stick, Bill," and he said: "You're right." So I took him by the arm and his face lit up with smiles when he came out. Except that he got overexcited and threw his arms high in the air to salute the crowd and started to fall backwards. I had to grab hold of him to stop him falling.

'He was an amazing bloke. After we beat Wolves once he didn't come into our dressing room. He went to the Wolves dressing room instead and commiserated with their players. It was some time before he got back to our room. "You didn't deserve that," he said to their players. How many managers would have done that? He was so honest, as honest as the day is long.'

Gary Mabbutt, for the younger generation, spoke without notes and reminded the audience that he, too, had 16 years at Tottenham. 'I remember the day when he rang me and invited me to talk about a transfer,' he said. 'I was in awe of him and was shaking when I came into the office. "My name is Gary Mabbutt," I said. "And my name is Bill," he replied. He didn't like being called Boss. He explained what he wanted from me, how Spurs played and what he wanted to do, and it was terrific. He drove me to Cheshunt and continued talking through the journey – it took me aback. But that was his way, what he felt was the right way to go about things. Even today, most managers like being called Boss, Gaffer and Manager as though they will lose respect if their players are too friendly. But Bill was one of the first to insist on being called by his Christian name.'

Linda wound up the speeches, ending with these heartfelt words: 'We know Dad loved you as much as you loved him. He did it with style and you will be always in our hearts.' The screen flashed up a sequence of a smiling Bill making his exit to the sound of 'Glory, Glory Hallelujah'. Julia Ward Howe's American Civil War hymn 'The Battle Hymn of the Republic', written in 1865, has stirred the hearts of millions, particularly in north London. This version was sung by Daniel O'Donnell, to the delight of Irishman Terry Neill and the words rang out: 'He has sounded forth the trumpet that shall never sound retreat; he is sifting out the hearts of men before his judgement seat.'

As Michael Hart, former football correspondent of the *Evening Standard* for 40 years, wrote: 'Sitting in judgement Bill, I suspect, would have approved. Glory, glory hallelujah!' There were tears running down the cheeks of so many celebrants, including his players, young and old. As the 75-minute service ended, 85 pigeons were released from white boxes to symbolise his 85 years. When the music died away and everyone got up to go, a lone, shaven-headed supporter shouted in a loud, gruff voice: 'Make sure we beat Arsenal on Saturday!' It was as if Bill had spoken – his last order.

For a time, there was silence then the fans started up their own song. They, and the club, had done him proud. Except that the result six days later, 4-5 to Arsenal, went the wrong way. With nine goals going in and entertaining the customers, Bill might have grunted a reluctant approval before criticising the quality of defending. His managerial career, of course, started with a 10-4 win in 1958. He loved goals, but they had to be good ones.

Afterwards Linda revealed: 'I was nervous, but as I was walking up to the mike, I suddenly felt it was okay. My mum was phenomenal – I was very proud of her.' Darkie lived for three years and three months after Bill's death, passing away on 30 July 2007.

Linda continued, 'There was a lot of emotion and it was all about love. The fans shared that feeling because Dad always said without fans there would be no game. He treated everyone the same, from the tea lady and the laundry lady to the players and officials and the supporters. He spoke to them in the same respectful way and he never brushed away anyone. He took an interest in them and that's why they loved him. He willingly gave his life to the club, expecting little in return.

'Yes, he worked long hours and his word was often arduous, but it gave such a lot of pleasure. It must be a great feeling to be paid for a job you love and everybody thinks you are really good at. He loved his work with his "other family" at the Spurs ground. He particularly loved the coaching side, and he really enjoyed working with the young players and helping them grow up into mature players.'

Shaun, Linda's son who played American football, said: 'Along this journey to fame, he realised there are a few things one must have to do well in life and he never hesitated to tell me what they are. If you want to do well at something and be better than most, you have to work harder and more often than most. He also instilled in me the value of honesty. He would say: "A coach and his players should be honest with each other. The truth may hurt at first but it saves more pain later on." Along with hard work and honesty, he said: "You should be nice to people, have confidence in yourself and your abilities and don't forget to have fun in life."'

The guests went upstairs to have a drink and a chat. Jimmy Greaves, with a glass of water in his hand, was in his most expansive mood. He pointed down to the playing pitch and said: 'Look at that! We'd have loved to have played on that. It would have suited our style, right up our street. Look at those pictures around the room. Most of them show mud pitches, not grass ones. Today a lot of games played in those conditions would be called off. The development of pitches is the biggest factor these days. They are made for passing. How much better we would have played! I can see it now, John White passes a great ball down the left, Cliffy Jones takes it on and crosses to the far post, Bobby Smith heads down and it's there! We'd have collected some more Doubles!'

In another part of the room, Pat Jennings was talking about contracts. 'Bill was such a great bloke that when my contract was close to ending he had me in and after a chat, I was happy to sign whatever he put in front of me,' he revealed. 'I am sure Bill was paid peanuts. In fact, I know he was. He looked on the club's money as though it was his own and he never threw it around. And he wasn't rich – he wasn't really interested in money.'

Mickey Hazard spoke of Bill's common touch. 'There was no

side about him,' he said. 'He would speak to anyone, the lowest or the highest; he treated everyone the same. He would talk to the fans as long as they wanted to listen. He was a wonderful, wonderful man!'

Doug Livermore was among the throng and he said: 'I've never attended such a fantastic and wonderful service, and I'll remember it for the rest of my life. The players spoke about Bill's belief that once the players get out onto the field they have to earn their money because the most important people in a football club are the supporters and they want to be entertained and that reflects my beliefs too.'

Livermore was the coach, then the assistant manager and co-caretaker manager of Tottenham, along with Ray Clemence, and he started his career under Bill Shankly's strict regime. 'The two Bills were similar in many ways,' he explained. 'They were great man-managers. Today people say that today's players are earning so much money that it's very difficult for managers to control them. If they don't like the manager, they can go off and join another club. But the Bills would be just as successful today – they were brilliant at using psychology.'

At the start of the service, chairman Daniel Levy made a speech, saying: 'Bill's time with the club was the greatest period in our history; it cascaded into a kaleidoscope of success after success. He did so much for the club and we must never let his legacy fade. He must be our inspiration as we strive to ensure a new era dawns at White Hart Lane.'

Whether a new 58,000-seater stadium emerges on the same site, or a new one in place of the Olympic Stadium, or even one somewhere else, has at the time of writing, yet to be decided. The chances are that the directors will want a lot of money for a brand name. How about naming the ground 'The [sponsor's name] Bill Nicholson Stadium'? It would be a permanent legacy, a true and deserved one. No man gave more, and took out so little, to compose and conduct glorious football that will never be forgotten.

Steve Mosby was born in Leeds in 1976. He studied Philosophy at Leeds University, worked in the Sociology department there, and now writes full time. He is the author of ten psychological thrillers which have been widely translated. In 2012, he won the CWA Dagger in the Library for his body of work, and his novel *Black Flowers* was shortlisted for the Theakston Old Peculier Crime Novel of the Year. He lives in Leeds with his wife and son.

www.theleftroom.co.uk
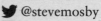 @stevemosby
/theleftroom

Also by Steve Mosby

You Can Run
The Nightmare Place
Dark Room
Black Flowers
Still Bleeding
Cry for Help
The 50/50 Killer
The Cutting Crew
The Third Person